Kingdom Come

RELIGIOUS CULTURES OF AFRICAN AND
AFRICAN DIASPORA PEOPLE

Series editors:
Jacob K. Olupona, Harvard University
Dianne M. Stewart, Emory University
and Terrence L. Johnson, Georgetown University

The book series examines the religious, cultural, and political expressions of African, African American, and African Caribbean traditions. Through transnational, cross-cultural, and multidisciplinary approaches to the study of religion, the series investigates the epistemic boundaries of continental and diasporic religious practices and thought and explores the diverse and distinct ways African-derived religions inform culture and politics. The series aims to establish a forum for imagining the centrality of Black religions in the formation of the "New World."

Kingdom Come

THE POLITICS OF FAITH AND FREEDOM
IN SEGREGATIONIST SOUTH AFRICA
AND BEYOND

Tshepo Masango Chéry

DUKE UNIVERSITY PRESS *Durham and London* 2023

Printed in the United States of America on acid-free paper ∞
Project Editor: Melody Negron
Designed by Matthew Tauch
Typeset in Arno by Westchester Publishing Services

Library of Congress Cataloging-in-Publication Data
Names: Masango Chéry, Tshepo, [date] author.
Title: Kingdom come : the politics of faith and freedom in
segregationist South Africa and beyond / Tshepo Masango Chéry.
Other titles: Religious cultures of African and African diaspora
people.
Description: Durham : Duke University Press, 2023. |
Series: Religious cultures of African and African diaspora people |
Includes bibliographical references and index.
Identifiers: LCCN 2022061111 (print)
LCCN 2022061112 (ebook)
ISBN 9781478019930 (paperback)
ISBN 9781478017226 (hardcover)
ISBN 9781478024507 (ebook)
Subjects: LCSH: Anti-racism—Religious aspects—Christianity. |
Black theology. | Liberation theology—South Africa. | Religion and
politics—South Africa. | African diaspora. | BISAC: RELIGION /
Christianity / General | SOCIAL SCIENCE / Black Studies (Global)
Classification: LCC BT82.7 .M37 2023 (print) | LCC BT82.7 (ebook) |
DDC 230.089/96073—dc23/eng/20230621
LC record available at https://lccn.loc.gov/2022061111
LC ebook record available at https://lccn.loc.gov/2022061112

Cover art: Abdoulaye Konaté, *Les Marcheurs* (*The Walkers*),
2006. Artes Mundi 2008 Wales International Visual Art
Exhibition and Prize. Photo by Jeff Morgan 10 / Alamy Stock
Photo. Courtesy of the artist and Gallery 1957.

To my father, MAAKE J. S. MASANGO, whose tenacity and courage has been a pathway.

To my mother, PAULINE SKOSANA MASANGO, whose love has been a refuge from which to flourish.

Thank you for being my first teachers and guides.

CONTENTS

ABBREVIATIONS

AIC	African-initiated church
AME	African Methodist Episcopal
ANC	African National Congress
AOC	African Orthodox Church
KCA	Kikuyu Central Association
KISA	Kikuyu Independent Schools Association
KKEA	Kikuyu Karing'a Educational Association
NAACP	National Association for the Advancement of Colored People
SANAC	South African Native Affairs Commission
UNIA	Universal Negro Improvement Association

TLHOMPO /ACKNOWLEDGMENTS

I am humbled by God, his grace, and the steadfast support of people who helped me birth this book. There is a Sesotho proverb that says a person is only a person through the presence and acknowledgment of others. It is my turn to give *tlhompo* to them. I am fortunate to have the most beautiful and gracious first teachers, life givers, and friends in my parents, Reverend Dr. Maake and Mrs. Pauline Masango. Your love, faith, and courage have sustained me. Thank you to you and our ancestors for courageously persevering so that I had the freedom to write this book. My research for and writing of *Kingdom Come* took many turns; this journey is reflected in the many thinkers, incisive editors, truth speakers, and exhorters who took time to usher my work forward. I started this journey because of the inspirational teachings of Debbie Miller, Christine Tibbetts, David Fowler, David Rich, and Alan Barksdale. One scholar, teacher, and mentor, Professor Mary Frances Berry, deserves my utmost respect. At each crooked corner, she turned me back to the archive, the writing, and the completion of this book. Thank you for never giving up the fight. Your intellectual rigor, generosity, and care made me a better scholar. You extended the support I received at Princeton University as an undergraduate where scholars in the Program in African American and African Studies cultivated so much in me. My thanks to Valerie Smith, Noliwe Rooks, Cornel West, K. Anthony Appiah, and Emmanuel Krieke, who made me believe that I could have a place in the academy. I must especially thank Nell Irvine Painter and Colin A. Palmer, whose words, food, and funds sustained me in hard seasons. At the University of Pennsylvania and beyond, Barbara D. Savage, Lee Cassanelli, Deborah A. Thomas, Harvey R. Neptune, Carol Ann Mueller, Stephanie McCurry, Stephen Hahn, Herman Beavers, and Tukufu Zuberi gave me invaluable training.

I am grateful to special colleagues at the University of Texas at Austin, the University of Houston, the University of Witwatersrand, and the University of Pretoria, who shaped my thinking by asking hard and important questions. My humble thanks to Edmund T. Gordon and Omi Oshun Joni L. Jones, who brought me to Texas and inspired me to see it as (an intellectual) home. To Daina Berry, Tiffany Gill, Kali Gross, Minkah Makalani, Nicole Burrowes, Keisha L. Bentley Edwards, Malik Edwards, João H. Costa Vargas, Xavier Livermon, and Kristin Smith, thank you for giving me steadfast wisdom and faith in the process. Samantha Pinto, thank you for pushing me along and holding me up when things got tough. To so many others, especially Toyin Falola, Niyi Afolabi, Bertin M. Louis, Kairn A. Klieman, Linda Reed, David McNally, Richard M. Mizelle, Abdel Razzaq Takriti, Leandra Zarnow, Gerald Horne, Ashlyn Strozier, Susanne Klausen, Karin Shaprio, Salim Vally, Piet Meiring, Graham Duncan, and Tshepo Moloi, and all the Garvey scholars, your scholarship and mentorship left an indelible mark on me. I have the deepest gratitude to archivists, especially Michele Pickover, Gabriele Mohale, Ann McShane, and Amy Evenson who offered sources without hesitation when travel seemed impossible. To Patric Tariq Mellet, your creative genius and insight strengthened the manuscript. Special thanks to Michael O. West; without some critical sources, some threads of this history might have remained a mystery. And to my scholar friends new and old, especially Jonathan Fenderson, Jeffery S. Ahlman, Jenifer Barclay, Tyler D. Fleming, Barbara Boswell, Dennis Tyler, Dave Nelson, and Dotun and Yemi Ayobade, thank you for reading my work and living life with me.

I have found family along this journey too. Philadelphia gave me brothers: Sean Greene and GerShun Avilez. My gratitude runs deep for Sean, who always breathed new life into seemingly old ideas and gave me the gift of family. There are no words for GerShun, who quietly cleared pathways for me to think, learn, and simply be in irrevocable ways. My thanks also goes to Victoria J. Collis-Buthelezi and Amanda Ellis, both sisters who opened portals of understanding and gave me the language to see things anew. To Robert R. I. Goldberg, you have brought me joy, peace, and rigorous insight since the first day of graduate school. To Jordan Gonzalez, you stand alone. There are no words to describe my gratitude for the ways you held and expressed the sacredness of my thoughts with delicateness.

In South Africa, I welcomed the embrace of the Masango, Skosana, Musengwa, Dikgale, and Maake families, who renewed me after seasons away from home and endured hardship. You gave back to me portions of myself through song, prayer, text messages, oral histories, and pure love, and I thank you. My thanks also extends to gracious strangers turned family. I am indebted to the Shannon, Huss, Bryde, Emmitt, Warrington, Anotine-Redondo, Chéry, and Lytle families. Special thanks to Colleen Shannon and Patrick Huss, who gave me so much love and courage for the journey ahead; to Walt and Louise Bryde, who offered space to learn and grow; and to Shirley and Daryl Lytle, who always made a home for me, as well as new family in the Warringtons and Chérys.

To family friends Belinda Curry, Donald Scott, Stewart Bertram, Betty Austin, Cristina Flores, Meredith and Curtis Duncan, Jenn and Russ Prentice, Anne Streaty Wimberly and Edward Wimberly, the Motswene family, the Siqbengu family, the McLendon family, the Bashman family, the Lalendle family, the Dube family, the Shai family, the Maake family, the Meaux family, the Harvey family, the Middleton family, the Brooks family, the Barnes family, the Pinson family, the Ness family, the Neumann / Jackson family, Angel Davis, Nekyla Franklin, Karole Holmes, and Orion Mosko, who picked me up from airports, drove me to strange places, sent me money, indulged me as I asked a series of questions about times past, cared for my children as if they were your own, rescued me from hurricanes, and whispered urgent prayers for me, you are appreciated.

I also remain incredibly moved by the generous support of administrators and staff who ensured that my scholarship advanced. My thanks go to Erika Henderson, Dan O'Connor, Paula Short, and Jay Neal as well as my departmental chairs, Philip Howard and Nancy Beck Young, for finding ways to let me pursue scholarship during a global pandemic. I am also indebted to a great deal of institutions that saw promise in my scholarship. I benefited from the financial support of the Annenberg Foundation, the Fontaine Society, the Marcus Garvey Memorial Foundation, the Carter G. Woodson Institute at the University of Virginia, the John Warfield Center at the University of Texas at Austin, the Institute for Citizens and Scholars, and the Underrepresented Women of Color Coalition.

I would also like to thank Duke University Press, the series editors for the Religious Cultures of African and African Diaspora People series, and my acquisitions editor. Dianne Stewart, Terrence Johnson, and Jacob Olupona, your thoughtful professionalism is unmatched. To Miriam Angress, my editor, thank you for imparting your brilliance, hard work, and compassion all while advocating for me in rooms I could not enter. To my anonymous reviewers, the meticulous and thoughtful ways you grappled with my work prove unparalleled. Thank you for your conceptual genius, keen editorial eye, and generous comments. You have made my book better.

I had hopes of honoring in person those who poured into me crucial lessons during life's highs and lows, but they have since passed on. This book is also in their memory. Thank you, Colin A. Palmer, Mable Lowman, Coretta Scott King, and my beloved (Uncle Des) Archbishop Desmond Tutu. These teachers taught me by sharing their lives with me. I owe them so much.

To my loves Nandipa Pauline, Ndileka Unathi, and Naledi Mohau, thank you for living with this book during your childhood. You always brought joy and passion amid hard research and writing seasons. Your perseverance living and dreaming across two continents has been a source of wonder and admiration. To Lisly, it's been a long road since September of freshman year when we met at Princeton. I never knew that you would selflessly create the space for me to delve into my people's past. Your love gave me permission to search for pieces of myself in this history. It has been the kindest gift.

Introduction

Thy Kingdom Come on Earth

I knew terror by the age of five. By 1985, Soweto, my home, was engulfed in flames. African people had made the country ungovernable by resisting apartheid, a racial hierarchy that framed every aspect of our lives. The state had effectively incarcerated, exiled, or killed many leaders of the antiapartheid movement but even still had failed to stop the movement. The government had not expected clergy and church leaders, such as my father and his colleague Archbishop Desmond Tutu, to intervene, organize, and lead resistance efforts in Black townships such as Soweto. Between boycotts and protest met with state violence, African people set decades of colonial order ablaze. The repercussions for rebelling against a colonial order were unbearable. The state sent the military to our townships, infiltrated political organizations with informants, shut off the water supply intermittently, and cut off electricity. Police entered our home on horseback, threw tear gas at me as I played in our backyard, and even detained my father for short stints. These hardships did not keep my parents from writing subversive documents, distributing banned books, and smuggling information and people to political camps outside of South Africa. My parents pressed on and consistently brought politically active religious leaders from as far as

Zimbabwe, Zambia, and even the United States to organize against apartheid. And yet through all of the political turmoil and violence, we found ways to survive, create normalcy, and dream of a different future.

In my family, bedtime stories countered chaotic life in Soweto. Stories recounted from children's books, created in the moment, or drawn from family histories not only offered an escape from the present but also served as the very space to imagine an alternative. My parents bookended our nightly story-time ritual with powerful prayers that carved out audible spiritual spaces of refuge, palpable sanctuaries against the sounds of gunshots, the sight of our homes alight, and the lingering caustic, peppery odor of tear gas. One night our prayers were pierced by the portentous wail of a young activist's cry: "*Tima mabone*" (Turn off the lights)!

The activist's words brought my neighborhood to a standstill. Darkness enveloped our street as families hid the illegal makeshift wiring that brought electric current into our house so as to avoid detection by the swiftly approaching security branch. We said our prayers in the dark that night. We prayed for freedom; the hope for freedom was our only sacred light. Though this all unfolded when I was very young, my memory of that night brings into sharp view the function and power of faith when enduring life under something as harrowing as apartheid.

A few months later, I was forced to flee South Africa without my parents. Intel from another young activist had been given to my parents and detailed the unthinkable. My parents' names and my own name were found on a hit list. This threat reflected a stage in the country's upheaval when the government attempted to silence leaders by assassinating their families, especially their children. Children often became casualties during the 1980s and 1990s even after there was an international outcry because of the 1976 Soweto Uprising, when the government killed hundreds of schoolchildren as they protested inequitable education. Somehow the government had picked up on my parents' activism even though it was often assumed that church leaders remained apolitical. My parents, however, drew their commitment to social justice from previous Christian leaders who felt that their faith compelled them to fight for freedom. Black Christians petitioned God for his kingdom to come "on earth as it is in heaven," a promise of freedom that a wider community of South African Christians had clung to for generations. Indeed, these clergy's faith-inspired activism was not new and did not begin in the 1980s but instead continued a century-old tradition of clergy leaders and other South African Christians declaring, envisioning, and working toward a kingdom on Earth that upheld their birthright to be free. *Kingdom Come* tells this little-known preapartheid history, when politically conscious Christians believed that the petition for God's kingdom to come was equal parts prayer and mandate. In doing so, they forged a politics of freedom within the church that was as spiritual as it was political, laying the foundations for clergy such as my father, Tutu, and many others to reclaim South Africa in the postapartheid period as a moral project and not just a nation-building one. Black clergy, church leaders, and Christians in South Africa and beyond worked together long before the antiapartheid movement to counter segregationist practices that later became established as apartheid.

Dreams of freedom seemed unattainable in a world where racial subjugation loomed large. Black Christians' passion for freedom was often ignited by struggles within their own denominations, where they experienced structural racism more intimately. Much of this conflict was part of a larger response to watershed moments in Western imperialism, beginning in 1884 with the partitioning of Africa at the Berlin West Africa Conference and ending with World War I and the establishment of the League of Nations. In South Africa, the British and the Dutch had organized their own colonies. The British implemented antislavery policies and anglicized as they established the Cape Colony in 1806; threatened, the Dutch left the region, forging a trek to the interior. The Afrikaners established the Transvaal and Orange Free State as their own colonies, an expression of growing Afrikaner nationalism. A decade later in 1846, the British cemented their presence through the Colony of Natal. Direct conflict came decades later with the discovery of and competition over diamonds and gold, one of the many impetuses for the Anglo-Boer Wars.[1] Almost a decade after the war, the Afrikaners signed the Treaty of Vereeniging, a symbol of reconciliation between the British and the Afrikaners that established a unified government. The all-white officials representing the Union of South Africa reconciled British/Afrikaner differences by crystalizing competing types of segregation in Cape Colony, the Colony of Natal, and the Transvaal and Orange River colonies, codifying the segregationist policies in the new government's legal system. Much of this legislation, especially the Land Act of 1913, dispossessed Africans of their land, relocated them into colonial ghettos, and restricted their mobility. And while Africans grappled with new material realities, their loss of land also meant the dislocation of their spiritual practices, an existential crisis.

During the interwar period, the South African government established a new racial taxonomy that essentialized Blackness by classifying certain multiethnic Africans as "Coloured" or of "mixed race." Faced with this European authoritarianism, African Christians strategized their response through the belief in God's promise that his kingdom could come in the here and now. Their vision for freedom insisted on its manifestation if not in their country then at least in their churches. This was collectively exemplified when South African Christians seceded from European-run churches ten years after Africa was officially partitioned by Europeans. This movement experienced the most growth just after the turn of the twentieth century, when Africans boldly created African-initiated churches under the banner of "Ethiopianism," including the Ethiopian Church, the African Church, and the Ethiopian Catholic Church in Zion, among others. The spiritual freedom that Black Christians cultivated produced future generations of clergy who, like Tutu, would serve as the bedrock of the antiapartheid movement. This freedom, I suggest, was rooted in the charge recited in the Lord's Prayer. The church leaders who catalyzed these shifts in Black religious life often were politically progressive and sometimes even radical but regularly relied on the Lord's Prayer to envision their politics. They included clergy, clergy wives, lay leaders, political organizers, community leaders, and local elders. Some were educated at local mission schools. Others studied at prestigious institutions in Europe and North America. Still others were working-class Blacks who were domestics and gardeners or had jobs at port city wharfs, railroads, and mines. Yet, across class and cultural milieux, they shared a common animating spirit in that their Christian faith drove their quest for freedom, their fight against darkness.

While the petition "kingdom come" became a revolutionary charge at home in South Africa, it also extended outward through the African diaspora and became a transnational response to oppressive political conditions globally. Many of these Christians found common cause with believers all over the world who were also facing racial persecution under European colonial domination. From South Africa to Zimbabwe and Kenya and on to the United States, Canada, and the circum-Caribbean, these people recognized their shared experiences of colonialism and white supremacy. As South Africans sought to worship and establish their own churches beyond paternalistic forms of white missionary supervision, Black Christians abroad shared similar experiences that cast dark shadows in the history of Christianity. Both the African Methodist Episcopal Church and the African Orthodox Church are examples of the way Blacks in South Africa and the United States forged their own sites of autonomous worship to combat their experiences of white supremacy. First established in the United States before taking root in South Africa, these US churches were composed of a mix of northern Black communities mingled with southern Blacks seeking refuge from the grip of Jim Crow and West Indian immigrants fleeing the collapsed sugar industry, hurricanes, and famine of their home islands. Together these transnational Christian communities, composed of South Africans, African Americans, and West Indians, created their own churches outside of white-run denominations, thus institutionalizing their desire for self-determination. In the 1920s, as some South Africans came to recognize the theological outlook they shared with US-based Christians, they sought connections despite the limitations of Black mobility on both sides of the Atlantic. Ironically, in the case of South Africans the assigned racial status of "Coloureds" actually granted some of them greater mobility than other Africans to travel to the United States, because the state did not imagine "Coloureds" to be part of Black politics. Radical Coloureds with the means to do so often relied on their privilege to travel and to forge relationships that linked them to other Africans and to African Americans in principally Christian networks.

Black Christians in South Africa had a similar transnational solidarity with Christians living in colonial Southern Rhodesia and Kenya. As Blacks in Southern Rhodesia and Kenya waded through their own consequences of colonial racism, institutionalized through the same British Land Act of 1913 that affected South Africans, they, too, saw land reclamation as a critical path to freedom. Africans turned to God to light pathways of resistance as they faced various kinds of land dislocation. Ethiopianists in Southern Rhodesia who sought to organize churches found themselves on the edges of cities facing the daunting realization that they couldn't build, much less gather, congregations in such marginalized spaces. Christians in Kenya who refused to accept land dispossession as a new colonial reality organized themselves to reclaim their land and create their own churches and schools outside of the purview of the European missionaries who ran these institutions. But when they joined the transnational network of Black Christians already linking the United States to South Africa, Christians in Southern Rhodesia and Kenya made this alliance specifically to defy missionary-imposed assimilative practices, even as British colonialism took hold in East Africa. Alongside South Africans and African Americans, Kenyan and Southern Rhodesian Christians helped imagine and circulate this larger vision of Black freedom predicated on God's promises for redemption in a dark world.

In the early to mid-twentieth century, South African Christians built and relied on a transnational network of Christians that drew persecuted Black people from across the diaspora to church; once there, they imagined freedom with no bounds. In reconstructing the lives, communities, and radical social visions of these men and women of faith—Tutu's predecessors—I show how transnational religious movements destabilized imperial forms of racialization and imagined freedom in and through church formation. *Kingdom Come* integrates scholarship on the field formation of the African diaspora; the history of racialization, particularly in South Africa; and religious expression, with work on Pan-Africanism, African nationalism, and Black liberation to assert that politically inspired religious and ecumenical radicalism begin long before it is traditionally imagined.

Kingdom Come positions Africa as a central site of discussion; it makes Africa much more than a site of dispersal in our understanding of diasporic religious studies, specifically, and diaspora studies more broadly. In this story, South Africans are the central point from which African Christians defined freedom on not only a local level but also a grander scale of transnational uplift. This history provides a way to contend with broader concerns about the place of Africa within field formation in African diaspora studies. Indeed, pioneering scholars such as Colin Palmer, Ruth Simms Hamilton, Paul Tiybeme Zeleza, Michael A. Gomez, Patrick Manning, Carol Boyce Davies, Kim Butler, and Robert Trent Vinson, among others, have posed critical questions about Africa's positionality within the diasporic framework. Africa is at the center of *Kingdom Come*; the book captures visions of freedom in South Africa, Kenya, and Zimbabwe and highlights the routes of dissemination from Africa to the West. Many scholars of the diaspora have focused on the opposite, the movement of ideas from the West to Africa. This work insists on illustrating the creative measures of faith that Africans relied on as they fought for liberation.

South African Christians' contribution to the country's politics are often retold through the lens of a historical metanarrative predicated on white oppression and Black resistance, with limited attention to the complex logic of race. *Kingdom Come* complicates the history of race in South Africa by telling the story of Africans who were classified as "Coloured" by the state. This book contributes to a burgeoning scholarship that interrogates "Coloured" identity in South Africa, accounting for more expansive Blackness on the continent. My examination of the colonial logic of race extends discussions by Zimitri Erasmus, Mohamed Adhikari, Vivian Bickford-Smith, Ian Goldin, Saul Dubow, James Muzondidya, and Zoë Wicomb, all of whom labored in different ways to provide histories of "Coloured" people while not always actively defining what was meant by the term.[2] My work defines the shifting contours of the term as defined by the state. But it also suggests that these South African Christians are the most representative of the modern African diaspora, in all the ethnic and spatial diversity that the identity encompasses.

The heart of *Kingdom Come* is a story of faith and the way it was employed for societal transformation. The book contributes to the scholarship on African diaspora religions by highlighting the impact of movement and migration on religion but, unlike most of the literature, centers on Christianity, an understudied theme within diaspora studies. *Kingdom Come* is indebted to the work of such scholars as George Shepperson, James T. Campbell, Robert R. Edgar, Morris Rodney Johnson, Joel Cabrita, Isabella Mukonyora, Afe Adogame, Michael A. Gomez, Yolanda Covington-Ward, Ras Michael Brown, and Tracey E. Hucks, among others, who developed our understanding of religion but also veered outside of the Abrahamic tradition.

Kingdom Come is about Christians who were engaged in various forms of racial uplift. Yet in many ways, the racial uplift ideology that these African Christians embraced was much more complicated than that defined by the largest Black mass movement of the time, led by Marcus Garvey's Universal Negro Improvement Association, that was an important feature and influence within these communities. Many members of these communities interpreted Garvey's call for freedom as one in which they would liberate and govern themselves. Garvey scholars such as Tony Martin, Rupert Lewis, Robert A. Hill, Claudrena N. Harold, Ula Taylor, Mary G. Rolinson, Adam Ewing, Natanya K. Duncan, Asia Leeds, and especially Robert Trent Vinson map the establishment of Garveyism worldwide, offering insight on transnational and regional working-class politics across the globe. Vinson's work is deeply instructive to my understanding of the ways Garveyism and, more broadly, Black nationalism circulated in South Africa but also remained hidden from the government. My work builds on Vinson's scholarship by highlighting further that Africans had already constructed their own visions of freedom well before they learned of the Garvey movement. Indeed, Africans did not simply depend on African Americans to define freedom; rather, they found resonance across diasporic lines. This book also stands in line with recent studies by scholars such as Adom Getachew and Quito Swan that show how liberation struggles engaged Black internationalism against colonial rule.³

South Africans both imagined and enacted their visions of freedom by cultivating global Christian networks that shaped the Black Christian landscape on the African continent and beyond. By focusing on South Africa as a politically generative place in a global diasporic context, I shift how scholars see, reference, and engage South Africa(ns), which tends to be exclusively through the lens of apartheid. Taking up the work of people of faith who fought against racial domination and violence long before the apartheid era, before the name Nelson Mandela was known around the world as a symbol of anticolonial struggle, this book is a call to consider South Africa and South Africans on their own terms. Black Christians in the first half of the twentieth century were searching for freedom, which they thought might only be summoned in a prayer for God's kingdom to come. That search extended to places and contexts outside of South Africa even as its leaders maintained that the country and its people needed to be the locus for that freedom movement going forward. Their stories establish the centrality of Pan-African mobilization in South African freedom struggles in ways that disrupt our familiar narrative of the South African and diasporic past during this period.

COLOURED, THE RECONSTRUCTED NON-AFRICAN

I also give sharp relief to the evolving and sometimes elusive practice of race making particularly in South Africa, where race governed all aspects of life. This exercise complicates the white/Black racial binary by considering the construction of "Coloured" identity. The divisive term "Coloured" encompassed people classified as "mixed race" by the colonial society. It was a racial description that eventually became codified by law.⁴ "Coloured" identity operated as an essentialized racial intermediary status between white and Black. Yet, it was much more. The term "Coloured" was the government's attempt to maintain uniform definitions of race as migration seemingly created a constant state of flux. As the government solidified its racial classification system, people, particularly immigrants, did not easily fit into the government-prescribed racial categories. The lack of uniformity made it difficult for administrators to define the group. Further, it reflected the larger impossibility of establishing a scientific or systematic basis of racial classification in South Africa or elsewhere, for that matter. Race was (and continues to be) socially constructed.⁵ Interestingly, the term "Coloured" included KhoiSans, Camisas, and Griquas but also Asians, Chinese, Indians, Malays, Indonesians, Malagasies, and English-speaking Blacks from the United States, West Africa, and the Caribbean, among many others. By tracing the oscillating and inconsistent definitions of "Coloured" identity over time, the fabrication of racial categories such as "Coloured" becomes overwhelmingly evident. The term's ethnic and racial capaciousness, as imposed by the government, was meant to connote that people defined as "Coloured" were something other than African. This ambiguous positionality, which obscured ethnic and racial distinctions, yielded relative privilege because "Coloured" presumed a distance from African identity and a proximity to whiteness even as many politically active Coloureds defined themselves as African.

GEOGRAPHIES OF THE BLACK ARCHIVE

Many characters fill this book, most of whom were classified as "Coloured" for one reason or another. Sometimes their classification was a direct result of their multiethnic heritage or because they are English-speaking Blacks from afar or simply because they travel well beyond the continent. A South African priest of the African Orthodox Church is one such example. Daniel William Alexander, who was identified as Coloured, found spiritual and political comradery as an African church leader in a larger global movement against white supremacy. His records show up all over the world, including Zimbabwe, Kenya, the United States, and the United Kingdom. Similarly, histories of the Ethiopian Church are accounted for in the public records of the United Kingdom. Indeed, the church shows up in multiple intelligence agencies in the United States and Britain, and sometimes the records bear traces of resistance movements among people of African descent worldwide. If we read each collection separately these records appear fragmented, but collectively they reflect the ways global networks of the African diaspora operated as a cross-continental archive of Black political organizing just waiting to be fully illuminated.

PRACTICES OF FAITH AND FREEDOM

Kingdom Come begins by providing the racial context of segregationist South Africa. The book moves beyond a history focused on a white/

Black racial binary to highlight the place of "Coloured" identity within a colonial racial matrix that the state continuously reshaped in an attempt to thwart African efforts of solidarity. Chapter 1 asserts race as a technology that is always building upon itself, stripping subjects of their humanity as it squeezes them into senseless categories to ensure the state's capitalist projects of coloniality. The chapter provides a historical context for the creation and evolution of the term "Coloured" as it traces the shifting legal and social status of the categorization. This term was much more than a racial description for "mixed race," as the South African government defined it from the segregationist period through the apartheid era. Instead, the chapter suggests that "Coloured" identity needs to be historicized as a colonial enterprise that used race making to maintain order. The consequence of these racist political frameworks was the collapsing of multiple identities and histories that then became invisible, an essentialism imposed by the state. Africans categorized as "Coloureds" had a relative advantage over other Africans, including increased mobility. "Coloureds" sometimes relied on these advantages to galvanize creative forms of resistance against a government that was crystalizing the racial hierarchy foundational to apartheid.

Chapter 2 introduces Ethiopianism, the secessionist movement that established African-initiated churches in South Africa. This chapter engages the spiritual and political convictions that African church leaders expressed while being attentive to the ways this pan-ethnic movement redefined the meaning of Black solidarity, particularly in the South African context. The chapter's focus on "Coloured" identity provides an opportunity to witness the ways Africans, whom the government defined as "Coloured," sometimes leveraged this colonial identity to disrupt the missionary enterprise for the sake of their freedom. The discussion demonstrates just how fraught the term was when some African clergy categorized as "Coloured" used it to position themselves above other Africans as the movement became more fragmented.

Chapter 3 highlights the work of Charlotte Manye (Maxeke) and her sister Kate Manye as they envisioned the future of African-initiated churches beyond the Ethiopian movement by connecting them with the African Methodist Church, an American church with a similar history of secession. These women placed South African theologies within an international framework. This chapter suggests that the Manye sisters' migratory existence—which took them from Uitenhage to Kimberly to London, then to the United States, and finally back to South Africa—allowed them to imagine a pan-ethnic religious experience that could become a promising platform for Black freedom worldwide. The Manye sisters had distinct skills and privileges that set them apart. These sisters' experiences forged new and increasingly important connections between South African and US-based Ethiopian movements, connections that would facilitate a 1920s racial uplift movement in both countries.

Chapter 4 uncovers the multifaceted layers of training and leadership that helped establish churches as part of the racial uplift movement in the 1920s. This chapter traces the paths of West Indian leaders, traveling from the circum-Caribbean to the United States, and is attentive to different kinds of training these church leaders took advantage of on their travels. This movement allowed them to build migrant communities in the United States and reconstitute new church structures. These multiple diasporas of people and ideas gave way to the Universal Negro Improvement Association and related organizations rooted in Black agency.

Chapter 5 suggests that the 1920s racial uplift movements led to the formation of new forms of Black religious expression. In particular, the chapter documents the establishment of the African Orthodox Church in North America. While it was a religious offshoot of Garveyism, it also functioned on its own terms such that, unlike Garvey's movement, it actually reached the shores of the African continent. The creation of this church, I argue, is a testament to the impact of the circulation of ideas within the global freedom struggle.

Chapter 6 tracks the remarkable growth of the African Orthodox Church in South Africa and Southern Rhodesia. This chapter positions that expansion as the culmination of transnational correspondence, organizing, and travel by Black Christian leaders such as Daniel William Alexander, whose highly effective actions were nonetheless limited by colonial surveillance that forced him to be wary of state reprisals.

Chapter 7 examines the different ways Africans advocated for and implemented spaces of agency in establishing their own African-run churches and seminaries, wherein we see the first earnest rumblings of a new kind of African anticolonial politics animated by the joint concerns of faith and freedom. Across their different race-based colonial and segregated contexts, Black Christians in South Africa, the Caribbean, the United States, and Kenya understood the shared injustice they faced from the perspective of a morally pure and ethically righteous Jesus Christ. They examined moments in Jesus's ministry to inspire them. These Black Christians were committed to a savior who confronted corruption in the overturning of tables.

They clung to a Jesus who spoke truth to hypocrisy. They believed that this savior was the king of the kingdom of God that they ultimately sought. So, they worked for a new world order and prayed together. This shared prayer, which called for God's kingdom to come, united them across space and reflected their singular mission. The spiritual, they believed, had earthly implications that could dismantle the religious, social, economic, and political insidiousness of segregation and colonialism. My father believed the same. The night that I listened to my bedtime story in the dark, my father lent me his faith. His theology insisted that hope coupled with activism would eventually overcome the evil fibers of apartheid. Turning to the historical record makes clear that a generation of Black Christians were forebearers to my parent's faith and politics, igniting his convictions and those of many others in the antiapartheid movement. They lit his spiritual path. And so, Black Christians in the early twentieth century turned their sanctuaries into freedom-striving spaces, spaces for organizing against white supremacy, enacting refuge, and strategizing anticolonial freedom as the fullest expression of God's will. It was in the church, here understood as an incubator of activism, often as hidden from the state as they were from the archive, that the practices of faith were irrevocably fused to the politics of freedom in ways that would shape Black African politics going forward.

ONE

"My Blood Is a Million Stories"

The Making of Coloured Identity

Krotoa, the first African baptized in South Africa, lived during a time when segregation was in its most nascent stage. Krotoa was initially a servant to seventeenth-century Dutch East India Company commander Jan van Riebeeck but later became an interpreter, intermediary, negotiator, and strategist to the Dutch as they laid claim to an Indigenous refreshment station at the Cape of Good Hope for ships traveling east.[1] Her Christian conversion, mastery of Dutch and Portuguese, adoption of European cultural mores, and, finally, union to a Danish soldier defied racially and religiously designated boundaries of African existence. Krotoa and her children straddled multiple worlds, racial, religious, and cultural; in doing so, they disrupted a tenuous race-based social order that white settlers had worked strenuously to establish in law and custom and equally strenuously to control. Centuries later when questions about racial classification among non-Europeans were raised, colonial administrations responded by assigning the label "Coloured" to people of the region who seemingly lived between worlds, such as Krotoa and her children.[2] This chapter traces the shifting legal and social definitions of the state-constructed term "Coloured." It is the story of how colonial governments simplified and ultimately attempted to erase the multiple identities and histories to pacify white anxieties of social mixing.

"Coloured" was a racial description for people classified as "mixed race" by the colonial administration. Coloured identity, as far as the government was concerned, encompassed people whose phenotypes, among other features, were not visibly congruent with whiteness or Blackness. Because the state espoused the idea that racial purity governed European (white) and African (Black) populations, Colouredness was facilely conceived as a mix between the two identities. It functioned as a racial alternative for those who could not be defined as white or Black. In the process, diverse groups of people were rudimentarily designated as mixed race. This not only encompassed many peoples but was also a label that accommodated diverse waves of immigrants continually being identified and integrated into society; the mixed-race designation was constantly being remade.[3] In its most complex examination, Coloured identity is much more than the result of biological processes; its hidden ethnic and racial expansiveness beyond a white/Black racial binary suggest that both the colonial and the apartheid government had it function as a repository for all people who did not easily fit rigid conceptions of Black and white identities.[4] Therefore, Coloured history, unlike Indigenous history, is not solely about South Africa's territorial expansion but is also a history of transoceanic travel and migration, a history of the sea, the land, and the interplay between them. We can access the changing contours of this state-imposed identity, one created to thwart Black solidarity through differentiation, a practice that would be integral to apartheid in the early twentieth century.

THE COLONIALITY OF RACE

Race governed the social, political, and economic landscape of both the British colonies and the Boer republics as a means of creating colonial order even before they formed the Union of South Africa in 1910. Discriminatory control was rather simple at first. Both the British and the Afrikaners resorted to articulating difference through broader binary classifications defined by Africans' relationship to Christianity such as Christian versus heathen.[5] They also included free or unfree and origin of one's ancestry (e.g., European, non-European) that later evolved into distinct racial divisions. The terms "Christian" and "heathen" gestured at the degrees of Christian adaptation between Europeans and non-Europeans during the height of the missionary enterprise in South Africa. Even the terms "European" and "non-European" signified a hierarchy of ethnicity that acknowledged European histories and cultures, while the term "non-European" lacked the same specificity. These terms also became racialized in that "European" became equated with whiteness, while "non-European" came to mean Black or nonwhite. Each of these terms also defined access to resources and privileges. It would be decades before colonial officials fully acknowledged ethnic complexities within Indigenous communities.

The terms "European" and "non-European" remained integral to identifying difference. Although "European" has a regional reference, it symbolized much more in the South African context. European identity represented foreign governance, with both the British and the Dutch having their own colonies until they created the joint Union of South Africa in 1910. Differences between the British and the Dutch became deeply accentuated when Afrikaner memories of scorched-earth policies and civilian internment embittered them against the British. These complex politics meant that European identity has often been limited to a British/Dutch binary history that has also been entrenched in notions of foreign governance. The term "European" has included colonial authorities, missionaries, and even other Europeans. The term was also extended to other white settlers, such as the Afrikaners who had long-established ties to the region. The term "European" was essentialist in nature because it rendered those who were visibly white as European even though some who were called European actually had (sometimes openly) African and Asian ancestry within them.[6] Rather, the term functioned to create a hierarchy between Europeans and all other races and ethnicities.[7]

The term "non-European" included all ethnic and racial groups that were not European. It extended to all people of color, including those of aboriginal, Coloured, and Asian descent. In fact, in the early nineteenth century, European society used "Coloured" interchangeably with "non-European." Non-Europeans/Coloureds included the Sotho-Tswana, Nguni, Venda, and Tsonga peoples as well as East Asians, Southeast Asians, and mixed-race people. Similar to the term "European," "non-European" encompassed a host of people, but these distinctions were masked by this appellation. Over time, Europeans acknowledged ethnic distinctions among these groups. For instance, the Sotho-Tswana, Nguni, Venda, and Tsonga people were also referred to as Kafirs in the nineteenth century, "Native" later in the nineteenth century, and finally Bantus in the mid-twentieth century. Coloureds and Asians, who also fell under the same umbrella of non-European, also had more specific nomenclature such as "mixed-race," "other," "Coloured," "Malay," and "Indian" to describe them. These specific distinctions would distance groups such as Coloureds from Natives/Bantus, who were at the bottom of the racial hierarchy. Even though alternative terms, such as "Native," "Asian," "Indian," and "Coloured," represented a growing degree of specificity, they did not accurately describe these groups of people. The term "Coloured" was the government's attempt to maintain uniform definitions of race because migration seemingly created a constant state of flux. As the government solidified its racial classification system, people, particularly immigrants, did not easily fit into the government-prescribed racial categories. The lack of uniformity showed the inconclusive ways administrators defined this group. It also reflected the larger impossibility of establishing a scientific or systematic basis of racial classification in South Africa and elsewhere. Race was (and continues to be) socially constructed.[8] By tracing the oscillating and inconsistent definitions of Coloured identity over time, the fabrication of racial categories is overwhelmingly evident.

COUNTING COLOR

In 1865, the first census was taken in the British Cape Colony. It relied on four identity choices (European, Hottentot, Kafir, and Other) to enumerate and record the population.[9] "European" described the foreign white population. "Hottentot" and "Kafir" were used to describe Indigenous groups. Nomadic hunters and herders known as the KhoiKhois, Sans, KhoiSans, or Bushmen, who occupied the western section of the colony, were officially recognized as Hottentots. "Kafir," an Arabic word meaning infidel or unbeliever, was used to describe the Xhosa people who lived in the eastern portion of the colony.[10] "Kafir" was also loosely used to describe other Nguni and Tswana-Sotho ethnic groups throughout the region. The classification "other" included all other non-Europeans. As the word suggests, it was a racial catchall that included Asians and mixed-race populations that did not facilely fit into the white European/Black African, or white/Black, racial binary. The group's composition oscillated and shifted dramatically over time as the Cape demographic transformed.

The use of "other," the category that would later be known as Coloured, was associated with the shameful (and, in the twentieth century, illegal) weight of miscegenation.[11] This notion, of course, reflects the larger history of sexual violation in South Africa. It is generally portrayed as a disheartening story rooted in the gendered oppression and sexual violence between Black women and white men for generations. These stories of interracial sexual violation defined both the historical and popularly accepted narrative of Coloured identity's origin. Yet, there are also other aspects of this history. The ways scholars often discuss the idea of Colouredness is rarely informed by these people's stories of active migration and movement. This part of Coloured history begins as early as the seventeenth century with sea travel. This movement of different people back and forth to the Cape ultimately diversified the population and simultaneously redefined the census's racial categories. Groups, such as Malays, who were the descendants of imported slaves from India, Sri Lanka, and Indonesia, along with mixed-race people, were considered part of this racial designation.[12] The category "other" emerged in this context.

Ten years later in 1875, the Cape census had acquired two new racial categories along with other subcategories. Six racial categories in total emerged: European or white, Malay, Hottentot, Fingo (*sic*),[13] Kafir and Bechuana, and Mixed and Other. Most of the categorical changes further described aspects of the non-European population.[14] Although these additions spoke to the government's wider recognition of African ethnicity, other factors underscored the change. "Hottenot" and "Kafir" remained stereotypical terms of African Indigeneity (even though the British acknowledged there were fewer and fewer "pure-breed" Hottentots in the colony).[15] The categories Fingo and Bechuana, which arguably could have been considered Kafir, actually became separate entities because of the ways each group had to negotiate their relationship with the British.

Each emerging racial category, moreover, directly reflected the colonial expansion of the British Empire farther into southern Africa. British records suggest that the Fingo people swore an oath of allegiance to the queen of England, Christianity, and education. But it seems more plausible that the Fingos had formalized an agreement with the British to gain protection during the Frontier Wars. In turn, the British claimed the Fingos not as subordinates but instead as actual allies in the cause of Christian civilization, hence their commitment to God and the queen that distinguished them from other Africans.[16]

The Fingos later identified with the Xhosas as British gratitude faded and Indigenous persecution became widespread, but prior to that the British had recognized an ethnic distinction from the Xhosas because of their alliance with and rapid assimilation to European Christianity and Western education.[17] Although the Bechuana people did not have such a prolonged history with the British, they too were introduced into the census because they readily espoused Christianity and its Western attributes.[18] The recognition of the Fingos and Bechuanas reflects the flexibility of government-imposed identity. It shows just how haphazardly notions of race and ethnicity were constructed. Political stature or collusion with colonial officials determined who was recognized in the government record. Thus, these coalitions were of great importance. In the spatial realm, they determined important issues such as land acquisition. In the case of the Fingos, access to land fostered a spirit of community and inspired a sense of collective culture, ultimately ensuring group solidarity. Residential patterns such as this engendered a similar sense of cultural communalism and solidarity among various groups. This was certainly true for Coloureds.

Another categorical change within the census concerned the ambiguous category of "other." "Other," which once encompassed all the racial identities not considered European, Hottentot, or Kafir, now specifically referred to "mixed and other." This meant that the government explicitly and openly acknowledged the mixed-race population as distinct from the subcategory "other." Additionally, Malay people were separated from the classification of "mixed and other." While census documentation did not explicitly suggest which groups of people "other" might include, sources outside of the census provide some clues.

Between 1872 and 1873, great numbers of St. Helenians immigrated to the Cape and other South African port cities. Economic downturns on the island encouraged farmers, artisans, and their families to make their way to South Africa via the Atlantic.[19] Newspapers from the island noted that "a good many St. Helen people . . . have emigrated to the Cape of Good Hope and many more are following."[20] These immigrants emerged in the historical record through newspapers and ship manifests that documented the journey of St. Helenians to South Africa. Although St. Helenians did not appear as a separate category in the census, both South African citizens and officials considered them "mixed-race" or "other." One South African newspaper described St. Helenians as people of "all colours— white, off-coloured, tawny, and several shades of black."[21] St. Helenians' varied phenotype placed them in an ambiguous racial position that could not be sorted by visible markers. The *Natal Mercury* reported that they were constantly compared to both Kafirs and Coolies (a pejorative term for Indians). At times, South Africans confused St. Helenians for English-speaking West Coast Africans, who also had a Cape presence and often tried to pass for St. Helenians. This inability to categorize St. Helenians led them to be considered a "little better than the native Kafir and on par with the Coolie."[22] This confusion is perhaps best exemplified by world-renowned South African singer Sathima Benjamin, whose grandmother protested being categorized as Coloured by a census taker. According to Benjamin, her grandmother refused to "sign away her identity" because she insisted that she was St. Helenian, and the census taker remarked, "There are no St. Helenians anymore, only Coloureds."[23] Many St. Helenians articulated a similar strong allegiance to St. Helenian identity throughout the nineteenth century and well into the twentieth century, as evinced by Benjamin's story. In the process, however, St. Helenian solidarity grew complicated by a growing cultural fusion and belonging that occurred between St. Helenians and other groups who were increasingly considered Coloured.

People who became classified as "mixed-race" and "other" also made their way to South Africa by sea. This included retired West Africans who had once served with the British Royal Navy, former slaves, fishers, whalers, and port workers, many of whom had originated from the Indonesian- and Swahili-speaking coastlines. Others, especially the Black sailors among them, had deserted American ships.

Although there were few African Americans in number, they had a profound impact on Black identity in South Africa. While African Americans were not fully recognized in the colonial censuses, their presence was acknowledged in other ways. Black sailors involved in various expeditions often landed on the shores of the Cape. As early as 1862, the Capetonians noted that African American sailors were on board the Confederate steamer *Alabama* that captured a Union ship in Table Bay.[24] Thirty years later, African Americans visited the Cape Colony yet again. This time the Orpheus McAdoo Virginia Jubilee Singers made their way to Kimberly in 1890. The singers were among the most well-known African Americans to travel to South Africa. Other Americans also pepper the historical record, including Horatio Scott, who migrated to Kimberly during the diamond rush.[25] John Ross was another American who lived and worked on the reef in the late nineteenth century. He was infamously known for accusing the South African government of assault when a white police officer mistakenly cited him for "impudence" and brutally beat him.[26] Other African Americans living in South Africa were activists, such as James King and J. G. Gumbs, both members of the Industrial and Commercial Workers' Union of Africa, which was affiliated with the Universal Negro Improvement Association.[27] The largest group of Black Americans in South Africa, however, was Christian missionaries.[28] Their goal, much like that of earlier European missionaries, was to proselytize and civilize their Native brethren. They included figures such as C. S. Morris of the African Methodist Episcopal Church and Caribbean American Kenneth Spooner of the Pentecostal Holiness Church.[29]

The government defined African Americans as Coloureds under their limited racial taxonomy, but American Blacks were constantly mistaken for Native Africans. Historian Robert Trent Vinson indicates that the American consulate insisted that all American citizenship be recognized on South African soil regardless of race. In fact, the South African government recognized African Americans as "honorary white citizens" to ensure that their phenotype did not keep them from enjoying their American privilege.[30] Often, this national distinction allowed African Americans to circumvent South Africa's race laws in ways that Blacks across the colonies could not access.[31] Despite pride in their own heritage, some West Indian immigrants strove to obtain the same legal privileges as their African American counterparts by taking on an African American identity. Indeed, many English-speaking Blacks were subsumed under this category. The system was even more complicated for West Indian mariners who entered South Africa by way of the United States. For instance, sailors such as Sydney Wilson, Peter Benjamin, and Will Brathwaith, all of whom had worked aboard African American explorer and millionaire Harry Dean's ship the *Pedro Gorino*, were often seen as American despite a migratory path that took them outside of the British colonies.[32] There were always exceptions and important complications. Henry Sylvester Williams, a young Trinidadian barrister, headed to South Africa with ironic hope that South Africa might serve as the Black utopia. In Cape Town, he lived and worked among those classified as Coloureds before leaving the country for London, where he organized the Pan-African Conference of 1900 often attributed to W. E. B. DuBois, who attended the conference. Perhaps Williams's education and profession protected him. However, for most English-speaking Blacks, American citizenship safeguarded them in strange ways from the racialized pitfalls of the country's legal system.

Regardless of these efforts, all English-speaking foreign Blacks were treated as "Coloureds"; subsequently, many of them came to view themselves as such. This becomes clearer in the twentieth century with figures such as newspaper editor F. Z. Peregrino from the Gold Coast (present-day Ghana). Peregrino moved to South Africa in 1900 and quickly established the *South African Spectator*. The newspaper's primary objective was to encourage "race pride," especially "in the interest of Coloured people."[33] Peregrino also established the Coloured People's Vigilance Society, which aimed to foster relationships among non-Europeans in South Africa. Peregrino, who at one time insisted that Coloureds refer to themselves as "negro," lived alongside people such as Wilson, Benjamin, and Brathwaith in the Coloured section of Cape Town.[34] Historian Susan Peberdy suggests that European immigrants who traveled to South Africa were "clandestine immigrants" and often easily integrated into South African society.[35] Similarly, black immigrants had clandestine identities, and many of them were simply considered Coloured. These English-speaking foreign Blacks, much like African Americans and West Indians, were considered Coloured by law, an argument also underscored by scholar Victoria J. Collis-Buthelezi.[36] And yet, legal sameness did not inhibit African Americans, West Indians, and West Africans from preserving their respective cultural and religious expressions. However, much the British colonial government in the Cape masked these differences through classification.

These migratory histories of St. Helenians, African Americans, and West Africans becoming "mixed race," "other," and eventually Coloured offers an alternative narrative to the popularly accepted history of Coloureds. In fact, stories of St. Helenians and African Americans also complicate the way sea travel has been racialized and gendered. Travel, in particular sea travel, has often been connected to European expansion and navigation. The history of Black sea travel has largely been limited to histories of slavery; only recently have Black mariners been added to this historiography. Very rarely do scholars fully enunciate the ways rootedness is read as immobility rather than stability. Rootedness is conflated with stagnancy and indigence.[37] In many ways, the historical narratives of stasis often pathologize people of color, particularly Africans, whose movement away from the continent is predominantly characterized as one that was authorized, guided, and controlled by Europeans. This has reinforced the notion that Africa is isolated and primitive. Coloured mobility, on the other hand, demonstrates the agency that people of color exhibited as they searched for employment, conducted their own philanthropic efforts, and seized entrepreneurial opportunities in the late nineteenth and early twentieth centuries. Evidence of sea travel implies that Coloureds actively engaged the world around them.

THE CENSUS IN SOUTHERN AFRICAN COLONIES

The rest of the colonies of modern South Africa did not consistently classify and enumerate their populations. The Orange Free State held censuses only in 1880 and 1890, and in both of these censuses the colonial officials were careful to make binary distinctions only between Europeans and Coloureds. In this context, Coloureds represented all non-European people. There were no records of mixed-race, other, or Coloured people in these censuses. It is important to note, however, that Orange Free State officials used the distinction between Europeans and Coloureds to indicate which part of the population was considered citizens and which was noncitizens. In the South African Republic (later known as the Transvaal), the census only kept account of the European population. Natal, on the other hand, had its first census in 1891, in which it estimated only the Indigenous population. While there is no full account of the mixed-race, other, Coloured, or Indian population in the census, historians, particularly those interested in Indian history, have been able to determine the size of the Indian population in Natal.

The majority of South Africa's Indian population would arrive on South African shores after 1860. As soon as indentured labor was introduced in Natal, many Indians would come to South Africa.[38] According to historian Maureen Swan, Indian men, women, and children were brought to South Africa on five-year labor contracts to work on sugar plantations in Natal.[39] At the end of their contracts, laborers could exchange their "free passage" home for a grant of the Crown land.[40] More than half of the 152,182 Indian indentured servants (from 1860 to 1911) remained in South Africa.[41] Before colonies fully disaggregated the Indians from the "mixed-race" and "other" categories, these Indians were lumped in with Coloureds. Immigrants from India and Mauritius, made up of elites and professionals who could pay their fare to South Africa and were referred to as passenger immigrants, also fell under the category "other."[42] However, as Indians grew in number and gained material success, colonial officials authored legislation that would limit Indian emigration to South Africa.

Equally relevant to this discussion is the inclusion of mixed-race people as European in Natal's census. In this instance, the "Coloured" classification was very narrowly constructed from the other subcategory of Asian or Indian. This subcategory was more subjectively based on phenotype, physical features, complexion, and perhaps even language (given the importance of language in separating "the true mixed race" from Indian). It was also likely that the inclusion of mixed race under the category of European seemed to be more about cultural assimilation than visible or physical evidence of non-European blood. It is imperative to keep in mind that the number of mixed-race people in this region was significantly smaller than in the Cape. Nevertheless, the inclusion of Indians as a subcategory of "mixed-race/other" and the incorporation of Coloureds as Europeans in the Natal census demonstrate the conflicting terrain of Coloured identity during the nineteenth century and makes evident the permeability of the color line in South Africa.[43]

UNIFIED RACE MAKING

Racial definitions remained in flux at the turn of the century, before the unification of South Africa. All four colonies used a census to identify, classify, and enumerate members of their populations. The racial categories commonly represented in the 1904 censuses were Europeans, Natives, and mixed populations. Asians also appeared in the census in all colonies except the Orange River Colony, which did not distinguish Asians from the mixed population.[44] While the terms "Europeans" and "Natives" were fairly established, the government wrestled to define the category of "mixed-race and other." For a long time, this category had included multiracial populations with African, European, and Asian ancestry. As previously mentioned, it even included English-speaking people of color. Yet, at the turn of the century the Asian population was officially separated from the "mixed-race and other" category. This decision was likely made because of the Indian and Malaysian colonial governments' commitment to account for their own populations around the world.[45] As a result, colonial officials in South Africa attached new subcategories to the term "Asian," which referred to Indians, Chinese, Syrians, and Malays. All of these groups were no longer considered "mixed-race and other." The "Cape Malays" were also included in this group. However, they would return under the category of Coloured in the near future, while the Asian category would remain separate and stable.

By the turn of the twentieth century, the Cape colonial government began to define the groups that were considered mixed race or Coloured. This move reflected the growing pressures for the colonial governments throughout the region to reach a consensus regarding the racial categories that would be officially recognized under the Union of South Africa. For the first time, colonies officially and explicitly defined "mixed-race and other" to include the following groups: (mixed) Natives, American (coloreds), and islanders.[46] The 1904 census is also one of the first instances when the government officially recognized the presence of "American coloreds" and "islanders," even though they had traveled to the region for decades. "Islanders" referred to various ethnic groups from the South Atlantic, such as the St. Helenian immigrants, but also included "West Indians" from the Caribbean. Even with more specificity, those people considered "mixed-race and other" always seemed dislocated from the South African racial terrain as the colonial government had structured it. Furthermore, while classification of race abounded, even colonial agents themselves did not consistently implement these state-prescribed distinctions.

A new system of racial classification was implemented in the Union of South Africa in 1910. As a barrage of racially restrictive and discriminatory laws emerged, the new government was not nearly as attentive to the complexities of race and ethnicity in census enumeration.[47] Instead, it worked to find a consensus among the former colonies that formed the new Union of South Africa. The government was constantly compromising with the former British and Afrikaner colonial governments in an attempt to reach a consensus. As a result, the complex classification was simplified not only for the sake of uniformity but also, more importantly, in the interest of instituting a simple and effective racial hierarchy. In the end, the government created three categories of racial enumeration: European/white, Native, and mixed/other Coloured, the same racial categories that had once reigned in the early colonies. These simplistic renderings of race reflected an empire-wide standardization of census practices.[48] These changes would actually engender pan-ethnic allegiance among Coloureds and would do the same among African Natives.

Mixed identity was simplified, even though the complex contours of who would be included in this group remained. For instance, Hottentots were reincorporated as Coloured, as they once had been in the 1875 Cape census. The logic behind this taxonomic change was to eliminate the seemingly superfluous distinction that had been made between Hottentots, Coloureds, and Natives. Further, government officials noted that pure-blooded Hottentots were rapidly declining.[49] The officials pejoratively declared that Hottentots' yellow skin color coincided with Coloured characteristics and therefore justified their Coloured classification. Indians, on the other hand, were once again categorized as mixed-race/other.

Between 1918 and 1941, the census recorded only the European population. The South African Act of 1909 had required a quinquennial census to determine the distribution of seats in the House of Assembly, an office that could be held only by Europeans. Therefore, Europeans were the only group enumerated in the 1918, 1926, 1931, and 1941 censuses. To be sure, European identity was fraught with its own set of problems, at least on a smaller scale. This was first exemplified in the nineteenth century when the South African Republic had determined European identity by barring anyone who had more than one-sixteenth non-European blood.[50] Even earlier, the Natal 1904 census had actually included Coloureds among Europeans. By 1911 and the Union of South Africa 's ratification, these issues had been mostly cleared up, and European identity hinged only on having "European descent."[51] In 1921, government officials insisted that to be considered European one must be of "purely European descent." If someone appeared European and presented himself or herself as such, then he or she would be considered European.[52]

There were, however, a few instances in which Europeans were reclassified as other races. One prominent example was that of Sandra Laing, who was born white (Afrikaner) and later reclassified as Coloured in 1955 as her phenotype appeared to darken. She was reclassified as white in 1967 when Population Registration Amendment Act No. 64 claimed that a child of two white parents could not be classified as any race other than white.[53] These echoed provisions in the Cape Colony that allowed Black elites in the nineteenth century to experience the elasticity of the law when their education, English-language facility, and property acquisition allowed them to be reclassified as white. While the South African government would always wrestle with definitions of race, identity would grow increasingly rigid in the mid-twentieth century under a new government regime.

COLONIALISM BY ANOTHER NAME

The National Party, the victors of South Africa's 1948 election, was the first to officially define and implement a system of racial categorization nationwide. In 1921 the minister of mines, Patrick Duncan, had unsuccessfully proposed that the government create a national population registry. Four-teen years later, the Parliamentary Select Committee made a similar pro-posal.[54] It would take another fifteen years before their vision would come to fruition, with the implementation of the Population Registration Act of 1950. The act fulfilled part of the National Party's campaign promises to secure white rule in a country where Blacks were the majority. The Pop-ulation Registration Act established a uniform definition of race and si-multaneously linked it to a governing racial hierarchy, with Blacks as the subordinate race. The state used this legislation and a string of statutes that followed to inject what the legal scholar Deborah Posel refers to as a "commonsense" racial rubric. The Population Registration Act made each South African "a white person, a coloured person, or a Native" overnight. Not only did it racially define them,[55] but they were also registered and were recorded in a national population registry and required to carry docu-mentation with their racial identity.[56] Now a racialized vocabulary extended beyond common parlance and was officially recognized. Posel suggests that through the implementation of the Population Registration Act, the Na-tional Party not only normalized race but also simultaneously connected it to social, economic, and political standing. This legislation's rigid set of criteria provided a racial index for government officials that quickly became accessible to ordinary citizens. In fact, ordinary citizens began to appropri-ate this nomenclature, and the illusive concept of race became a tangible category of difference in the everyday life of South African society.

Three racial categories governed the South African racial landscape under the Population Registration Act of 1950: white, Coloured, and Na-tive. In theory, the act would immediately supersede all legislation that once pertained to race even if the statutes still existed in the books. In prac-tice, however, it would take substantial time to realign all the racial statutes. Government officials such as magistrates and judges were still able to de-fine whiteness and Europeanness without much legislative guidance. They had primarily determined European identity through imprecise physi-cal or social markers. Important politicians such as future prime minister Hendrik French Verwoerd openly championed the notion that race could not be biologically determined. His training and experience as a sociolo-gist at Stellenbosch University had informed his opinion that Caucasian identity was characterized by advanced cultural civilization rather than an-cestry.[57] These terms would guard many Afrikaners from the embarrass-ment of having to disclose their non-European ancestry. Therefore, a white citizen was described in the Population Registration Act as someone "who in appearance is, or who is generally accepted as, a white person."[58] Under this law, whiteness was visibly evident and socially reinforced.[59] This generally made racial divisions, especially those between Europeans and non-Europeans, quite clear.

Non-European identity, particularly the distinction between Natives and Coloureds, however, was unclear and practically ungovernable. In fact, state officials recognized that to govern, "it would be impossible to determine with any certainty which people are natives and which people are Coloureds."[60] These distinctions would never be definable. In fact, government officials knew that it would be nothing short of an "uneconomical waste of time and money to try . . . to determine a person's race with precision." For practical reasons, they resorted to a rudimentary racial rubric. Natives were described as people "of any aboriginal race or tribe of Africa."[61] Coloured identity, on the other hand, was malleable. The government stated that "a coloured person is a person who is not a white person nor a native."[62] These exclusionary terms meant that Coloured identity operated in comparison to white and Black identity. This lack of defined characteristics perpetuated the popular myth that Coloureds had no distinct culture. Legally, it presented a great number of obstacles. Without any identifiable characteristics, it represented an intermediary position, what historian Mohammed Adhikari calls a "buffer between whites and blacks."[63] Depending on one's phenotype, certain Coloureds were able to build an identity as either a white or a Black person. In some cases, passing for white could potentially earn them political and economic advantage, while claiming a Black identity could be a disadvantage.[64] It also meant that based on physical characteristics alone, people in the same family could clandestinely pass for white but be designated Coloured or Black. The subjective means by which race was determined could potentially divide families, friends, and communities based solely on appearance.

Racial designations became a site of government authority and surveillance. In fact, this attempt to catalog all South African citizens along racial lines set the administrative tenure of the National Party regime. The Population Registration Act of 1950 was in no small measure the introduction of a system of racial scrutiny that would become known as apartheid. According to Posel, it demonstrated the National Party's commitment to combating white fears of "die swart gevaar [the black menace]."[65] During the 1948 election, one of the dominating issues was the fear that Blacks could and would engulf cities. The National Party had successfully countered these fears by proclaiming the importance of "racial purity" through

the Population Registration Act.[66] Notions of white supremacy continued to reign over political discussions even after the 1948 election.[67] One
speaker declared, "We should have one aim and purpose . . . the preserva-
tion of white civilisation in South Africa."[68] The Population Registration
Act made good on the National Party's election promises to fully establish,
protect, and maintain white supremacy by establishing "jackal-proof fenc-
ing" between the races.[69] In short, the government's mission was to establish a sharp demarcation between races that would ensure racial order and
stability.[70] Racial identity would no longer be a site of confusing conflict
or contest especially among Coloureds, who had elided these divisions in
the past. Coloured identity, much like the other identities, would take on a
superficially stable meaning under the segregationist regime insofar as this
stability and the coherence of the term "Coloured" rests on destabilizing
ethnic difference. The Population Registration Act of 1950 signaled monu-
mental change: the crystallization of a South African racial order.[71] These
documents reflect the confluence of cultural, ethnic and even national
identities that comprised Coloured identity over time, making it clear
that Coloured identity could not accurately be defined solely in relation to
white and Black identities. Even though the government hoped to instill a
level of distance and separation between Coloureds and Blacks, there were
social, cultural, and political overlaps that pervaded these racial divisions.
In fact, many Coloureds in the nineteenth century aligned themselves with
Blacks in an effort to combat the prejudice, discrimination, and racism that
also affected them. These coalitions come to light in the late nineteenth-
century Christian secessionist movement in which Black and Coloured
clergy seceded from European-run missionary churches. This movement,
known as the Ethiopian movement, has been narrowly depicted as driven
solely by Black clergy. In what follows, I uncover Coloured contributions
in the Ethiopian movement that thus far have been underexplored.

TWO

Faith of Our Fathers

The Ethiopian Movement and
African Identities

My father is a good storyteller. One story he told me transformed my understanding of Ethiopianism in South Africa and its leader, Maake Mangena Mokone, as well as my own positionality in pursuing this research on religious agency. Ethiopianism was a nineteenth-century secessionist movement led by African evangelists from mainline Protestant churches. Historians have attributed Ethiopianism to Mokone because in 1892 he wrote a fourteen-point letter-of-resignation-turned-manifesto that inspired African Christians to leave European-led denominations. One of the most poignant parts of Mokone's letter—his statement that segregation within the churches "shows that we can't be brothers"—prompted his resignation from the Wesleyan Society. For many years, scholars such as Bengt Sundkler, George Shepperson, George Wallace Mills, Christopher Saunders, J. Chirenje Mutero, Robert R. Edgar, Richard Elphick, James T. Campbell, Elizabeth Elbourne, Philippe Denis, and Graham Duncan have pieced together the histories of Ethiopianism.[1] This scholarship puts into perspective the stakes of the rupture, from the vocational limitations to access to church finances, and explains shifts of power within the missionary enterprise in South Africa. Over time, these scholars wrestled through tensions in the motivation of the movement—the place of politics within the movement—and examined the transnational networks forged by African Christians.[2]

By drawing from an archive that stretches beyond South Africa to the United States, Kenya, and Zimbabwe and with attention to influences from the Caribbean, my understanding of Ethiopianism is distinct. I veer away from categorizing it simply as a movement that was a powerful yet undeveloped plan for African ministers to eschew disciplinary action, secure institutional control, and, of course, rise in professional stature.[3] Nor do I comprehend it as a springboard for African sociomobility, motivated by personal circumstances.[4] Yet, these historians' deep archival work has offered me an understanding of the way African church leaders presented their grievances, making them legible to the missionaries they had long served with little acknowledgment and compensation.[5] Their scholarship relied on missionary diaries, church papers, and even Mokone's letter that had vanished from the archive long ago.

When I told my father these histories of Ethiopianism after an archival trip, he responded by telling me a story about Maake Mangena Mokone's baptism. My father told me that Mangena's father had resisted Christian conversion because it required renaming his son with "a Christian name, a process that rendered him [Mangena] bereft of ancestral guide."[6] Empathizing with Mangena's father, my father noted that renaming Mangena undermined the "the deeply entrenched notion in [southern] African culture that each person's name proceeds them and seals their fate."[7] The terms of Christian conversion stripped Mangena of both identity and legacy. Critical to my father's retelling of the story was the meaning of Mokone's name, Maake, which was actually a family surname meaning "warrior."[8] When Mangena's father eventually allowed his son to be baptized, he insisted that his son keep his name. Family legend has it that Mangena's father raised his spear when he heard the missionaries say "Maake" as they baptized his son. Mangena's father had not heard that the church had also bestowed his son with another name: Jonathan. Still, Mangena insisted on using his name Maake.

Finally, my father concluded the story by pointing to Mangena's "new surname," Mokone, stating that "had the missionaries been aware that the name Mokone derived from family totem, they might have cringed; the ancestors outwitted them all." I wondered about this story, my father's conclusion, and this textured bit of history left out of the archives. When I returned to it years later, I finally made the full connection that Maake Mangena [Jonathan] Mokone was my father's namesake (and that I stood within this familial genealogy I studied). When I queried his subtlety, he said he trusted that even in sifting through the archives, I might consider who is bearing witness (Tshepo) and that the purpose of my own name, meaning "hope," would be guide enough to rescue portions of this story resting outside of the documents. Read and heard together, these scattered archives raise questions about (un)belonging, Ethiopianism as refuge, and its intersection with a more expansive definition of what it means to be African. Mangena, like his father, raised his spear in battle, but also critical to the history is who would heed the call and how they chose to define religiosity on their own terms.

The aim of Ethiopianism seemed simple. The late nineteenth-century movement was about prominent African evangelists such as Nstikana ka Gaba, Nehemiah Tile, and Maake Mangena Mokone establishing their own churches independent from European missionaries in South Africa. It was an attempt to gain religious autonomy, one of the only forms of freedom accessible to Africans in an increasingly racialized society. This chapter explores Ethiopianism as a project of religious liberation that was complicated by not only race but also ethnicity. By paying special attention to the ways ethnicity shaped African clergy, especially among those considered Coloured, the chapter examines the emergence of this racialized battle between Black church leadership and white missionaries. This focus on African ethnicities suggests that this movement was possible only because African leadership united across ethnicities to include Sotho/Tswanas, Xhosas, Zulus, Tsongas, Ndebeles, and Coloureds, among others. These clergy understood the shifting racialization of Coloured identity within the legal realm but did not accept it as true. Instead, the Black clergy regarded Coloureds as part of an African brotherhood of church leaders that did not undermine Black spiritual solidarity. The chapter also highlights how cross-ethnic solidarity among African church leaders ignited hysteria in which missionaries to South Africa worried that Ethiopianism might incite a revolt much like the Haitian Revolution. This geography of hysteria illuminates the circulating discourse of fear across the Atlantic among white settlers. From the United States to the Caribbean to South Africa, racial self-determination cemented memories of violence among whites.

Most historians begin the history of Ethiopianism by focusing on some of the most prominent clergy: Reverend Nehemiah Tile and Reverend

Maake Mangena Mokone, the progenitors of Ethiopianism. Tile is best known for establishing the Thembu Church in 1872, the first church established by an African, what scholars call an African-initiated church (AIC). This church, perhaps more so than others, openly resisted efforts to colonize the Thembu people in the Eastern Cape. Twenty years later in 1892, Mokone established the Ethiopian Church after leaving the Wesleyan Methodist Society; this church served as the main organ of the movement early on. Mokone's fourteen-point letter-of-resignation-turned-manifesto inspired many African leaders to leave their missionary stations. His letter and subsequent resignation began the movement. Leaders such as Tile and Mokone have become critical vectors for understanding the ways African Christians made an autonomous place for themselves within South African churches. However, these stories obfuscate some earlier organizing efforts for religious agency among African Christians that occurred decades before Tile and Mokone even began their own ministries. It is this longer contextual history that I turn to next.

THE EARLY GROUNDWORK FOR ETHIOPIANISM

African Christians' collective departure from European-run churches and their establishment of their own churches truly laid the foundations of the Ethiopian movement. In 1839, about one thousand former slaves broke ties with the Presbyterian Church in the Cape Province. This is very likely the first documented secession from European-run missionary churches in South Africa. Presbyterian Church records show that these ex-slaves, who had been integrated into South African society as Coloureds, established an independent congregation with the help of a German Lutheran minister, Reverend Georg Stegmann, who also left the church.[9] Although this group of about fifty ex-slaves did not submit a formal letter of resignation, they did sign their names on a document labeled "abandoned Coloured members."[10] These members simply could have left the Presbyterian Church as many before them and even after them had done. However, signing this letter of resignation was a documented collective act in which former slaves imagined a new religious destiny beyond the Presbyterian Church. It was a clear pronouncement from their congregation that also reflected on the denomination. But because the resignation coincided with their freedom, resigning from a European-run missionary church that was not organized around their own religious needs both marked their status as free people and freed them from spiritual bondage. These former slaves wanted this moment documented for posterity. They wanted their act of defiance from mission churches to be part of the church's written record. And further, these former slaves also wanted it known that they would create their own church. Fifteen years later in 1854 another group of former slaves also established their own church, perhaps another precursor to the freedom movements to come. The historical record doesn't say much about either of these groups. Rather, what is emphasized is their racial status and classification. In both instances, the African congregants are described as newly freed slaves whom church officials disparagingly label as Coloured, which seemed to distance them from the Ethiopian movement.

These two moments shift our understanding of the Ethiopian movement. First, the moments point to a collective discontent that African Christians expressed well before the late nineteenth century, when most scholars believe Ethiopianism began. By taking a closer look at how these stories affect the periodization, we see that the movement began under the helm of those who would be deemed Coloured in the mid-nineteenth century rather than the late nineteenth century. And while Coloured identity is ethnically expansive, in both of these instances the congregations were all composed of people who were once enslaved. This suggests that their oppressive existence motivated a deliberate act of freedom from the only institution African people were tied down to under slavery. Their resignations were also a collaborative decision that was very likely discussed and planned among church parishioners rather than solely envisioned by the individualized desires of a church leader.

African laity were critical facilitators of this Black Christian movement, not merely ancillary figures. They not only imagined but also created a religious space to exercise power and authority. Further, as Africans built their own autonomous institutions, beginning with the church, their efforts demonstrate the ways Africans negotiated as well as leveraged their multiethnic and multiracial identities to justify their own ecclesiastical self-governance in a society that was becoming increasingly racialized. Perhaps it was the freed slaves who inspired the first set of African clergy to submit letters of resignation. By the time the Ethiopian movement gained momentum with the well-known resignation of Mokone, African clergy had found ways to articulate their grievances through formal letters of resignation rather than simply the signatures of formerly enslaved people. Before the Ethiopian movement officially began, these congregations led the struggle for religious control. In fact, African laity, not African clergy, were the first to secede from mission churches. Their efforts laid the groundwork for Ethiopianism. Perhaps they, like Krotoa, recognized the unspoken ways that the church controlled them—from baptism to lifestyle to the institution itself—and wanted true freedom.

REVEREND MANGENA MAAKE MOKONE: A CENTRAL FIGURE IN ETHIOPIANISM

Ethiopianism was marked by the rapid resignation of church leaders from the Wesleyan Methodist Missionary Society, the Berlin Lutherans, the Paris Evangelicals, the Moravians, the Anglican Church of the Province, and the London Missionary Society, among many other mission churches. Hundreds of clergymen and evangelists left. Most letters of resignation confronted issues of unequal mission assignments, low wages, poor living conditions, and limited training opportunities as reasons for leaving European-run churches. Racism loomed large in these discussions of inequality. The historiography of Ethiopianism does not fully engage the role of race or ethnicity beyond acknowledging the ways this movement over church control was racialized. The movement was described through a white/Black racial binary that has also been referred to as a division between Europeans and Africans or, more broadly, between Europeans and non-Europeans. The overwhelming focus on white missionaries and Black leadership has often obfuscated the complicated African identities of the clergy. This white/Black binary not only is unique to describing the Ethiopian movement but also serves to uphold a larger metanarrative of white oppression and Black resistance in South African history. Therefore, to identify groups that fall out of this racial and ethnic purview is to question the fixed ways race has functioned in the historiography. To acknowledge Coloured identity would require unpacking the colonial term "Coloured" within the context of this church history. It would also demonstrate its legal arbitrariness, as its definition changed over time, while simultaneously showing that Coloureds experienced forms of oppression similar to oppression other Africans experienced.

Even without always making these ethnic distinctions, Mokone's letter of resignation demonstrated the many forms of discrimination that African leaders faced. Mokone is most famous for his letter of resignation, a detailed discussion of the professional and personal indignities non-European clergymen experienced in mission churches.[11] He complained that in non-European district meetings, the church required a white chairman and secretary and that, to make matters worse, their word was considered infallible. Beyond his issues with white supervision, he stated that non-European district meetings were "more or less barbaric."[12] Furthermore, non-European clergy were not even given district minutes or the denomination's annual report, and ordained Native ministers were stripped of some of their most sacred rights, from serving communion to officiating over weddings. They were never "placed in a position of trust." Mokone discussed the clergy's deplorable living conditions, lower salaries, smaller family stipends, and inaccessibility to church resources as compared to his white colleagues. To add insult to injury, non-European clergy were not treated with authority or respect despite their clerical standing and labor. Mokone declared that from baptisms to weddings, white clergy were nowhere to be found. Worse yet, Mokone asserted, they "don't even know the members of their circuits." Mokone's demands made clear that these grievances extended to the larger church. He concluded his letter with the following questions: "Where is Justice? Where is brotherly love? Where is the Christian sympathy? God in heaven is a witness to all these wrongs."[13] He insisted, "No Native minister is honoured among the white brethren. . . . This [racial] separation shows that we can't be brothers."[14] These infamous words suggested that racial separation in the church contradicted the tenets of brotherly love that were integral to Christianity. It is this hypocrisy that propelled Mokone to action.

Mokone's letter inspired African clergymen. They followed suit and broke away from their own denominations, quickly becoming a movement of Christian secession. Nevertheless, many of these clergy still remained dedicated to Christianity on the African continent. They had to find creative ways to practice their vocation outside of the mission churches they had actively built. Their first objective was to secure their own religious institutions. Mokone led the way. As I mentioned, he established the first church initiated and governed by Native clergy, the AICS.[15] Mokone called it the Ethiopian Church, which reflected its African origins. Ancient Hebrews referred to Africa as "Cush" or sometimes "Ethiopia." Mokone was inspired by the nation-state of Ethiopia itself and the favor it was shown in both the scriptures and politics. The most cited reference to Ethiopia is Psalms 68:31: "Princes shall come out of Egypt and Ethiopia shall stretch her hand unto God."[16] In this scripture, King David claimed that Ethiopia would submit only to the power of God. By the late nineteenth century, this prophecy materialized right before Mokone's very eyes as Ethiopia maintained its sovereignty from European forces through their victory over the Italians at the Battle of Adwa. With spiritual eyes, this victory was a divine confirmation of God's promises for African autonomy. In the context of the church, this scripture informed Mokone's demand for African control. The name of the church signaled the spiritual and political sovereignty Mokone and others reclaimed from European missionaries. Its reference to a collective group of people, a place, and a nation-state also drives home the idea that Mokone desperately wanted to reclaim African authority and sovereignty not just for himself but also for his people. This was never an individual exercise but rather one he did for his people. And therefore, the Ethiopian Church wasn't just a church that Mokone established for his own glory but instead became the center of a political movement for African Christians.

RACIALIZED ACCOUNTS OF ETHIOPIANISM

Ethiopianism sought to empower non-European clergymen in the church. Its leaders imagined their movement to be a racial awakening of sorts, but whites denigrated its objectives by calling it both a Black peril and a new danger.[17] The Natal governor called Ethiopianism the root of all "native disturbance."[18] Reverend Allen Lea, a missionary and scholar, also believed it to be a troubling movement. He vulgarly declared that Ethiopianism's preoccupation with "a black God, a black Saviour and black angels," was "unchristian and niggerish."[19] "This black peril," he continued, is a "foolish desire to get rid of the white man's control." These descriptions of Ethiopianism demonstrate the way a growing race consciousness among Africans stirred white anxieties even beyond the religious realm. Churches such as the Ethiopian Church were especially threatening because they functioned without government-sanctioned missionary supervision. Therefore, even worship services held in cramped quarters seemed particularly subversive. The movement's politicization pit European missionaries, church leaders, and government officials against Native ministers, evangelists, and even Christian lay leaders. However, these concerns did not deter Natives from supporting the Ethiopian movement even when missionaries and colonial officials launched an attack on their work. The Ethiopian movement was not only deemed unruly and sinister; it also became depicted (and continues to be described by many contemporary scholars) as a racial struggle between Black local church leaders and white foreign missionaries.

Those Africans who were identified as Coloureds also worked alongside other African clergymen such as Mokone to secure their ecclesiastical independence from European missionaries. Their absence from the historiography is a reflection of both the scarcity of sources and the underdevelopment of the study of Coloureds in South African history. Snippets of their presence can be found in the records of the South African Native Affairs Commission (SANAC) from 1903 to 1905 as British and Afrikaner government officials aimed to consolidate and create a new government. These years, sometimes called the era of reconstruction, were also a moment when the British and Afrikaners attempted to construct a normative whiteness governed by a tightening grip on African people, even those who were deemed pious. The commission, comprised of British and Afrikaner leaders who had served in their respective Native administrations, examined various aspects of non-European life in the colonies. Morality was at the forefront of their evaluation. They believed, much like their forefathers, that morality was tied to race. The commission based its conclusions, however misguided, on its members' readings of the interviews that took place with African clergy nationwide. And thus, the interview questions make clear, there was a need for the government to divide Africans in newly racialized ways. Government officials recognized Coloureds and Africans to be different people, and as such these legal divisions (as arbitrary as they were) are reflected in the ways they discussed African religious life, especially Ethiopianism. In fact, government officials included portions of the interview transcripts in their report. These findings provide an understanding of the racial and ethnic contours beyond what white officials simply called "the dark peril." The interviews illuminate the diversity and ethnic complexity among African clergy. And as such, the SANAC hearings reinforce the idea that Coloured identity was just another African ethnicity with its own distinct culture and language, among other ethnic experiences.

SANAC was created in preparation for a new government that sought to unite British and Afrikaner colonies. As the commissioning body examined policies from the Cape, Natal, Transvaal, and Orange River—the four colonies that would make up the Union of South Africa in 1910—they sought to reconcile a range of Native laws into a common policy. After two years of extensive research, SANAC amassed evidence from witnesses who "were either invited or in response to advertisement, proffered their evidence."[20] The final report represented the views of officials, politicians, ministers of religion, missionaries, lawyers, educators, landowners, farmers, traders, municipalities and other public bodies, employers of labor, and "natives of all classes." Their oral testimonies and written responses touched on all aspects of Native life from labor to land tenure. Above all things, however, the commissioning body concluded that "there is available no influence equal to that of religious belief" among Natives.[21] And so, African morality was at the center of Europeans' colonial project of both Christianity and civility.

SANAC launched an investigation on Christian morality to evaluate the reception of Christianity, assess its impact on Native civilization, and determine the effectiveness of the missionary enterprise in South Africa.[22] Concomitantly, SANAC examined the ensuing "church separatist movement," also known as the Ethiopian movement, which it believed was unraveling missionary endeavors and the progress toward Native civilization in South Africa. SANAC's findings reinforced popular sentiments that Ethiopianism was driven by Native clergymen's desires to undermine European missionaries even decades after the movement began. Most Europeans echoed these conceptions of the movement, calling it "anti-missionary," "anti-European," "anti-white," and pure and unadulterated "race-hatred."[23] These accusations about Ethiopianism and its followers permeated South African society. Missionaries in particular resented the secession because they lost some of their most respected and capable ministers alongside other African evangelists, church leaders, and whole congregations. To missionaries and now to SANAC members, these rapid resignations threatened the future of the church in South Africa.

Missionaries bitterly complained that African clergymen poached members of mission churches rather than converting non-Christians to join their ranks. Missionaries argued that Ethiopianists were "enlarging on racial differences" to recruit members to their churches.[24] For instance, Reverend J. White, the general superintendent of the Wesleyan Church in Southern Rhodesia, claimed that Ethiopian clergy would simply "disaffect people against their European ministers."[25] D. A. Hunter, a longtime member of the Free Church of Scotland and editor of the *Christian Express*, voiced the same concern when he angrily exclaimed, "I think the Ethiopians are sheep stealers."[26] It is their practice, echoed another minister, to "try to upset the work of European missionaries and clergy." Their battle cry, Reverend White continued, is "down with everything white." These angry declarations about membership loss expressed missionaries' concern about the ways Ethiopianism ultimately stifled European ministry.

Their greater concern was that they would lose control over Christianity throughout Africa.

Missionaries were in the midst of two battles. The first was over European secularization, and the second was to secure their position of authority in African churches. Consequently, missionaries recognized Ethiopianism as a personal attack on their very existence. Missionary anxiety and anger were rooted in their own displacement from the church. By the turn of the twentieth century European missionaries had Christianized Africa, but concurrently, "dechristization and secularization of much of western Europe" was underway.[27] Perhaps it was Europe's waning dedication to Christianity that inspired missionaries' evangelization in new geographic territories such as Africa and Asia. On the continent of Africa, church leaders were particularly successful in the South African mission field, where they obtained high conversion rates.[28] European missionaries very much wanted to retain this religious territory, especially as Ethiopianists threatened to take it over. Their motivation, however, was not solely African salvation. They feared that displacement in South Africa, or Africa as a whole, would render them entirely powerless. They would not have a base of Christian governance in Africa, much less Europe.

Missionaries' reactions to the movement reflected their own discomfort with their position in the Christian Church writ large. As the Ethiopian movement gained currency, South Africa, like Europe, started to seem like an unstable space for a thriving mission field, much less a host country for Europeans. Having witnessed the religious transitions in Europe brought on by industrialization and urbanization, missionaries feared similar changes in South Africa. This emotional context made it easy for missionaries to imagine African clergy's secession from mission churches to be a product of industrialization. Missionaries could reduce the Ethiopian movement to be solely about African clergy's economic mobility rather than larger issues of church governance and structure. Missionaries processed and understood this shift among African church leaders to be secular in nature, a reflection of a socioeconomic experience in which the missionary industry did not survive. Ultimately, Europeans struggled to maintain religious control and worried about the way political and social power as well as modernity reshaped Native and Coloured lives.

For Reverend White and Mr. E. H. Hogee, the Native magistrate and commissioner of Transvaal, the Ethiopian movement extended beyond the church. Hogee feared that its supporters would "drive the white man into the sea."[29] He had heard an Ethiopianist minister preach a sermon insisting that Natives "should not go and work as servants for the white man."[30] The minister demanded that Natives "let the white man rather go and work as servants for them." Mr. Hunter of the Free Church of Scotland recalled hearing a similar claim. "I have heard a native say: 'This is my country, these are my farms and mines; why are we not working them for ourselves and for our own benefit?'"[31] Mr. Shepstone, a member of the Transvaal Agriculture Union, also expressed his discomfort with the looming overthrow of the government by Ethiopian enthusiasts. In his testimony to SANAC, Shepstone nervously clamored that Ethiopianists wanted the entire country for themselves and were willing to launch a full-scale revolt. He testified, as Hogee had, that the movement's proponents were convinced "white people have no right here at all, that Africa is for the black race and not for the white."[32] Reverend James J. McClure reiterated this point, stating that "the movement was to give the native back the land, and in fact, to turn South Africa into a negro state."[33] Their objective, he asserted, was to "establish a South African Native State or a country purely of South African natives."[34] Panic and instability characterized these testimonies. Many whites believed that Black autonomy in the church could lead to Black political rule.

Elwin Neame, editor of the *Rand Daily Mail*, came to the most damning conclusion about the Ethiopian movement. Neame declared that Ethiopianism would transform South Africa into a modern-day Haiti. He vigorously asserted that "the rapidity with which a native church may descend, when free from white control, is shown by the horrors of Hayti."[35] Reaching back to the Haitian Revolution, Neame suggested that Ethiopianism stirred a deep fear among Europeans. On par with the Haitian Revolution, the Ethiopian movement frightened whites because they believed that this church conflict could erupt into a national crisis. This narrative of Black revolt recirculated along with the Ethiopian slogan "Africa for the Africans" during the interwar period, when Marcus Garvey's US-based movement gained popularity in South Africa.[36] But for now, these common themes of African governance and redemption were a local manifestation of race consciousness. These new religious expressions galvanized European anxieties over non-European autonomy and what they believed would be a threat on the racial order. Historians have favored European voices and their perceptions of the Ethiopian movement, even though Native and Coloured testimonies appeared alongside those of Europeans in SANAC's final report. These testimonies countered the tales of insurrection and disorder, but such non-European perspectives hardly figure into most historical accounts of the movement.

Non-European clergymen approached SANAC with a specific set of objectives. While gaining European respect was a goal for some, most hoped that by testifying at the commission and presenting themselves as a non-threatening entity, they might earn government recognition. As a result, most non-Europeans who testified were usually educated and respected clergy. When SANAC invited testimony from clergymen, many presented intensely researched statements of faith, constitutions, and other church documents.[37] This process of approval was an important step in establishing a new church recognized by the government, and most clergy thus tempered their responses to SANAC. With government recognition, their "religious independence" would no longer be associated with a "mischievous political agenda."[38] This, they hoped, would divorce them from the grandiose tales of insurrection that had long been associated with the Ethiopian movement.[39] State recognition also meant that churches would be scrutinized and harassed less.

As more clergymen left mission churches and created new AICS, government officials developed reservations about the religious legitimacy of these leaders and their churches. The evaluation process grew increasingly cumbersome as hundreds of AICS came into existence, quickly splintered, and in some cases became reconstituted under various names. Church leaders actively established many new religious institutions, all within five years of the first formal secession and the creation of the Ethiopian Church.[40] Many of them who led these churches—including the African Church, the Ethiopian Catholic Church of Zion, the Bapedi Lutheran Church, and the African Presbyterian Church, to name a few—testified at SANAC. Close to fifty clergy were Coloured.[41] Even Coloured ministers who could not appear before SANAC found their way into the written record in various ways. Some Coloured clergy provided the commission with a written account of their church history instead of making the arduous and expensive journey to testify. Others responded to a set of prescribed questions from SANAC.[42] A strong contingent of Coloured ministers from various parts of the nation pledged their support for the Ethiopian movement in their testimonies. While their religious and political activities are not all clearly documented, it becomes evident that some Coloured Christians used the church to advance their own political desires. For instance, the Coloured-led African Orthodox Church, which grew out of the Ethiopian Church, had strong ties to the Garvey movement. Their intention was to bring Garvey to South Africa and set up a Black empire. These political rumblings did not appear in the SANAC proceedings. However, Coloureds' decision to support Ethiopianism was undergirded by race consciousness and, in some instances, Black nationalism. Yet, all the while, SANAC and, subsequently, the larger European community wholly overlooked Coloured engagement in the Ethiopian movement.

As the commissioning body sought to understand the larger Ethiopian movement—its mission, its key leaders, its following, and its potential political impact—they suspected and speculated that African solidarity drove it. Colouredness was dislocated from ideas of racial rebellion in southern Africa. Thus, the commissioning body focused on collecting evidence on Native rather than Coloured churches. Church leaders from decades earlier such as Ntiskana and Nehemiah Tile relied on ethnic solidarity among Xhosa clans to propel their own forms of Indigenous Christianity.[43] A similar phenomenon of ethnic solidarity occurred with the Griquas (who were also categorized as Coloured) when they strove to create an independent nation and an affiliated church.[44] Historian Paul S. Landau charts this history when he shows that Christian Griqua in Kimberly, Cape Town, Fort Beaufort, Kokstad, and Mount Ayliff expressed similar aspirations to Ethiopianists mere decades before the Ethiopian movement. This history of the Griqua was not contextualized or even recalled when SANAC members evaluated the Ethiopian movement. They evoked the more dramatic religious and political histories of Ntiskana, Tile, the Haitian Revolution, and the Morant Bay Rebellion in Jamaica to cast Ethiopianism as a movement of radical Black Christians.

These colonial leaders fixated on the racial dimensions of the crises in Haiti and Jamaica rather than the complex entanglement of class, race, and ethnicity that galvanized the Ethiopian movement. Ethnicity, race, and, perhaps more poignantly, the trope of an unwieldy Black revolt became the primary lens through which to examine the religious changes taking place in South Africa. As a result, colonial authorities throughout the colonies and even SANAC officials diligently searched for points of racial solidarity to explain what they perceived as a direct response to anti-European sentiment rather than race consciousness. Some of the savvier colonial authorities also searched for intraethnic collaboration similar to the kind of Xhosa nationalism that had bolstered Nstikana's and Tile's ministries. These assumptions enabled colonial officials to overlook other types of alliances.

SANAC and the larger European community failed to fully recognize the diverse body of Christians who supported Ethiopianism. The Ethiopian movement was a pan-ethnic, cross-regional, and interracial religious movement in South Africa. This meant that Native clergymen with various ethnic origins—Pedi, Xhosa, and Zulu, to name a few—found common cause with other church leaders throughout the four colonies. Seemingly unlikely coalitions between Coloured and other African ministers also played a hand in the movement. Despite their ethnic differences, they shared common experiences of racial oppression in the church. They aired some of these grievances in their letters of resignation as they withdrew from mission churches. Such grievances ranged from desires for greater clerical control to concerns about low wages and allowances. However, most of their circumstances were directly related to their status as non-European clergy.[45] African ministers (including those identified as Coloured) coalesced as racially oppressed people; their complaints were a specific response to missionary authorities and the increasingly segregationist government and society. This pan-ethnic coalition that included those identified as Coloureds went largely unnoticed.

STRATEGIC DEPLOYMENT OF COLOURED IDENTITY

Careful examination of the commission's proceedings sheds light on those Africans likely identified as Coloured within the Ethiopian movement. From Reverend Thomas Maitland of the African Church to Reverend Peter Serfontein of the African Catholic Church, Coloured ministers from large and small congregations, whose settings spanned bustling towns to rural outposts, offered their testimony to SANAC.[46] They openly distinguished themselves from Natives by describing themselves as "Cape boys," "Creoles from Mauritius," "Cape coloureds," "Griqua," and very simply "coloured." These racial descriptions set them apart from Africans and reflected the ethnic, cultural, and national diversity among Coloureds themselves. In other words, this governmental term flattened the myriad and diverse African origins of these African clergy, and because the clergy knew these simplistic racial definitions, they leveraged the term as they sought to build their churches with government approval. The goal was government support so as to gain approval for their plans. It seems clear that many clergy used their various identities to their advantage even if they understood themselves to be African. Reverend Serfontein, who identified as Coloured, was one such example. In his testimony Serfontein explained, "My father was Creole from Mauritius. My mother was a Cape coloured woman."[47] Despite his own explanation of his diverse identity, SANAC and colonial authorities simply categorized him as Coloured. Serfontein's ancestral details, however, illuminated an extended cross-cultural network that was available to him that included the South Pacific as well as southern Africa. Similar networks could be found throughout his congregation. Serfontein had attracted a massive following of Coloured Christians in his branch of the African Catholic Church. Among them were Cape Coloureds, Mauritian Creoles, and even Indigenous Griquas and Khoisans, all of whose ethnic complexity was undercut by the classification of Coloured. But perhaps critical to this ethnic diversity was the lingua franca that often functioned among these African Christians: English. These ethnic divisions within churches were largely practical in that language often made one church Coloured and another church African in the government's eyes. This complex racial and national web was as common among Coloureds as it was among other Africans, but perhaps the distinction for Coloured Christians was that it often directly linked them with other subjects of the British Commonwealth. And while government officials failed to recognize or acknowledge these cultural markers, Coloureds were cognizant of ethnic and cultural differences among themselves and other African ethnic groups.

Some clergymen limited discussions about their ancestry in their testimonies by simply referring to themselves as Coloureds or, even more colloquially, as "Cape boys." Charles Demas of the African Methodist Episcopal (AME) Church described himself as a Cape boy but offered more detail about his identity. "My parents and grandmother were Coloured people and my grandfather was a Frenchman."[48] Reverend Thomas Maitland of the African Church in Germiston also called himself a Cape boy.[49] Reverend Brown, Maitland's colleague at the African Church, identified as Coloured too.[50] Peter August, L. P. Jacobue Smith, Joseph Rulph, and others also testified to being Coloured.[51] A. C. Van Diem, founder of the Christian Evangelist Mission Church, called himself a Cape boy, as did Andrew Piet Oliphant of the Apostolic Faith Mission Assembly of South Africa.[52] "Cape boy" embodied a particular type of racial politics; it was a geopolitical marker that distinguished them from other Coloureds. While the government might have ascribed a level of subordination to the idea of Cape boys, sometimes clergy were simply trying to jettison racial labels for geographical ones. Further, as historian Vivian Bickford-Smith has pointed out, the idea of the Cape Province was often connected to a space and politics of the Cape's (seemingly) liberal tradition.[53] To this end, ministers professed their Coloured identity for both its political and racial status if it might translate to their church's government approval.

SANAC records also reveal that entire AIC congregations were made up of Coloured Christians. These testimonies demonstrate that Coloureds were not simply present in these independent churches but were also constitutive of them. At the Christian Evangelist Mission Church, which was founded by A. C. Van Diem, for example, the membership was "equally divided between Cape Boys and Natives."[54] Diem eventually left the same church to establish the Griqua Independent Church, which the Griquas had been trying to create along with their own separate nation.[55] While they never officially established either an independent nation or an affiliated church, the Griqua Independent Church did attract Indigenous people in the Highveld region. Other testimonies briefly referenced Coloured congregations. Native clergyman Abel Mnsangu boasted that his Coloured colleague Charles White had attracted 365 Coloured members to his Bloemfontein church.[56] Another prominent minister, Reverend Davies Boksburg, also cultivated a substantial Coloured following.[57] It seems clear that these references to Coloureds were a type of political negotiating that church leaders drew on to appease government authority rather than an expression of racial consciousness that refused solidarity with Africans.

Many Coloured Christians flocked to Coloured-led churches such as those established by Diem, White, and Boksburg. For instance, the African Church had at least three Coloured pastors in the Johannesburg area, all of whom had amassed formidable Coloured followings.[58] The AME Church also attracted Coloured congregants because of its Coloured leadership. When African American bishop Henry Turner visited South Africa in the late nineteenth century, "about thirty native and coloured ministers were ordained at the conference held in Queenstown, Bloemfontein, and Pretoria."[59] These ministers drew hundreds of Coloured members, making it a foundational denomination among AICs in South Africa.[60] Coloureds also joined the African Mission Church, which, like the AME Church, was not exclusively Coloured. In fact, the sub-Native commissioner of Pretoria was well aware of the racial demographics of this church even though he referred to all of its members as Native. His rationale was that a Native was "any person male or female who is a member of the aboriginal race or tribe in Africa" and that this "shall further include any company or other body of persons corporate or unincorporated . . . who have a controlling interest therein are natives."[61] In other words, Coloured Christians who became full-fledged members of the church had "controlling interests" in church Native affairs. He said that because they had Native interests, they too should be presumed Native. Other colonial officials might also have diverted to this logic even as the government drew clearer distinctions between Coloureds and Natives, making it more difficult to parse out the Coloured support of the movement. Further, this suggests that many Coloureds (and white officials) recognized themselves as part of a larger Black community. In this case this community, which strove to gain religious freedom, meant that Coloureds were fighting white oppressive structures within the church by creating their own. While it is not clear that most people considered Coloureds to be Native during this period, this rationale could have made Coloured contributions to Ethiopianism indistinguishable from Native efforts and, as a result, largely overlooked.

Coloured clergymen demonstrated their ambivalence to the term "Coloured" when they leveraged different identities at different moments. For instance, when a SANAC official asked former Anglican priest Samuel Jacobus Brander about his identity, Brander simply stated, "My father is Mokhatla of this country but I was born in the Cape colony."[62] He did not indicate that he was Coloured. Instead, Brander emphasized only his paternal ancestry, which categorized him as Sotho. Brander claimed the Mokhatla people, who were Sotho royalty of Basutoland. Yet, he is known to have associated primarily with Coloureds of West Indian origin in the Cape Colony. Perhaps Brander mentioned the Cape as a type of regional identity marker, using the Cape's liberal tradition to indicate his social and political stature as a multicultural South African. Either way, it appears that Brander presented himself as a non-European of great importance and privilege. At SANAC, he positioned himself as a Native elite from Cape Town. However, his mother was African American, and by default Brander was classified as a Coloured South African.[63] By the turn of the century, the Cape had become the home of numerous English-speaking foreign Blacks, including African Americans. It was not uncommon for foreign Blacks from America or parts of the British Empire to settle in Cape port cities.[64] These English-speaking foreign Blacks and their descendants were classified as Coloured, and Brander was among them.

Brander did not mention his multicultural ancestry during his SANAC proceedings. He disclosed only his transnational ancestry in his own official church documents that circulated among his colleagues and parishioners. In "The Constitution and Canons of the Ethiopian Catholic Church of Zion" (Brander would finally lead the church), he described himself as an offspring of "a Mosuto of the Transvaal and . . . an American Negress."[65] This identity, rather than the one he'd provided during his SANAC testimony, more comprehensively reflected his racial and ethnic background. Beyond his own racial heritage, Brander regularly associated primarily with other Coloured ministers, a likely indicator of his self-identification. This was evident by the constitution's frontispiece, where Brander was pictured with the leading figures of his church who all had West Indian origins and were classified as Coloured. This stately photograph of Brander and his wife along with other clergymen graced the front of the church constitution and canons.

Brander's protégé, Daniel William Alexander, was among those photographed. Alexander, who was the vicar at Bertrams of Johannesburg in the Ethiopian Catholic Church of Zion at the time the photograph was taken, had an equally complex heritage that extended to the Caribbean.[66] He was also considered Coloured. Like Brander, Alexander had seceded from the Anglican mission church. He initially supported Brander's efforts to establish the Ethiopian Catholic Church of Zion before breaking away to establish his own church. These leaders strategically deployed their Coloured identity at key moments as they were testifying about their churches in order to gain government approval. This leveraging of African identities was a common practice as clergymen worked to obtain their own religious institutions.

Clergymen such as Brander also contributed to the idea that those classified as Coloureds understood themselves to be African when they leveraged different parts of their ancestry. The type of government documentation carried correlated to the racial classification of the clergyman. In some cases, clergymen chose not to identify their race before the commission. Sometimes all that appeared in SANAC's written record of non-European clergy were their surnames and church affiliations. In other instances, clergy shared their government-related documentation such as their pass status, an internal passport system that regulated and even segregated African movement. This information still offers a great deal about the non-European clergy and might have determined a clergyman's racial identity within colonial terms. Surnames that were not Nguni, Sotho, Shangaan-Tsonga, or Venda were likely of Afrikaans or English origins, the two main languages ascribed to Coloureds.[67] Surnames read alongside government documentation provide important information about clergy's racial status. SANAC documented both meticulously. The commission diligently recorded the type of documentation that all interviewed clergy-men were required to carry whether it was a pass, a certificate of exemption, or no documentation at all.

The South African pass system worked to control African people by separating populations, restricting Native travel, and racially managing urbanization to the benefit of white people. Colonial government required all Natives to carry documentation when they traveled throughout the colonies. The *British Parliamentary Papers* stated, "All natives domiciled in the Colonies shall be required to carry passes."[68] Passes were government-authorized labor papers reserved for travel. They were dispensed by or on behalf of European employers to grant their Native employees permission to travel. These passes helped missionaries control Native movement outside their prescribed residential or labor reserve. They worked to enforce racial order by regulating and limiting Native mobility.

Non-European clergymen had slightly different regulations. Their extensive mission work would often cause them to travel outside of their residential and labor reserves, beyond their primary mission station, to more remote substations to serve other Africans. Therefore, the government did not require all recognized non-European clergy to travel with passes, bestowing them with certificates of exemption.[69] Yet, a clergyman still had to present his certificate of exemption to government officials as he conducted his work. Coloureds, on the other hand, were fully exempt from carrying any documentation. Because they were not required to possess passes or certificates of exemption, it was easy to determine which clergy-men were Coloured. Coupled with a diligent examination of surnames, this information made it relatively simple to distinguish Coloureds from Native clergy. For instance, Reverends J. L. Mont and Fred Heighel of the African Church in Edenberg and Johannesburg, respectively, did not carry passes or certificates of exemption.[70] It is likely that both were identified as Coloured. The same circumstances applied to Reverend Le Roux of the African Christian Baptist Church of South Africa,[71] Reverend Stephen Hotsnaal of the African Congregational Church,[72] Reverend John George Philip of the Christian Apostolic Church in Zion of South Africa,[73] and many more. Even though most of these clergymen do not have substantial records they did appear in brief testimonies, and others were simply referenced in other hearings or church clerical rolls submitted to the commission. These records reveal moments in which Africans adopted Coloured identity to ensure certain privileges, especially those related to mobility.

Brander was among the first non-European clergy to secede from European-run mission churches. While leading historians such as James T. Campbell and George Frederickson have described the Ethiopian movement as a unique configuration of circumstances that led individual ministers to leave mission churches for various reasons, non-European clergymen openly coalesced around the notion of religious independence and self-determination. Historian Christopher Saunders understands these proclamations to reflect those very tenets.[74] While no evidence has shown that any non-European minister—identified as Coloured or Native—made any forthcoming declarations of nationalism, it remains certain that many expressed their desires for control of their own religious institutions even on government documents.

Some clergymen made these declarations publicly to the commission. For instance, when asked the reason for his withdrawal from the Church of England, Reverend Maitland stated, "I personally left the church eleven years ago because I preferred to belong to and work for a church with the same doctrines, but controlled by one of our own colour and race."[75] Maitland claimed that his secession did not hinge on theological orientation but instead was solely related to the need to control his own religious destiny. His request was not uncommon. In fact, Native clergymen made similar arguments, claiming that European missionaries had promised transference of power from European missionaries to non-European clergy as they became more exposed to Christianity.[76] Like Maitland, Craig Davidson also believed that churches were ready for non-European leadership. Davidson argued that he "preferred churches led by people of his own race."[77] Other Coloured clergy, including Archbishop D. Abrams of the Ethiopian Catholic Church who proclaimed that he wanted to have a "church controlled by one of our own race and colour," reiterated this point.[78] Solomon Mndaweni noted that his Coloured colleagues from the African Cathedral Episcopal Church had left not only the Church of England but also the American-based AME Church for similar reasons: "We preferred a church controlled by our own race and colour."[79] These calls for non-European church leadership and governance were especially interesting because Coloured and African clergymen alike officially demanded them together. Mndaweni was among many ministers who did not distinguish between Coloured and African clergy, suggesting that Coloured identity was simply just another African ethnicity; he believed that Coloureds were of the same race and color and were fighting for the same religious and political freedom.

Other clergy claimed that their desires for non–European-governed churches reflected a failure on the part of European missionaries to maintain and govern churches. For instance, a minister simply listed as Reverend Jacob left the mission church because, as he stated in his testimony, "We are dissatisfied with the management of the Church of England in South Africa." He also wanted to be under a church that was controlled by "someone of the same race and colour."[80] Another Coloured-identified clergyman flatly cited racial discrimination as the impetus for establishing independent churches, yet another indicator of the shared experiences of oppression. He noted that "having observed a colour distinction predominating[,] we abandoned them."[81] In short, he chose to escape racism by starting his own church. John George Phillip of the Christian Apostolic Church in Zion of South Africa shared similar desires. Phillip explained that he wanted no part in his former mission church because it was "a church under white control."[82] He and many others thought that non-European clergymen needed to take the future of the church into their own hands.

Coloured ministers added to the chorus of African dissatisfaction with mission churches. A Coloured clergyman from the Cape simply cited the following as his reason for leaving the Anglican Church: "I was not satisfied with the manner in which I was treated by the European Ministers of the former church."[83] Discrimination continually emerged as African clergymen's reason for leaving mission churches. Reverend Serfontein, on the other hand, did not recount why he joined the African Catholic Church. Instead, he provided SANAC with his founder's reasons for leaving the mission church. Serfontein claimed that the mission church had "treated him [Andrew Oliphant] more like a servant than an equal," and as a result he established the African Catholic Church.[84] One of his ministers, Ephraim Munyane, noted that the issue of equality was also paramount to Oliphant and claimed that Oliphant left his mission church because "he did not receive a fair wage for all the work he did."[85] In his own testimony Oliphant cavalierly asserted, "I left because I felt like doing so."[86] Oliphant's words mirrored those of Mokone almost five years earlier, who famously declared to his district superintendent that "I hereby give you notice that . . . I will leave the Wesleyan Church and serve God in my own way."[87]

Oliphant's and Mokone's statements made it clear that the mission church did not appreciate them or satisfy their callings. Nor did it satisfy Reverend Lucas Thomas of the African Christian Baptist Church of South Africa. Thomas echoed many of the previous grievances by citing specific issues. He explained that "we were persecuted under white leadership, including no ordination and no participation in communion, and many other things."[88] His testimony is striking because it is one of the few that explicitly accuses white missionaries of limiting the clerical authority of non-European ministers. Unfortunately, even outside of missionary churches, the government continued to block non-European clergy from dispensing sacraments. In other words, non-European clergy were not able to fully serve their congregations.

Joel David, another minister classified as Coloured, echoed similar distrust of white church leadership. David, who resigned from the Anglican Church, claimed that the Church of England mismanaged money,[89] arbitrarily reassigned ministers, "treated the complaints of *black* office bearers unsympathetically," and did not attend to the needs of their congregations, whether it was to give communion or bless a marriage.[90] He concluded his testimony by stating that non-European Christians "needed a church of our own race and colour." David's testimony reveals the pervasive inequality that affected non-European clergy and laity in the Anglican Church. Further, despite his racial classification as a Coloured man, David identifies as a Black clergyman who has suffered under the rule of European missionaries. This is one of the few moments in the SANAC hearings when a Coloured church leader overtly positions his oppression as part of a larger Black subjectivity. David's testimony as well as the testimony of many others demonstrates the pan-ethnic coalition built among church leaders. However, it should be noted that as Coloured identity became more entrenched in South African society, those who identified as Coloured waged separate campaigns for Coloured rights. Some of these campaigns were led by elite organizations such as the African People's Organization, but even allegiance to these associations did not preclude Coloureds from supporting movements with Black nationalist undertones. David was one example of many clergymen who defended Black rights and freedom in the religious realm. Nearly two decades after he gave his testimony, he found his religious freedom as a priest of the African Orthodox Church.

Clergy sought to establish their own churches not just for their vocational advancement but also for the betterment of their people. An unnamed Coloured-identified minister from Pretoria claimed that his "aim is to preach the word of God to the descendants of Ham, to uplift them in Christ, and to build churches and schools for the young—far and abroad."[91] This bold statement resonated with the Black uplift rhetoric circulating globally at the time. His statement embodied the core of Ethiopianism: Black progress and advancement among his people had to be centered in Christ.

Brander also worked to uplift his people. He originally left the Church of England to help Mokone establish the Ethiopian Church.[92] Reverend James Dwane, another former Anglican priest, joined the Ethiopian movement shortly after Brander. These three figures were the cornerstones of early Ethiopianism. They worked endlessly to canvass and recruit discontented ministers, evangelists, and church members from myriad Protestant denominations to the Ethiopian Church. After four years, Mokone sought affiliation with the US-based AME Church.

The AME Church, which had grown out of its own Ethiopianism movement in America, was very appealing to South African clergymen because they shared a great number of tenets and precepts. Within ten years of the affiliation, however, Brander and Dwane declared that African American authorities had not lived up to their promises and started their own churches. Brander established an Anglo-Catholic Church called the Ethiopian Catholic Church of Zion.

Both Brander's and Dwane's departures from the AME Church have repeatedly been explained as part of the period when AIC's grew rapidly. However, a closer look at clerical rolls suggests something else. In the case of the Ethiopian Catholic Church in Zion, Brander took with him numerous Coloured clergymen to lead the church's congregations. Daniel William Alexander was among them. According to Brander's SANAC hearings, he left the AME Church "on account of the promises they gave us not being kept."[93] But when corroborated with Alexander's personal papers, it seems that a number of Coloured ministers were growing discontented with their locally based Native counterparts. Alexander cited Native "ignorance" as the main reason for the mass exodus of Coloureds,[94] adding that "this ignorant and uneducated bunch have no vision and will never have the potential to uplift natives or my people." Several years earlier SANAC had similarly described Ethiopian clergy, claiming that Ethiopianism stemmed from "discontented and restless spirits . . . of the misdirected leadership of ignorant men and misguided men." These unsuitable men, they declared, could not "direct the fledging ideals of a people just emerging from ignorance and barbarism into a state of semi-enlightenment."

According to Alexander, these men were uncivil, ignorant heathens who could not possibly conduct the important task of mission work.

Alexander's comments about his colleagues reflected a growing uneasiness between other Africans and Coloured church leaders. Despite their smaller numbers, Coloureds were an integral part of the Ethiopian movement. As a result, Coloured clergymen make modest appearances in the historical record. Beyond Brander, Alexander, and, to a lesser extent, David, very few Coloured clergymen emerged as leaders of Ethiopianism. One must diligently search to find them. But even in clear view, it appears that Coloured clergymen had a complicated relationship with their other African counterparts. While they often made statements about their allegiance and commitment to Ethiopianism, it seems that by the turn of the twentieth century quite a few Coloured clergymen had distanced themselves almost entirely from their Black colleagues. They had relied on other African clergymen to create the foundations of stable religious institutions and then branched out to govern churches on their own. Many motives could have propelled this development, including language and culture among the obvious reasons. Or perhaps it was much more than cultural differences. By the time Brander broke away from the AME Church, he had amassed a Coloured following. But even Brander's consolidated Coloured denomination did not last long. Both Alexander and David would leave the denomination, Alexander seeking affiliation with the African Orthodox Church in North America and David joining his efforts once Alexander's branch of the African Orthodox Church was established in South Africa.

What remains clear is that as the Ethiopian movement developed, so too did Coloured identity. Initially, those Coloured-identified ministers, evangelists, and laity labored and fought in solidarity with their Black colleagues, although this multiethnic coalition was short-lived and would only pick up again during the antiapartheid struggle. Together these clergymen articulated their desires for a religious and political freedom found in their shared faith. Understanding Ethiopianism in these ways highlights the participation of additional historical actors who were central to the movement, namely people who came to be understood as Coloured but had been excluded from the movement's history. This illuminates the collective nature of the movement and collaborations that have been obscured in the historiography of Ethiopianism. And it provides deeper insight into the complex motivations behind the creation of the movement that cannot just be explained within a Black/white racial binary or strictly through desire for individual gain.

THREE

In the Name of the Father

The Manye Sisters and Church Formation

Charlotte Maxeke (née Manye) and Katie Makanya (née Manye) critically shaped Indigenous church formation in South Africa, yet their contributions are hardly documented as evidenced by scarce traces of their history found in archival sources. The two sisters imagined and articulated a new vision for the Ethiopian Church, founded by their uncle Mangena Mokone. During their twenties, the Manye sisters had already traveled throughout Europe with an ensemble of talented African singers. At the end of the tour Charlotte enrolled in Ohio's Wilberforce University, while her sister returned to South Africa. The Manye sisters had once relied on letter writing to maintain contact throughout their lives; this period in which Charlotte studied in the United States and Katie tended to her family in South Africa was no different.

In a letter Charlotte penned to Katie in 1895, she dreamt of connecting the African Methodist Episcopal (AME) Church in America with the Ethiopian Church based in South Africa. Charlotte's dream of a new religious institution was an incredibly unusual aspiration for a person so young, much less a woman. Her experience of the AME Church's commitment to racial uplift and self-governance likely resonated with Charlotte, reminding her of her uncle's church back home.[1] Katie—who lived far from her uncle in the Transvaal—made a considerable effort to share Charlotte's vision to expand the AME Church to South Africa with him. This process of letter writing, reading, and sharing between the sisters to establish the church in South Africa has been underexplored largely because the letters do not exist in the archival record yet persist in cultural memory. Nevertheless, historians acknowledge the existence of the letter that established the church but do not give significant analysis to its memory. Consequently, this oversight invites us to parse through the limits of any given archive and forces us to consider the ways race, nation, and gender continue to conjoin in ways that shape our study of South African and Afro-diasporic history. Commentary about this important letter shared between sisters also surfaces in denominational commemorations and in South Africa's national public discourse. Without the material correspondence, however, historians are unable to fully recognize, examine, or question the Manye sisters' contributions to African-led churches during the colonial period.

Of the two sisters, historians have focused on Charlotte because, apart from being the first Black South African woman with an undergraduate degree, she established both the Bantu Women's League (the forerunner of the African National Congress Women's League) and the National Council of African Women and also supported the creation of the Industrial Workers and Commercial Union through her political organizing and institution-building prowess. Charlotte has been described as "the mother of the black freedom struggle."[2] The acknowledgment of Katie's existence, much less her contributions, only gained further national attention with the release of her memoir, *The Calling of Katie Makanya*, at the dawn of South African freedom in 1995. Even so, Charlotte's recognition is still limited. Thozama April has illuminated that Charlotte's postapartheid positioning as "the mother of the nation" detracts from our understanding of her as an "intellectual, theorist, feminist, or nationalist."[3] To April's list I add "religious authority," because Charlotte's faith was central to her life and politics.[4] In this chapter, I am concerned with the period I mark as formidable to the sisters' personal development and faith between 1871 and 1903. There are instances in which I move the narrative forward past this time to reflect on how the sisters imagined the church and then how it was subsequently implemented.

Many historians have written on the Manye sisters—mostly preoccupied with Charlotte—but very few have rigorously engaged their faith with the exception of James T. Campbell's comparative history of the AME Church in the United States and South Africa. Within his book *Songs of Zion*, Campbell provides a biographical profile of Charlotte along with other South African students sponsored by the AME Church for undergraduate study in North America. His reading of the archive suggests that this "transatlantic traffic," or network of students, drew from the Christian elite. Campbell argues that these students, much like the men who established the Ethiopian movement, reflected a particular form of African elitism that actually maintained colonialism rather than opposed it.[5] Campbell's scholarship accounts for Charlotte's education and mentions the oft-referenced letter that escapes the written archive even though it inspired church expansion.

To note, though, Campbell's research warrants more sustained engagement with how gender shapes what we can know about and how we come to understand the Manye sisters. Veit Erlmann's *African Stars* comes to similar conclusions through his discussion of class. Erlmann emphasizes the way class informs the Manye sisters' relationship with religion, asserting that the unidirectional flow of people and music from South Africa to the United States forged distinct musical expression. Erlmann and Campbell both conclude that this group of African Christians never found political solidarity with African Americans. Erlmann explains it this way: "Christianity was primarily a premise of their involvement in colonial society and only rarely a weapon against its unpleasant side effects."[6] In other words, African elites relied on their identity as Christians to socioeconomically position them to take advantage of an ongoing transnational network. Though this conclusion is certainly provocative, I depart from Erlmann and Campbell to turn more pointedly to the Manye sisters' faith, the specificities of their upbringing, and the curious significance and role of the ephemeral remnant and memory of the letter that remains and lingers in our imaginary yet does not materially exist.

In this chapter I also trace these circuits of people and ideas by turning to the Manye sisters' underexamined early lives, suggesting that this transnational vision for a church was only possible because of the Manye family's expressions of faith, embrace of a pan-ethnic cultural identity, and migratory experiences that informed their commitment to religious connectivity. I consider the ways the Manye sisters' lives and family's labor history reflect the significant impact that mobility, migration, and travel had on their vision for a transnational Christian network and church in Africa. To ask a new set of questions about the Manye sisters' contributions to church formation, I knit together slivers of the archive[7]—newspaper articles and church pamphlets—alongside biographical fragments and even the memory of this fabled letter. Several questions animate this chapter: Who were the Manye sisters? How did they navigate the world they lived in? Which experiences might have informed their understanding and their impulse to envision a transnational practice of Christianity?

More broadly, their limited presence in the historiography renders the Manye sisters' work unimportant, fleeting, or even coincidental at best and obfuscates our understanding of women's contributions to Christianity in South Africa.[8] The Manye sisters' absence from narratives of church formation invites us to write important African women such as them back into the metanarrative of African history.[9] Women were not only active in the church, but as Charlotte and Katie's story shows us, they also fundamentally shaped these spaces, and without them the church would not exist.[10] Amathembile Masola translates the stakes of this work beautifully for us in a South African context when she recounts the saying "oomama bayidiesel yecawa—mothers are the diesel of the church—implying that without oomama, the church would not exist."[11] Almost one hundred years after the Ethiopian movement, Charlotte's vision manifested when the Ethiopian Church merged with the AME Church before it splintered again to forge new churches.[12]

The Manye sisters' letter-writing practice, a seemingly mundane yet crucial aspect of life during the Victorian era, recorded the multifaceted ways these women negotiated their racial, ethnic, class, and gendered identities within the shifting social climate of South Africa and beyond. It also was an intimate space from which to consider the future of Black Christianity in South Africa insofar as it was the means by which the sisters maintained connection across time and space. Their letter challenged the long-held assumption that only established male evangelists and ministers contributed to the Ethiopian movement, and in the process Charlotte and Katie envisioned what religion throughout Africa could become. The Manye sisters—two young, single, and well-traveled African women—also cast visions for Black Christians; they, too, were engaged in church building, planning, and envisioning what the church could become. Indeed, the sisters' correspondence charts a complex web of domestic and international travel that eventually helped them imagine a global network that reshaped their life trajectories even as it tethered them to the church in South Africa. The Manyes' Black diasporic network connected them to Christians throughout Britain, the United States, and southern

Africa. Such connections demonstrate the sisters' commitment to their faith alongside their family's deep intergenerational allegiance to Christianity and the European-dominated practices that accompanied it. Captured on paper, these familial intimacies connected and grounded the two sisters in a cultural and political world quickly changing beneath their feet, one that was vast but linked through fellowship that sustained the entire family across oceans and continents.

WRITING FROM VAST PLACES: TO BE FINGO AND PEDI AMONG THE XHOSAS

One of the most obvious ways gender complicates our ability to understand Charlotte can be attributed to her name. Although the Manye family called the Cape Colony home, an area mainly occupied by the Xhosa people, sometimes Charlotte is inaccurately imagined as part of a cadre of Xhosa political leaders who dominate the historiography of many South African freedom fighters. Charlotte's married name, Maxeke, was Xhosa, but she actually hailed from a multiethnic family of Christian Fingos and Pedis. Alfred B. Xuma, a respected South African doctor and longtime friend of Charlotte, described her identity. Charlotte was born in 1871, "a Basuto woman by nationality but born among Xosa tribes. Through her mother, a Xosa woman[,] she had already acquired a strong blood tie with those people. This blood tie would be made stronger later in marriage."[13] Xuma's description, albeit slightly inaccurate since the Manye sisters were Pedi rather than Sotho, points to Charlotte and her family's ethnic distinction within a largely Xhosa society.

In actuality, the Manye family navigated and crossed many ethnic divides even within the specificity of their own immediate nuclear family. Their ethnic hybridity meant that the family did not belong; they were outsiders. Their religious and ethnic identity meant that Charlotte and Katie had to navigate and leverage to their advantage different identities, coupled with the specificity of their gender. In turn, as we examine their lives and legacy, we are more poised to understand how remarkable they were. The Manye family skillfully bridged overlapping ethnic divides even as white settler society increasingly policed African ethnic divisions in its creation of a new colonial order. During the late nineteenth century, two regions of Xhosa speakers—the Ciskeis and the Transkeis—divided the Eastern Cape. A white corridor consisting of urban areas with settler populations such as East London, King Williams Town, and Queenstown separated these Xhosa-speaking enclaves.[14]

Most biographical accounts of Charlotte's life claim that her mother, Ana Manci, was of Fingo origin, a subethnic group among the Xhosas described as refugees during Shaka Zulu's establishment of the Zulu kingdom and its territorial expansion.[15] Xhosa leader Hintsa kaKhawuta was best known to have welcomed the Fingos during his reign between 1820 and 1835.[16] According to Xhosa accounts, the Fingos took Hinsta's safe haven for granted, and Hintsa kaKhawuta died at the hands of the British, with whom the Fingos cultivated a partnership. The Fingo-British agreement undermined the Fingo's support of Hinsta's Gcaleka and Rharhabe clans, and many deduced that the Fingos were complicit in Hinsta kaKhawuta's death. The period between 1834 and 1835, known as the Fingo Emancipation (from Xhosa oppression), also signaled a moment in which colonial agents constructed the very idea of Fingoness.[17]

On May 14, 1834, the Fingos made an agreement "to obey the Queen, accept Christianity, and educate their children."[18] The British declared it an emancipation day for the Fingos from the Xhosas, but it was likely a mutually beneficial arrangement. In return for their support of frontier wars, the Fingos were rewarded with confiscated Xhosa land. This exchange ultimately transformed their relationship with land. A budding agrarian culture made the Fingos amenable to a settled colonial life that was legible to Europeans and illegible to the pastoralist Xhosas. Fingo identity therefore was constructed to fit into the colonial order. By design, it differentiated Xhosa speakers from one another and worked as a form of division outside of the colonial framework undergirding African identities. Historian Poppy Fry describes this process of categorization within the context of the Fingos by suggesting that the term "Fingo" (rather than the heavily used anthropological term "Mfengu") calls into question the veracity of this ethnic history by emphasizing its constructed nature.[19] As such, the Fingos can be understood as displaced Xhosas whom the British had turned into contract laborers following the Xhosa War. The Fingos' integration into the Cape Colony came out of desperation for stability within a shifting social and political terrain as the colonial frontier expanded.

Some Xhosa people, particularly those of the Rharhabe clan whose rivalry with the Fingos stretches back to various frontier wars, suggest that "Mfengu" was not even the name of a clan but instead evolved from the word *siyamfengu*, which means "we are hungry and seeking shelter," an allusion to their vulnerable misfortune. In essence, rather than refer to a subethnic group, the term "Mfengu" describes an experience of Nguni displacement and conquest.[20] Charlotte and Katie's grandfather emphasized this history and its damning implications when he explained that the Fingos became "the dogs of the Xhosa . . . because we wandered about in a land that was not our own."[21] Their grandfather's description suggests that the Fingos (and other Nguni groups) ventured farther south and adopted the Xhosa language, culture, and way of life but must have never felt part of this culture or identity. As a result, many clans questioned the Fingos' Xhosa identity, an indictment that still has social ramifications among Xhosas and Fingos today.[22] This minor detail about Ana Manci's Xhosa ethnicity surfaces in official historiographies, political pamphlets of her time, and church commemorations, which makes the sisters' Xhosa identity information commonplace. However, these accounts also placed Manci living in the Ciskei, away from the hub of the Fingos in the Transkei, as she raised her family. Even if the Ciskei was more ethnically heterogenous than the rest of the colony, most Xhosas looked down on the Fingos and alienated them from Xhosa identity.

Charlotte and Katie's father, John Kgope Manye, was from the Batlokwa Tswana-speaking people, a group found outside of the Cape in the Transvaal. Again, most historical accounts simply mention that the girls' father was a Tswana-speaking man or even describe him as "a primitive mountain man."[23] Their father was the son of a Batlokwa headman based in Pietersburg, which is also the place my own father's people call home. According to Katie's memory, her father fled Pietersburg for the Eastern Cape in search of weapons to fight the British. Although there is no letter on record about his travels, Katie recounted the story of her father's migration west. She remembered him telling her of his journey, saying "a Boer farmer in the Orange Free State saw me and gave me some trousers and put me to work" and "also gave me a piece of paper." As the sisters' father transported harvest from the farmer to a shopkeeper, he carried with him a note that had recorded the amount of produce he had in tow. The shopkeeper used the letter that marked Manye's travel to hold him accountable for having consumed a piece of fruit out of hunger along the way.

As her father concluded the story, he intimated how preoccupied he had become with the letter. He told his children, "I was afraid of paper. I thought it was magic."[24] While the note was not his own, it recorded his journey, at once horrifying him and inspiring him to learn how to read. Charlotte had taken the story as a charge, saying "I'll go to England to study what white people are taught. Then I'll come back to teach our people."[25]

Most of her family, including her mother, dismissed Charlotte's musings, but her father, who was always a proponent of his children's education, suggested that "perhaps all this will come to pass." Their father's letter, which captured in it the hardship of colonial encroachment and the trauma of fleeing his homeland, inspired not only him but also his children to learn how to read and write; these would be the tools that the Manye sisters relied on to maintain their own correspondence of travel. What is important to notice here is that even though education was certainly part of the colonial project, from early on John Kgope Manye and his family members understood literacy as a critical tool with which the Manye sisters could interrupt the workings of power.

Katie's description and periodization suggest that Manye left during the frontier wars as the British encroached on Batlokwa land. The letter, albeit not written by him, reminded Katie of the distance her father had traveled in an attempt to flee the frontier wars, find labor, and resettle in a foreign place with only the security of the Christian community he found in the Eastern Cape hundreds of kilometers from Pietersburg. Through the story, we also learn that her father and his people identified themselves as Presbyterian. When I initially read these details, I found it fascinating if not coincidental that my father's people from the same area claimed roots in the Presbyterian Church for generations. Perhaps these details—his Pedi origins, homeland in Pietersburg, and Presbyterian affiliation—stood out to me because I shared them. The point is, it was glaringly obvious to me that he did not belong in the Cape. John Kgope Manye's family history is one of many refugee stories of the Pedi/Sotho/Tswana-speaking peoples alienated from the land and pushed out of Pietersburg during the mid to late nineteenth century.

John Kgope Manye's migration to the Cape—much like the way the Fingos fled Xhosa territory and conveniently aligned themselves with British missionaries—was not a unique occurrence. I have wondered if John's and Ana's stories of displacement brought them together. However, the historical record does not offer this insight, nor does it give any details about John's early life in the Cape. Amid the absence of other scholarship, the work of Fiona Vernal is instructive for imagining John's life. Vernal explains that Christian mission stations offered refuge and grounded many displaced from the Fingos to the Sotho-Tswana–speaking peoples in Christian mission stations.[26] Vulnerability drew these peoples to mission stations, where they often found security and stability. Christianity became a critical anchor in how many people connected to the missions identified themselves, constructed new communities in multiethnic communities, and fortified themselves against a changing world. The implications of both Manci's and Manye's arrival is critical to our understanding of Charlotte and Katie. The Manye family did not neatly conform to either Xhosa identity; they lived a pan-ethnic life bound together by their religious identity. The esteemed couple was an unusual ethnic pairing, and the Manye sisters, along with their siblings, likely lived in communities where they didn't share cultural mores. Charlotte and Katie would have felt these sociocultural differences even more starkly had Christianity not been an identity they shared with others in their communities. My point here is to underscore the ways their unique intersectional locations and identity as Christians forced them to forge connections in situations that were far from comfortable.

The Manyes started their married life in Fort Beaufort, but it remains unclear whether Charlotte, their first child, was born in Fort Beaufort or in Ramakgopa, the birthplace of her father and his people, and located near Uitenhage. Because Xhosa tradition dictates that a woman return to her home village so her family of origin can assist her with childbirth and its corresponding rituals, it seems less likely that Charlotte was born in Fort Beaufort.[27] Regardless, Charlotte spent her early years living with her parents in Fort Beaufort. There, a heterogeneous group of Xhosa speakers lived southwest of East London and close to the town of Alice. From Fort Beaufort, the Manyes settled in the small provincial town of Uitenhage (about sixteen kilometers from Port Elizabeth), referred to as the "center of the Cape Christian elite."[28] Though the Manye family later relocated to the bustling diamond city of Kimberly and eventually to the rural outskirts of Pietersburg, Uitenhage served as the Manye family's home for much of the eldest children's most formative years.[29] At Uitenhage, the family established a homestead on the rolling hills of this small provincial town in the Eastern Cape. There Charlotte, Katie, and their four siblings lived their early lives in pastoral bliss. Even though their linguistic facility granted them some access into such communities, their ethnic origins often differentiated them from their neighbors and fostered a distinct close-knit family culture that didn't seem to always draw from Fingo or Tswana traditions.

John and Ana met and married each other as their people, Pedis and Fingos alike, eked out a new existence in this segregationist climate. Operating beyond their ethnic origins, they remade themselves. Because missionaries embraced vulnerable Africans, they also actively worked to help them reinvent themselves within the new world they inhabited alongside white settler missionaries and even colonial agents. As a result, Christianity became the cornerstone of this recrafted identity. European missionaries and African refugees rallied around this newly formed identity for different reasons. Because the entire group of people had dedicated their lives to the civilizing mission, missionaries held up Fingos as the ideal example of African respectability. For displaced Africans, however, these new identities legitimized them within the stability of the new colonial order. The Fingos' political, spiritual, and culturally strategic decisions reinvented them as model colonial Africans.[30] Much like the Fingos, Ana and John Manye centered their marriage and family on the Christian life they had found among the British missionaries. In the process, their new identity as Christians made them more legible to other Xhosa speakers who might have shared the same faith or had witnessed other Xhosas undergo their own religious conversions. Ana and John also embodied the success of the "civilizing mission," the focus on converting African life, culture, and spirituality to one that mirrored Western Christian mores, an objective that medical missionary and explorer David Livingston had proudly claimed as his Christian vision. "Civilized" Africans, such as John and Ana, were those who had committed to the church, education, and Western culture and ultimately integrated more easily within the region's settler society.

Journalists and community members often described Ana and John as the African elite in part because their education, both formal and informal, allowed them to transcend European ideas about Africa and its people. Yet, Ana and John represented much more than good colonial subjects. They had learned the colonial registers, especially foregrounding the importance of education, that they relied on as a tool to navigate colonialism. Ana and John are among the African Christians cultivated in the Eastern Cape, some of whom migrated north near Kimberly's thriving diamond fields. Campbell describes them as having "the devotion to education, the preoccupation with respectability, the ambivalent feelings of duty and distain toward their 'uncivilised cousins,'" all what he considers shared characteristics of their class.[31] The British, especially those who described themselves as espousing the liberal tradition, proved willing to engage with and consider African Christians as the first fruits of the British Empire in South Africa. In many ways, this was true. The emergence of an African elite meant the destruction of economic, social, and political African life, a subversion of African social order. The crumbling of this social order meant that various African ethnicities would be remade to fit a new social order undergirded by a project of Christianity, civilization, and capitalism. Yet, Ana and John were much more than good colonial subjects.

Prior to years of formal education, the Manye family already had to leverage their multiple identities alongside their linguistic and cultural facility and wisdom as they navigated a world whose boundaries of difference came into sharp relief more and more each day. While the ethnic divisions, especially those being crafted in the Cape, seemed to work against their identity, Charlotte, perhaps even more so than Katie, used it to her own advantage. Katie remembered, "Customs differed from one household to the next, depending on whether the family was Sotho or Xhosa or Swazi or Fingo, whether they were African or Coloured, Christian, or heathen. But Charlotte moved easily among the different peoples."[32] The difference that Katie described not only articulated ethnicity, race, and religion but also demarcated the growing colonial schema the state imposed on non-Europeans. Katie was also pointing out different languages, customs, and diverse spiritual constellations embodied in such superficial expressions as embracing Western clothing and robust displays of Christianity through liturgical customs of prayer over food. Charlotte's uncanny facility of social communication—the use and understanding of a variety of languages, religious cosmologies, and cultural registers—enabled her to traverse myriad spaces. It is very likely that the family's movement throughout the region allowed them to develop various connections and perspectives of different cultural mores. The sisters used this knowledge to help form relationships with a variety of people, including the Pedi-speaking Manyes and the Xhosa-speaking Mancis, and extended these connections similarly in the communities they lived in throughout the country. They found common cause with people they could communicate with and built lasting relationships, especially with people connected to the church.

FROM RAILROAD TO PULPIT: MIGRANT LABOR, URBANIZATION, AND CHRISTIANITY

The Manye family's movement reflected John's labor patterns, which followed African men's changing relationship with labor as colonialism crystalized. John Manye likely secured his position as a railroad foreman for the British South Africa Company because he had worked for a road construction company before moving to the Eastern Cape.[33] Like most economic migrants, employment opportunities set his path. Manye had left his hometown of Ramokgopka on foot amid the Pedi-Boer Wars that began in the 1860s with the plan to work in Kimberly, whose urban center provided many economic opportunities for young men.[34] He gained professional experience during his journey south to the Cape, a move typified by many African men who fled Pietersburg at the beginning of frontier wars in that region. African men responded to the structural transformation within African societies that were increasingly becoming dependent on frontier wages as a way of life.

The railroad company was owned by business magnate Cecil John Rhodes, who envisioned a transcontinental "Cape-to-Cairo railroad . . . to cut Africa through the centre," from the south of the continent to the north. Rhodes sought to connect British-controlled Cape Town, South Africa, with its British counterparts in Cairo, Egypt, and even possibly the Mediterranean in the future. Imagining it as part of the British empire-making initiative, Rhodes appealed to the British-run Cape government to fund the "all-red railway." Though Rhodes had his own interests, the railroad allowed him to implement a telegraph system for business communication. While his endeavors were likely dictated by the backlog created from the Matabele Rebellion and the emergence of the infectious livestock disease rinderpest, he believed that the railroad would best serve British interests whether led by government or business.[35] With it, his company (and presumably other companies) could use the telegraph system to compete with those British companies whose submarine cables facilitated communication between Great Britain and Africa. Government interest in the venture was not as clear-cut, especially due to the waning British interest in the African continent caused by decreasing colonial profits. Nevertheless, the government agreed to fund the first part of Rhodes's vision by building an 834-kilometer railway between Cape Town and Kimberly at an estimated fifty pounds for every kilometer.[36] It's likely that the government agreed to fund a domestic railway to facilitate much-needed internal communication within the Cape colony. John Manye was part of these early efforts to build the railway from Cape Town to Kimberly.

Manye's work as a foreman was steady employment for a growing family even though it was marked by oppression. Katie described the oppression vividly, noting that sweat still "darkened the khaki shirts of Boers shouting orders to black men [such as her father] unloading the train."[37] Katie's description of her father's work makes evident the way coloniality imposed a racial hierarchy on all forms of labor. This means that Black men always took up some form of menial labor regardless of any supervisory position they might hold. For instance, despite Katie's father being a foreman, he was still subject to the commands and demands of white supervisors who lorded over him. She lays bare for us an entire system of extractive labor that affected all African men working the railroad. Besides Charlotte and Katie, the Manye family had four other children—Philip, Henry, John, and Mary-Ann—to support, and it didn't seem like his wife's teaching wages went very far. In fact, Katie vividly remembers that her mother had to resort to subsistence farming to supplement their income. John Manye's work on the railroad proved critical to their existence, yet his work in the church seemed to be his true calling. Manye was a Presbyterian lay preacher, a church leader who was not ordained within the denomination. Despite his job on the railroad, his devotion to Christianity encouraged him to seek an education. Much like his cousin Mokone, Manye attended night school to obtain seminary-like training. Though Mokone became ordained in the church, Manye, like many other African church leaders, became a lay preacher. Manye learned to read and write through his Bible courses in the nearby night school, where Ana Manci taught.[38]

Both John and Ana served as important models of adulthood for Charlotte and Katie. Charlotte obtained formal training to become a teacher like her mother, who also became a visible role model of African femininity within a Christian context as she juggled her profession while being both a wife and mother. Charlotte relied on her observations of her parents' ministry to congregants years later when she served as the first lady and subsequent president of the Women's Missionary Mite Association, where her husband, an ordained AME minister, led the church. Though Charlotte's formal training as a social worker proved pivotal to her role as first lady, she was nonetheless bound by the cultural norms and the limitations faced by Christian female leaders.

John and Ana's work reflected the newfound ways educated Africans engaged with the burgeoning colonial state, mediating the gap between the colonizers and colonized by educating them in schools, introducing them to Western forms of organized religion, and working to build other forms of colonial structures such as the railroad. The intermediary roles "functioned somewhat paradoxically, as the hidden linchpins of colonial rule."[39] The British relied on the Fingos to do much of their colonial work in the Cape. They channeled them into professions such as clerks, traders, and teachers, such as Manci, because their allegiance to the British made them seem like dependable parts of the colonial structure. Colonial forces also positioned the Fingos to take on a variety of professions to keep Africans within the colonial structure in order; Ana's work as a teacher and John's work as an evangelist were among the positions that advanced the colony's civilizing agenda. Yet, the Manyes recognized their work within a cornucopia of Christian discipleship. Manye was among a large number of African evangelists in the nineteenth century. Some of the most notable included Tiyo Soga and the Xhosa poet/evangelist Ntsiksana. Manye's commitment to Christ and his vocational calling distanced him from his Tswana-speaking people, who had long resisted Christianity, and the British missionaries who insisted on undermining Batlokwa life and customs. Even so, his work in the church became the familial cornerstone of faith across generations. He and his wife, along with his cousin Mokone, became critical to conversion efforts. It is no wonder, then, that John's daughter, Charlotte, would later bring the AME denomination to southern Africa and spearhead an AME ministry with her husband, Reverend Marshall Maxeke. Charlotte followed in the footsteps of her mother and father and carried out a call in the name of the Father.

On the railroad and in the pulpit, John Manye's work shaped his children's lives. As a foreman with the British South Africa Company, he traveled as the company developed throughout the region. The Manye family's move from Fort Beaufort to Uitenhage and then to Kimberly was a function of Manye's work. According to Kate's memoir, *The Calling of Katie Makanya*, the family's Cape migration was an intentional form of economic migrancy that moved the family across urban cities to Ramokgopa, where Manye's ailing father lived. Manye had hoped that when he returned to Ramokgopa, he'd have the kind of economic stability that would ensure both his family's and his extended family's livelihood. This worked well for Rhodes's British South Africa Company, which depended on the willingness of skilled workers such as Manye to advance their construction projects. For the Manyes, the move was spurred by familial obligation that reconnected them to the Tswana-speaking people. For Rhodes and his railroad company, Manye's willingness to move rendered the company a stable enterprise as it relocated its workers across the region.

Migrancy also meant that the Manyes routinely reckoned with what it meant to be ethnically illegible as they moved from place to place. The family's migratory patterns reflected their parents' attempts to negotiate their multiple identities but also gave their daughters models from which to think about their own identities. Additionally, the Manyes hoped their children would recognize travel as a form of agency amid a government that increasingly restricted Africans' movement. The family gained the strategic competency to navigate a complex cultural sphere in the British-governed Cape and Afrikaner-ruled Transvaal as well as among the African people living there and beyond. Moving became a strategy they employed to negotiate their multiple identities. Consequently, the movement made evident their parents' attempts to secure economic stability while also allowing their father to fulfill his important role as an adult son within Pedi culture. This simultaneously fortified their children to consider travel as a strategy.

Charlotte in particular later leveraged her various identities—as a Black British colonial subject; a Black and, more particularly, African performer abroad; a South African student within an enclave of students from the colonies; and a Black Christian seeking ecclesiastical freedom—to make a life for herself not only at home in the Cape but also abroad in Britain and then the United States. Finding her place in the seemingly mundane parts of life, Katie would choose to retire from her work as a performer to become a Christian wife, a homemaker, and later an interpreter for an American mission's physician. The sisters' movement across the country fundamentally altered their relationship to community. The sisters' expansive appreciation for diversity and the methods they used to ensure their belonging gave them an in-depth understanding of community. The constant traversing across the country might have been destabilizingly heartbreaking, but it gave them their capacity to make Christianity a space of true belonging and unification across geographic, linguistic, and ethnic strictures.

WRITING FREEDOM: GENDERED NARRATION
AND SOCIAL MOBILITY

The Manyes passed on their Christian identity to their children. They passed down the missionary ideals of Christian life through Western education by encouraging all of their children, even their daughters, to attend school. Their parents, particularly their father, found it paramount that they attend school. Zubeida Jaffer, journalist and author of *Beauty of the Heart: The Life and Times of Charlotte Mannya Maxeke*, suggests that education was a family more. John Manye very much aimed to shield his children from the ruthless ways Africans needed to engage with an emerging colonial economy that hinged on formal education. Their father found his way by attending night school, where he had learned to read and found a wife in the process.[40] Formal education presumably also sharpened his biblical knowledge and preaching ability, because most mission-funded schools depended on African evangelists to proselytize. The impact of Manye's conversion and education proved fairly sizable. When he fled Pietersburg, his people had not yet converted to Christianity and only did so when he returned trained as an evangelist at the turn of the twentieth century. In fact, it seems that John and Ana Manye recognized Christian education to be the cornerstone of conversion so much so that they even committed to educating their daughters, which was a fairly unusual commitment for an African man in the nineteenth century. Though it may be enticing to interpret the Manyes as assimilated and indoctrinated subjects, I invite you to wrestle with the ways faith is leveraged by people to pave their fates and destinies in ways that are unanticipated by colonial projects.

The Cape colony was the birthing center of African education. From the late nineteenth century until about 1920, missionaries worked vigorously on developing education as an attractive pipeline to Christianity.[41] Only one-third of the South African population lived in the Cape by 1920; it was home to 60 percent of African schools, teachers, and students. Strangely enough, African females outnumbered males in African schools even though African women were channeled into a particular type of feminine domesticity that mirrored British practices of relegating women to the home space.[42] A comment made by Natal's prime minister Sir John Robinson aptly expressed gendered expectations for Africans within the colony. Robinson encouraged African schools in his region to turn out "the good old-fashioned, true English type of woman who had made England what it was."[43] He hoped that missionary schools would educate a class of African women who could adequately support white settlers in their endeavors to remake England in southern Africa. Missionaries echoed this idea, but they also wanted these educated women to function within a "civilized" African society that they could police. Margaret's Home for Native Girls in Pietermaritzburg suggested this in its mission statement with its pledge to train girls "to be useful servants or wives for native Christians."[44] The point was simple: the British, whether working for the colonial administration or missionaries, did not think that African women could ever fully occupy the space of British femininity in the ways Robinson intimated. Rather, British settlers hoped that the reliance on African women could extend the possibility for white women. To that end, many British administrators stressed an industrial education that prepared African women to work within the colonial domestic sphere by teaching them sewing, cooking, and laundry work. At the one premier institution, African students were even encouraged to take on industrial habits such as the wearing of European clothing, the development of agriculture, and the use of money all in an effort to become fully integrated into colonial society.[45] Sir George Grey, the Cape governor in the mid to late nineteenth century, even went as far as suggesting that Africans might become part of a colonial society with "common faith, common interests, useful servants and consumers of our goods, contributors to our revenue."[46] Grey's comments intimate the inextricable ways that the colonial state and the missionary enterprise worked to transform African society sociopolitically, economically, and spiritually. Historian Deborah Gaitskell further notes that African women found themselves in an educational system that worked to produce much more than African wives and mothers fit for a civilizing mission; rather, it pushed a colonial economy in which African women functioned as useful employees in white homes.[47] These expectations of African women work to crystalize a racial order that began in the private sphere where white women would govern at home, displacing African women from their own homes and making them work to safeguard settler family life, a system that would extend well into the apartheid era. However, this oppressive racial order doesn't preclude us seeing Charlotte and Katie as thinking subjects and agents who actively built the church. Christianity, like their education, though constituted through colonial processes, has an impact that we are unable to fully understand or anticipate.

Charlotte and Katie's father as well as a burgeoning educated class imagined it differently. They believed that education might render them citizens of the British Empire to which they had already pledged their allegiance.[48] Africans had long believed that education might elevate their standing. Twenty years earlier, many had believed that meeting the stipulations of the Cape Franchise of 1853—which secured voting rights for educated African men—recognized their agency. By the time the Manye sisters were of school-going age, however, the possibility of Cape Franchise had long collapsed under the weight of an increasingly segregationist society. Education, though, continued to hold a central space in African imaginations of freedom, especially among those who embraced Victorian Christian ideals. This proved especially true of the Fingos, their mother's ethnic group, which had long considered education a critical tenet of their mores when they promised to live as exemplary Christians. Thus, John and Ana maintained this way of life in their own family by sending all their children to school, even the girls.

Between 1877 and 1885, Charlotte and Katie attended a nearby school in Uitenhage run by Reverend Isaac William Wauchope during their primary years.[49] Wauchope and his family made an important contribution to the Manye sisters. Not only did Wauchope teach the girls, but he also exposed them to the power of writing. Wauchope and others, such as writers and activists Sol Plaajte, Mphilo Walter Rubsana, Isiah Bud-Mbelle, John Langibele Dube (whom Charlotte would meet in the United States), and Richard Msimang, were among the many politically oriented Africans living, writing, teaching, and organizing near the Manye sisters. Charlotte and Katie grew up and were educated in an ethos that inspired Wauchope and other Africans like him to pursue political and ecclesiastical initiatives that put them on equal footing with whites. Uitenhage—and the Cape region in general—was a hotbed of activity prompting African freedom fueled by African Christians.

Wauchope descended from a long line of Christians. His great-grandmother, Tse, was a devout follower of J. T. van der Kemp. Van der Kemp was a pioneering Dutch missionary—trained and supported by the London Missionary Society—who believed in racial equality (so much so that he married a Malagasy slave girl).[50] Tse's daughter, Mina, also followed in her mother's footsteps, becoming a devout Christian and a congregant of van der Kemp. She followed him to Bethelsdorp, where he established a prominent mission station. From there, Mina and her husband established their own mission station and family. Their daughter, Sabina, married Dyoba, bringing Isaac William Wauchope into this world. This family, like Ana and John, had crafted their legacy on their Christian faith and their lives on the mission station. And while much of this family history is tied to the church, it is also tied to the growing class of educated Africans that emerged from these mission stations. Reverend Wauchope's robust and varied career makes this point clear.

Though best known for being the minister aboard SS *Mendi* when it sank in 1917, Wauchope also had a career as a teacher, an interpreter and clerk at the Magistrate's Court, a sports coach, an entrepreneur, a philanthropist, and a political activist. One of his greatest legacies was his writing, as he relied on writing to imagine and articulate a new future for African people free from white settler control, a practice the Manye girls witnessed regularly. Wauchope developed a writing culture even before he attended the Lovedale Missionary Institute, one of the most prestigious mission schools for Africans. Much like his more well-known predecessor Tiyo Soga, Wauchope used his writing to comment on various forms of white control and oppression that he experienced. Soga expressed his desire to acknowledge, examine, and preserve Xhosa culture in Lovedale's official newspaper *Indaba* (Xhosa for "news"), and later *Isigidimi* (meaning "the Christian Express"), which he hoped would be a "lovely dish of holding safely the legends, news, and sayings of home."[51] Soga resisted missionaries' attempt to civilize Africans by limiting their power; he instead leaned on spirituality and writing as a way to reframe African futures. It would be only twenty years after Soga made the appeal that John Jabuvu would ultimately garner a space for Africans to fully express themselves in print. Jabuvu founded and became the editor of *Imovu zabantsundu* (Black Opinion), another outlet for African thought and expression. In the next few decades, other Xhosa publications such as the *Izwi labantu* (Voice of the People) emerged beyond the purview of European missionaries. Xhosa writing and opinion was developed, expressed, and disseminated in this medium. Soga, Wauchope, and many other Lovedale alumni relied on writing to resist many restrictions imposed on Africans. Wauchope perhaps went one step further to create and cultivate different forums to express his desires for African freedom.

Uitenhage and the surrounding area became a base of some of this activity. And by 1879, Wauchope established the Native Educational Association. Shortly after in 1882, he played an instrumental role in forming Imbunda Yamanyama in Port Elizabeth, a political organization created in response to the Afrikaner Bond, an Afrikaner organization founded on ethnic pride. In all his endeavors, Wauchope implored his people to examine their current condition, write down their grievances and petitions, and organize institutions of resistance. He was not the only African leader taking on similar work. Throughout the Cape, the Manye girls were exposed to an array of African leaders and their legacies that sought to build institutions of change. The establishment of these platforms, in which educated Xhosas found expression through writing and institution building, became critical models of African intellectuals' insistence on freedom and equality as a necessary mode of existence. It is no wonder, then, that seemingly innocent letters between sisters would index thoughts and opinions concerning church formation on the horizon.

The prevailing mood among these educated Africans was a demand for a new kind of future. Jeff Opland, one of the premier scholars of Xhosa literature, declares this period as one during which a new generation of Xhosa writers "fought with pen and paper rather than assegai."[52] Opland frames Wauchope, the Manye sisters' teacher, as one of the most prominent among them. Charlotte and Katie may not have been old enough to understand writing as the form of resistance that Africans such as Wauchope, Soga, and Jabvu relied on to fight white settler control, but being educated within this legacy may have influenced the Manye sisters' understanding of writing as a form of political organizing largely engaged in by African Christians. Charlotte would first write to her sister during her schooling and again when she went abroad to perform and would also write papers and speeches to support her work as a social worker and political activist. Katie would join her sister in an exchange of letters for their family but would later rely on memoir writing to document the details of their extraordinary lives. Both acts of writing were a transformative paradigm of African resistance that bound families and political causes together. As a result, Charlotte's simple act of writing, even a family letter, should be regarded as a revolutionary act not only influenced by a Black global project of liberation but also inspired by local teachers such as Wauchope who made the path possible. The Manye sisters lived within this network of radical African Christians who relied on each other rather than on European missionaries to educate and inform themselves about the world around them.

When Charlotte and Katie matriculated from Wauchope's school, they sought entrance into the esteemed Edward Memorial School in Port Elizabeth shortly after 1885. There Charlotte and Katie received musical instruction from Mr. Paul Xiniwe, a matriculate of the highly regarded Lovedale Missionary Institute, and the sisters both joined the school choir.[53] This advancement in their schooling required Charlotte and Katie to live on the outskirts of Port Elizabeth. Charlotte was the first one to leave the family home to earn her keep as a domestic and nursemaid for Ms. Hutchinson, a young white mother needing assistance. When Charlotte matriculated, Katie entered Edward Memorial School and took over Charlotte's domestic work. Hutchinson, though, did not value the sisters' employment as the Manye family did: a means from which to educate themselves. Hutchinson believed that their work as domestics was the highest possible aspirational goal for African women. Truth be told, their steady employment was aspirational for many but not the Manyes. They comprised a select group who sought professionalization. Even as late as 1935, less than 5 percent of African students were able to attend school up until Standard IV (the equivalent of sixth grade).[54] Hutchinson, on the other hand, considered their employment in her home as free vocational training for their future employment as domestics, perhaps in more well-to-do homes. Hutchinson had a number of other African workers supporting her household. While these other African workers marveled at the privilege of Charlotte and Katie's education, they also thought the pursuit of education was frivolous and impractical for African life. All too often, they snidely pointed out the racialized limitations placed on Africans while highlighting the socioeconomic privilege their own steady work in Hutchinson's home brought them.

Katie in particular felt the social and even cultural alienation of being an educated African even among her own people. Much of the alienation came in the form of criticism and claims about her shirking her potential rather than choosing to develop her family. To be sure, their African counterparts were right. Historian Deborah Gaitskell showed decades ago that African girls were often limited to employment as paid maids or unpaid housewives and mothers within their own marriages.[55] In more promising scenarios, educated African women in the late nineteenth century became primary school teachers like Charlotte and her mother. At the turn of the twentieth century, they became nurses like Katie had once aspired to become before Charlotte explained that African women could not pursue this line of work.[56] Charlotte had exclaimed, "You can't be a proper nurse[;] . . . the nursing schools are only for white girls. If you go to work in a hospital, you will just be a servant, mopping floors and cleaning up after the Europeans. If you really want to do important work, then you must study hard and become a teacher."[57] Katie always thought that "all her cleverness was in her hands."[58]

But professional aspirations were not the only limiting factor. Charlotte faced the frustration of feigning ignorance around Hutchinson in order to preserve her colonially bestowed position of superiority. In other words, as educated and ambitious African women, Katie and Charlotte were forced to maintain a delicate symbiosis that kept the Hutchinson household operating within the racialized bounds of white South African domesticity, the very project that white settlers in the colonial administration and the church had articulated. The Manye sisters would consider the place, the expected role, and the ways African women defied these cultivated roles of controlled African domesticity for years to come. Both sisters carved out different paths to freedom. Katie sought freedom out of the purview of the state through a carefully selected marriage. Charlotte educated herself and then assessed her own position in both the private and public domain to consider the pressing concern of the time, the "Native question" from a gendered lens. Charlotte's circumstances were critically unique in that in both the private and public domains, she performed the role of an exemplary Christian wife by virtue of being married to a clergy man. But beyond that highly esteemed position, she also considered African women's identity from her trained vantage point as a social worker. Her conclusion, as she unequivocally expressed throughout the years, was that African women deserved to live a full life marked by morals but also a life that cultivated their gifts and talents. For Charlotte, this always required as much education and training as possible.

This formidable period of training served to teach Charlotte and Katie the importance of self-reliance through employment, but they also each learned to advocate for and make space for their education despite pressure to quit from threatened whites and even skeptical African counterparts. Both sisters excelled at their studies even in the face of financial and sometimes personal obstacles. Also during this period, both girls cultivated some skills that they would depend on for their entire lives. Beyond developing their love for and commitment to choral music, fragments of the written record suggest that Charlotte pursued writing in various forms. It is during this point that she published an article for an American journal in which she wrote about African life and Christianity. While there doesn't seem to be enough evidence to find the actual article that she wrote, it still serves as an important marker of the ways Charlotte relied on various writing genres to assess and document her experiences. This kind of writing functioned differently for missionaries. For them, articles such as Charlotte's were evidence of their effectiveness in establishing mission education among students. Rather than the usual church reports to the metropole, African students' own writing demonstrated the importance of mission education.

Yet, for young women such as Charlotte, articles such as this one allowed her to assess her society almost ethnographically while giving her opportunity to process her own thoughts. Nonkutela Dube (née Mdima), Charlotte's contemporary and friend she met in the United States, wrote a similar article. Dube, like Charlotte, made a critical impact on South African education, music, and politics, establishing the first African school with her esteemed husband John Langalibalele Dube, the cofounder and first president of the African National Congress (ANC). Nonkutela and her husband became the first Black South Africans to start a school, the

Ohlange Institute, an important part of their legacy. Nonkutela, like Charlotte, wrote an article in her adolescence that was published in missionary reports.[59] Her essay still survives as an example of the ways African Christians engaged in the practice of writing so as to critically (re)consider their world. Simultaneously, this meant that figures such as Charlotte and Dube actively worked to use writing, whether in article form or letter, as a way to document their lives and share it with loved ones far away.

Nonkutela published her article, "My Home," in the *Rice Country Journal* of Northfield, Minnesota, produced by Reverend W. C. Wilcox, who was a missionary to South Africa by the American Board of Foreign Missions. Nonkutela's article was a nuanced examination of Zulu life, Ida Belle Wilcox wrote in a note to her mother.[60] While "My Home" seemed ethnographic in nature because it described Zulu life, it also had a moral subtext. Nonkutela wrote that within her ethnicity there were both "good and some wicked people." She continued on, saying "some are rich and some are poor. Those who are poor are jealous for the things of those who are rich." This moral judgment bestowed by an adolescent girl was one that Ida Belle Wilcox, wife of Reverend Wilcox, seemed to position as working in tandem with people's salvation. In other words, Nonkutela's assessment of African living standards was not simply an issue of class but also one of civilization and morality. This critique of Christianity's impact on African life continued to inspire Nonkutela and her husband's other articles as well as fundraising speeches in an effort to point to missionaries' effectiveness in Natal. For missionaries such as Mrs. Wilcox, Nonkutela's starkly contrasting description of African Christians and nonbelievers further emphasized the impressive inroads of missionary work. Wilcox's note to her mother made this point clear when she wrote, "This week I will send you a copy of an essay written by a girl who has been here but about three years." Her final point to her mother was that a student such as Nonkutela reflected the possibilities of missionary education. Wilcox made a more general argument for African education writ large: "These girls do not know a word of English before they come here. Of course, the essays of the graduates will be much better English for they have been here five or six years." Her point is that Nonkutela, whose critical assessment reflected their effective teaching, was also emblematic of the possibilities of missionary work.

Likewise, articles such as this one and the ones that followed rendered Nonkutela (and Charlotte) an exceptional African woman. These types of women would not only write with each other, but they also would write on behalf of their people. Charlotte and Dube did indeed do so.

The two later wrote together with Nina Gomer Du Bois (esteemed African American scholar W. E. B. Du Bois's first wife) in a book that shared insight on African life while also allowing them to provide their perspective on American life.[61] Furthermore, this practice of examining and writing about African lives and experiences would fuel a form of letter writing that documented so much of these women's everyday lives while living abroad.

Before Charlotte and Katie left South Africa, they shared many years of writing letters to their families while also routinely assessing and giving commentary on their lives; much of it would document the love for music they cultivated while living away from home. Their love for music was inspired by their school's choral director, Paul Xiniwe. Both Manye sisters were star performers during their tenure at Edward Memorial School. Charlotte and Katie also became drawn to choral music when African American choirs that were touring Kimberly, most notably the McAdoo and Jubilee Singers, sang for African audiences. Charlotte and Katie were privileged enough to hear them perform, and in the Kimberly audience was also Daniel William Alexander, leader of the African Orthodox Church. Kimberly became an important organizing space in which African musicians established their own choirs similar to those the Manye sisters had seen perform.

FAITH, FATE, AND THE FORGING OF POLITICAL NETWORKS

The Manye family had moved from Fort Beaufort to Uitenhage and finally to Kimberly through the girls' most formative years. In the process, the sisters had been exposed to the growing industrialization as their family grew closer to the bustling city of Kimberly, where diamonds had been discovered. It is in Kimberly that the girls joined the African Choir. The choir, which claimed to use the tour as a fundraising effort to build technical schools, exposed the Manye sisters to so much of the country. These travels gave them exposure to a host of ethnic groups.[62] While this might seem insignificant, their parents' pan-ethnic marriage between a Pedi and a Xhosa, in addition to moving from the Eastern Cape to the Northern Cape, meant that the girls learned much more than a number of languages. In fact, Katie noted that by the end of her second year of schooling she spoke "English, Dutch, Xhosa, and Pa's Sotho."[63] The sisters' travels also meant that they learned how to coexist beyond established ethnic tensions. This ability to negotiate across ethnic lines prepared them for tour with a multiethnic choir that visited many spaces, including England, Scotland, Ireland, and finally the United States. Their rich experience as outsiders and as people who moved from region to region was crucial to their willingness to stay in England even when the African Choir fell apart. Charlotte and her sister Katie outstayed other choir members by an extra year. In particular, with Charlotte focused on funding her study in the United States, she extended her visit to England to consider this option more fully.

In England, the Manye sisters encountered a new side of European cultures and perspectives with a range of people from ordinary citizens to dignitaries, including, in England, Queen Victoria; Henry Thurstan Holland, 1st Viscount Knutsford; Baroness Angela Georgina Burdett-Coutts; and suffragist Emmeline Pankhurst.[64] Despite the important audience it kept, the choir still faced nasty bouts of racism. The choir's manager had even considered changing its name from the Jubilee Chorus to the Kaffir Choir. He exclaimed to the group that "the English know about kaffirs and will be curious to hear you sing."[65] Mr. Xiniwe, the choir's director from back home, had challenged this derogatory language, insisting on keeping the original name. Some British newspapers had more generous descriptions, stating that they were "Black as black could be, but the men splendid in physique, of gentle manners and charming address; the girls also 'black but comely,' with a charming modesty and conscious dignity about them that attracted and won immediate sympathy."[66] Whether the choir was portrayed in an unsavory or favorable light, the Manyes learned about the pervasiveness of racism.

Pankhurst seems to have had the most profound impact on the Manye sisters; some scholars argue that Pankhurst introduced Charlotte to feminism. The exchanges between Pankhurst and the sisters are indeed powerful, perhaps attractive to the Manye sisters because they had come to England already examining systems of power through a gendered lens. Katie remembered Pankhurst's exchange with her sister. Pankhurst had shared her excitement about just having elected a woman to the London Country Council. According to Katie, when Pankhurst "opened the door, she said, 'But one small victory is not enough. We have to keep on fighting for our rights.'"[67] Pankhurst went on to explain to Katie, "We're just trying to educate the public . . . that we women want the vote." Katie thought it strange that "English women had no rights, yet they lived in a country that was ruled by a woman"—the queen of England—who had been a captive audience of the African Choir. While meeting Pankhurst might have given

Charlotte the vocabulary to contextualize her own experiences within the contours of feminist rhetoric, Charlotte also came with her own experiences and knowledge that made Pankhurst legible to her. This seems clear largely because the Manye sisters left South Africa advocating for themselves and their future well before they met the British feminist.

Charlotte is considered a foremother of African feminism. She emerged as a pioneer for women's rights after she became the first African woman to earn an undergraduate degree in South Africa. At home, she not only worked as a social worker and probation officer but was also the founding member of the Bantu Women's League of the leading political party, the ANC. People knew Charlotte from her political work, where she advocated for women's and girls' rights, gave speeches, and offered advice about women's role in African society. Her work made such an impact that the esteemed A. B. Xuma, who served as president general of the ANC from 1940 to 1949, even wrote an essay, "What an Educated Girl Can Do."[68] Xuma relied on Charlotte's educational and professional impact to make an argument to promote education for women. In fact, the Manye sisters attributed their success to their highly supportive parents, who very much wanted their daughters to make their own path. For Charlotte this meant pursuing higher education, but for Katie it would mean marrying and establishing a Christian household. Their parents welcomed these seemingly contrasting lives largely because their daughters determined their own fates.

Furthermore, the Manye sisters' exposure to Black people from within the British colonies also served as an important point of exchange in which they shared their experiences living as subjects of Britain while enduring their subjection. Among the most memorable meetings were those with West African female medical students and West Indian sailors as well as an interracial American performing group called the Bohee Brothers. The trio encouraged Charlotte to study in the United States even as the African Choir began to fall apart. The American Bohee Brothers spent a lot of time helping her understand the US university system. She imagined that they might sponsor her education like the McAdoo Singers had sponsored her friend Titus Mbongwe's education at Hampton University years prior.[69] Her conversations with the performers left her thinking that Black institutions such as Hampton were her best option for pursuing her course of study. As Katie remembered in her memoir, "Charlotte was not willing to leave London, until she had found some way to continue her education. She could not forget what those Bohee Brothers had told her about the colleges for black people in America." Charlotte had declared, "There's one called Wilberforce University and that's where we'll go."[70] But Katie knew that "whatever she wanted to do, she did without hesitation."[71] In the end, before attending the university, Charlotte was forced to return home to South Africa while the African Choir reorganized for a second iteration of the choir with replacement South African singers. This second choir performed in the United States.

Meanwhile, Katie decided to return home rather than go to the United States. She worried that if should did not return to South Africa, she would not find a suitable Christian suitor. While she did eventually marry, she struggled to adjust to South Africa's hardening racism after having performed and received such acclaim before British dignitaries. Katie gave up her opportunity for musical training in order to retain cultural ties in South Africa. Subsequently, this also meant that Charlotte was able to keep abreast of family life through her correspondence with Katie, a practice they had adopted earlier when Charlotte left for schooling. There are no details about how many letters were exchanged between the sisters, yet there is a rhythmic reference that begins in Charlotte's adolescence, around 1885, through her young adult years, around 1901. Katie recalls the importance of these letters in her memoir well before 1894 and 1901 when Charlotte attended Wilberforce University, where she earned her BSc with distinction.[72] Xuma's publication "Charlotte Maxeke (Mrs.): What an Educated Girl Can Do" suggests that it was Reverend R. C. Ransom who had a "vision flamed into his mind" that the six choir members get an education when their choir director abandoned them in Cleveland, Ohio.[73] Yet, Charlotte had already made her intentions to secure an international education when she inquired about studying in the United States during the Virginia McAdoo singers' visit to Kimberly in 1890. She gained more courage and vigor when her choir toured England and she met the Bohee Brothers, who encouraged her to pursue her education in the United States. Charlotte had seen the blueprint to study abroad when Ransom was ignited by his own vision, which aligned with hers. Ransom only made manifest Charlotte's prayers and her father's belief that it all "will come to pass."[74] Should we as scholars take religion more seriously, we might see the same sacred network of prayers and declarations that Charlotte and her family witnessed and believed made miracles possible. The power of prayer and declaration, a practice Charlotte shared with her African American community, are the same spiritual tools she relied on to cement her work as an institution builder.

Religion brought Charlotte to Wilberforce University in Ohio. In addition to being the first Black college in the United States, its Methodist foundations very likely resonated with her because of her work as a Methodist teacher earlier in Kimberly. Likewise, the Christian charity of the AME bishop, who read an article about the abandoned choir members, offered her support in Ohio close to the university.[75] Charlotte excelled under the guidance and tutelage of Pan-Africanist W. E. B. Du Bois and his first wife, Nina Gomer.[76] Upon her completion, Xuma wrote, "her education translated into service for humanity."[77] He continued that it has been "a God-send for our people." In fact, he hoped that his writing about Charlotte might inspire more interest in women's education, but he also hoped that the work would inspire "spiritually and materially for the redemption of Africa." At Wilberforce, Charlotte wrote the letter that her sister Katie would share with their uncle, the leader of the Ethiopian Church. Overall, the Manye sisters' travels and, more specifically, Charlotte's time studying at Wilberforce University, an institution established by the AME, likely reminded her of her Ethiopian roots back home in South Africa. Charlotte's ability to recognize these connected threads of racial uplift inspired her to fortify lines of religious solidarity from the United States to South Africa.

The letter was an important institutional marker, but it also charted the sisters' different trajectories. Charlotte returned to the West with the hopes of being educated in the United States, while Katie left for South Africa in search of a viable Christian union. The act of writing the letter was not all that different from earlier moments in which the sisters exchanged letters that bridged their distance. Yet, the sisters' genius was that they recognized fellow South Africans' desire for ecclesiastical freedom and the ways that this independent African American institution could be a means to fully establish their own independent church. The sisters were the ones who envisioned and instituted the transnational church connections between Africans and African Americans. They were not timid about expressing themselves as leaders because they'd had enough practice on account of living with their family of origin, earning a South African education, gaining an informal education by way of touring, and then finally obtaining higher education in the United States. They immediately recognized this familiar Black global project of ecclesiastical liberation as practiced by the AME Church. And their ability to connect these projects challenged masculine framings of African Christianity that had long been tethered to other male Christians within their network such as Mokone and, even earlier, Soga and Ntsikana. Charlotte and Katie were invisible radicals who knew that their vision of a new and independent African church could only come to fruition if it flowed through the patriarchal leadership structures that underpinned the church.

But if this chapter wrestles with and contextualizes the memory of Charlotte's 1895 letter to show how she and her sister laid out plans for an entire denomination, it makes another argument about the singular life and work of Charlotte. Beyond her formal training as a teacher, musical performer, and social worker, Charlotte was also an institution builder, a strategic thinker, a global ambassador, a Pan-Africanist, and a feminist, a reflection of her lived experiences. Indeed, Charlotte's grandmother had once intimated that "she is not like us,"[78] and her sister Katie had stated that Charlotte had a "knowingness and deep thoughts."[79] Charlotte's early experiences helped develop not only her leadership abilities but also how she imagined a different world of transcended liberation, a geopolitically expansive church. At the time of the letter writing, Charlotte was a capable and recognized leader. As her letter stated, she aimed to produce a body of believers who would make anticolonialism, anti-imperialism, antisexism, and pan-Africanism integral to their Christian faith. Katie's observations from decades past proved prophetic when she explained that once "Charlotte was gone away . . . there was nothing left of her except [the memory of] the letters."[80] Like the Manye family did so long ago, we must meditate on all that is left. This practice of re-membering—the pulling together of archival slivers alongside the members of stories captured—resuscitates the lives of young women who built, extended, and institutionalized the Body of Christ.

FOUR

Ministries of Migration

George McGuire, Robert Josias Morgan, and the Transformation of Black Churches in the West Indies and the United States

Between 1914 and 1924, some members of the Ethiopian Church abandoned affiliations with the African Methodist Episcopal (AME) Church, the African Church, and the Ethiopian Catholic Church of Zion and eventually founded the African Orthodox Church (AOC). With each merger and split, clergy and laity sought to envision, define, and enact freedom. The establishment of the AOC in South Africa, a US church founded and inspired by Black nationalist politics, was a new example of the ways Black Christians declared their freedom. Reverend George McGuire's sermon at the 1920 Universal Negro Improvement Association's (UNIA) Fourth Annual Conference in New York—where he called upon Black Christians to "forget the white gods" and establish "an international day when all the Negroes of the world should tear the pictures of a white Madonna and a white Christ out of their homes and make a bonfire of them"—was the initial charge to create a church grounded in Black nationalist theologies.[1] Reverend McGuire's questioning of the seemingly inextricable ways white culture enveloped Christianity acknowledged the multiple colonial projects undergirding the church even as he urged Black Christians to imagine an alternative space where Black religiosity was also concerned with questions of race and political well-being.

In essence, Reverend McGuire's call precedes the voices that arose in mid-twentieth century movements that sought to dislodge Europe's centrality to questions of being, including but not limited to questions of spiritual and religious practice, voices that would later openly declare Europe to be "spiritually indefensible."[2] McGuire's message and his subsequent founding of this church represents new aspects of political theology that consider the place of race, politics, and power. This subfield is marked by the work of such scholars as Vincent W. Lloyd, Corey D. B. Walker, Keri Day, George Shulman, Ted A. Smith, Emmanuel Katongole, Charles Villa-Vicencio, and Allan Boesak, among others.[3] Together, they move beyond the seminal work of Carl Schmitt's concern with the religious in European political theory to rigorously engage race and the social practice of religion, and in doing so, they expand more traditional theopolitical questions to consider the specificity of racialized political subjectivity. Clearly, in thinking about the Black Church throughout Africa, a "more appropriate focus then, it is argued, should be on political subjectivities whose bodies are riddled with the scars of the misgovernance of nation-states in both their colonial and postcolonial incarnations."[4]

This chapter, which is attentive to the specificity of Reverend McGuire's racialized political subjectivity, traces the establishment of the AOC through the migration of its founder along with church leaders he encountered as critical to his imagining a new sacred space marked by a particular kind of refusal. This refusal animated McGuire's ability to imagine an alternative site of worship and political organizing for Black Christians globally and echoes scholars Corey D. B. Walker's and Allan Boesak's theorization of new and alternative conditions for freedom, what Walker calls the "political theology of freedom."[5] Boesak declares it as part of the "hermeneutics of protest and liberation."[6] These scholars emphasize the condition of possibilities or religious alternatives that overturn hegemonic expressions of faith outside of the established church. Ultimately, these alternative expressions call into question the "difference between those who always seek ways to negotiate with the hegemonic powers that rule society and those drawn to and gathered around Jesus of Nazareth, the defender of the poor and powerless, the revolutionary teacher who exposed and resisted."[7] Read together, Walker's and Boesak's findings shed light on a connective project of freedom across religious geographies.

The AOC and its transnational leaders—spanning the Caribbean, North America, and eventually southern and eastern Africa—offer critical spaces to imagine an alternative site of worship and political organizing for Black Christians globally. When Reverend McGuire made clear his mission to decouple European culture from ridged codes of Christian morality, he did so for the sake of not just the delegates attending the UNIA conference but also those who would read a transcript of his sermon in the pages of *Negro World*. Put another way, McGuire and countless others "rejected the anemic, inadequate theology of accommodation and acquiescence, of individualistic, otherworldly spirituality foisted upon us by western Christianity that taught us to accept the existing unjust order as God-ordained. [They] embraced, rather, what we called a 'theology of refusal,' a theology that refused to accept God as a God of oppression, but rather as a God of liberation who calls people to participate actively in the struggle for justice and liberation."[8] Readers met Reverend McGuire, UNIA chaplain-general of the executive branch, but they also heard a prophetic vision for Christian believers. The sermon ordained him as a sacred visionary even though McGuire had been officially bestowed with religious authority through formal training and experience. Through his service as an ordained priest in the Caribbean and Central America before becoming a missionary in the United States, his travels armed him with a transnational perspective on Black sociopolitical life, one that inspired him to consider political liberation as a fundamental part of Black spirituality. McGuire's reclamation of familiar Christian religious iconography such as household images of the Madonna and Child reflected Garvey's program of racial uplift and also fostered synergy among those in the Ethiopian movement on both sides of the Atlantic.

Scholars have tended to limit their understanding of Reverend McGuire to his work in the UNIA as the founder of the AOC, a religious offshoot of the UNIA. Yet McGuire's work reached much farther. McGuire drew from a set of theologies that were self-consciously contextual; it was part of his lived migratory experience as a Black man. McGuire relied on his position as chaplain-general for global reach, but it was his migratory experience that surely captured a transnational readership that was familiar with the plight of African Americans from the US South, economic migrants of the Caribbean, or labor migrants of colonial Africa. When he announced the building of a new religious order, sensitive to the overlooking forms of oppression Black people faced, readers of *Negro World* were indeed receptive to this call for spiritual agency.

McGuire's iterant ministry throughout Central America, the circum-Caribbean, and the United States distinctively shaped McGuire with a global-scaled vision for his ministry. His witness of racism and xenophobia—overlapping experiences of oppression unique to English-speaking Black workers from the British Caribbean as they labored and lived in the Spanish-speaking countries of Honduras, Costa Rica, and Panama—inspired him to offer Christianity as refuge for the marginalized even when he arrived in the US South. This practice of creating a space of Christian refugee, a practice he carried over in his work in the Anglican community as a leader of the US Episcopalian Church, is an application of Christianity that Walker defines as "a critical confrontation between the contemporary elaborations of forms of theological thinking and a critical understanding of the function of race."[9] Walker claimed that from this understanding of the intersecting dynamics of religion and race grew the possibility of radical forms of freedom that McGuire eventually created. Indeed, much like Charlotte Maxeke's travel to the United States and return to South Africa to expand the AME Church, McGuire's migration and ministry prepared him to establish his own church, a distinctive contribution to the growing transnational network of Black Christians.[10] And as a Caribbean migrant in particular, his work highlights the hidden importance of considering Black diasporic migration and the impact of Black migrants on the development of North American Christianity. Such an exploration is crucial for elaborating our understanding of early twentieth-century Black Christian culture and belonging, a subject that remains underexplored especially during the interwar period.

THE COMMUNION OF COLONIALITY

In the decades that followed the American Civil War, American bishops invited Black students from all over the world to study theology and gain their ordination in the Episcopalian Church.[11] Some of these foreign Black seminary students remained in the United States to serve Black parishes in both the North and the South. While George McGuire did not study in the United States, he did become part of a cadre of newly ordained foreign Black clergymen to serve in parishes, especially in mainline Protestant churches with smaller congregations of Black Christians. With the promise of a recognized ordination and the escape from a destabilized Caribbean economy, many aspiring priests offered their services to the Episcopalian Church in North America. A steady stream of West Indian Anglicans soon filtered into these churches, and with them came men familiar with and raised in the Anglican doctrine.[12] These men's familiarity with the long-established Anglican Church in the Caribbean and its doctrine made them efficacious students.

In fact, these students became the backbone of Black Episcopalian clergy in North America. Between the end of the American Civil War in 1865 and the beginning of World War I in 1914, 45 percent of Black clergy in the Episcopalian Church were from the British West Indies. The church preferred these students, too, largely because their British training made them critically attuned to the theology, liturgy, and practices of the Anglican Church, a form of High Church that was rarely practiced in the denominations with high concentrations of African American Christians. One Episcopalian archdeacon in the Deep South during the interwar period described the arrangement best when he said Black priests "affiliated with the church's mission are from the West Indies where they have had most excellent church training."[13] The archdeacon's comments were largely a reflection of the ways British colonialism in the Caribbean was imbued with a long-standing commitment to the Anglican Church.

West Indian clergy contributed to the development of the Black Episcopalian Church worldwide. Their British training meant that they often brought with them a penchant for a High Church or Anglo-Catholic worship style, which emphasized priestly authority, rituals, and sacrament, extensions of Catholic Christianity.[14] British missionaries to the Caribbean who were from the Society for the Propagation of Foreign Parts, an arm of the Church of England, had converted numerous people from the Caribbean. This society's mission was "to provide a chaplaincy for Englishmen overseas, and to evangelize African slaves as well as indigenous people."[15] Most of these missionaries were sent to the West Indies and West Africa to proselytize. In the process, these missionaries transmitted the High Church worship style, which starkly contrasted the Low Church worship style that neither follows a proscribed order of worship or developed liturgical patterns, rituals, and ceremonies nor makes use of all the traditional worship accoutrements such as vestments. This minimizes the emphasis on priesthood, sacraments, and ceremony to highlight evangelism.[16] The High Church worship style among Caribbean people would ultimately influence the type of churches West Indian clergy established in North

America. Raised and trained in the highly ritualized and ceremonial Anglican Church established by the Society for the Propagation of Foreign Parts, McGuire was no exception.

When McGuire completed his training for the ministry in 1888, the Anglican Church in the Caribbean had a relatively small Black following throughout the region.[17] In its heyday, the church had been the exclusive domain of the white settler population.[18] The Anglican Church—unlike the Moravians, Baptists, and Methodists—did not extend itself to the Black population until supporting abolitionist efforts in the 1820s and 1830s.[19] During the postemancipation era, however, the Anglican Church drew a steady Black membership primarily because of the support they provided former slaves. Yet, the colonial church's connection with the denominational headquarters changed because of the shifting relationship between the British metropole and its colonies. In the past, the bond had been economically driven by Caribbean islands' primary commodity: sugar.[20] Toward the mid-nineteenth century, however, the global economy that had once depended on the British Caribbean for sugar had found other sources. Cuban and Brazilian sugarcane production had eclipsed that of the "old colonies" of Jamaica, Barbados, and the Leeward Islands, not to mention the alternative sugar beet production that was also flourishing in Europe during this period.[21] A series of natural disasters in the form of hurricanes, earthquakes, and droughts further extinguished economic prospects in the British Caribbean. With no promising industry, the British government abandoned its colonies in the Caribbean. The social implications for the demise of the sugarcane industry were devastating; high rates of death, infant mortality, and malnutrition became commonplace. West Indians responded by fleeing from their home islands.[22]

A petition to the British government from 1899 aptly sums up the crippling conditions faced by all British subjects, especially for the proletariat: "Her Majesty's black and coloured subjects in the West Indies have to choose between death from starvation in their native islands or suffering in ill-treatment [abroad] . . . because their homes are merely Islands of Death."[23] The petition's author, it seems, hoped that by explaining the British subjects' very dire circumstances, he might convince the Queen to intervene and provide aid for her Caribbean subjects. Yet, with the British cultivating economic interests elsewhere, British West Indian subjects would not be rescued from their distress and hunger anytime soon. Samuel A. Haynes, a West Indian journalist in North America, reiterated the impact of economic suffering taking place in the islands even three decades later. Writing in the *Philadelphia Tribune* in 1930, Haynes, like the earlier petitioner, lamented the economic situation in the West Indies.[24] After fleeing the region for the United States, he was able to more accurately compare Black life in the Caribbean with Black life in North America: "I for one, can see no difference between being lynched by the neck in the United States and being lynched through the stomach in the West Indies." The overwhelming economic conditions drove many away from the Caribbean. Those who remained, suggested Haynes, lived only to eventually starve to death.

As the British Empire's Black colonial subjects struggled to survive, so did the churches. The British government simultaneously stripped the region of its spiritual centers. The economic downfall jeopardized many denominations' investment in the British West Indies. The Anglican Church—the unofficial state church of Britain—was particularly vulnerable to the economic turmoil and uncertainty. As a church predicated on colonial presence, it collapsed, and the British government no longer supported the Anglican Church in this region. In 1883, the British gave Anglican leaders in the West Indies full autonomy by establishing a separate synod for the Caribbean diocese.[25] The new synod gave Caribbean leaders self-determination. It also reduced the clerical appointments from Britain to the Caribbean. The Anglican Church in Britain encouraged Caribbean people to foster their own leadership. This made it imperative for the church to create a new generation of clergymen and leadership from its own ecclesiastical population. The most pressing challenge, however, would be how to adequately train West Indian evangelists and candidates for ministry without the institutional support of the denomination.

The establishment of a separate synod of the Caribbean diocese had significant economic consequences too. The transfer of power ultimately meant that the British were no longer held accountable for their Caribbean counterparts, and the Anglican Church throughout the West Indies could no longer rely on the British church authorities to bankroll their efforts. The British authorities even terminated the biannual imperial subsidy of £20,000 they had provided the Anglican diocese since 1824.[26] Such subsidies and grants continued to be checked in the following decades, as declining revenues and escalating costs in social services and public works tied up British funds. These changes to the earlier relationship between West Indian churches and British colonial administrations not only limited the resources available to the Anglican Church in the West Indies but also drove many churchgoers in the British West Indies out of the region to more economically promising places such as British Honduras, Costa Rica, and Panama, where they would work as plantation laborers at the United Fruit Plantations or the Standard Fruit Company (later known as Standard Fruit & Steamship Company) and its subsidiaries. Others braved the seas and moved to bustling cities such as New York. Altogether, thousands of Anglicans left the British Caribbean in search of a better life. Faced with declining membership, a lack of trained leadership, and diminishing financial resources, many churches shut their doors.

MIGRATION OF A DIFFERENT KIND

Before he helped support a campaign to secure Black clergy for Episcopalians in the United States, Reverend McGuire revitalized Anglican leadership in the Caribbean. As a son of devout Christians, he spent his most formative years in Antigua in the Anglican Church, of which his father, Edward Henry McGuire, was a member.[27] Reverend McGuire's mother was Moravian, but upon marriage the family identified as Anglican. McGuire had an active Christian life. During his childhood, he was both baptized and confirmed as an Anglican. He earned his tertiary education from a branch of Mico Teacher's College,[28] where he attended the satellite campus in Antigua, which eventually closed in 1902 after its board redistributed educational funds.[29] After completing his studies at Mico, McGuire left Antigua for St. Croix, in the Danish West Indies, to pursue specialized training in theology. In St. Thomas he studied at Nisky Theological Seminary, a Moravian-governed institution. It was there in St. Croix where he would take his first post as a pastor, serving a small Moravian congregation in Frederiksted, St. Croix, between 1888 and 1894. In St. Croix, McGuire gained invaluable religious training and experiences that he would rely on when he later began his US ministry. Like most West Indians, McGuire's migration from his smaller town of Swetes, Antigua, to St. Croix would be the first of many moves. The young clergyman would eventually settle in New York, another island of sorts, where he would join the UNIA. Unlike most West Indian immigrants during that period, McGuire had been formally educated, and his theological training at denominational institutions made it easy for him to move to North America because the denomination recognized his professional experience even if it also meted out subtle forms of discrimination. While McGuire's vocational study and training guided his individual migratory path, he also followed the same routes that many West Indians took before making their new home in the United States.

In the United States, Reverend McGuire immediately found community among West Indian migrants. One of the most important new contacts was Robert Josias Morgan, an Anglican priest. Morgan, much like McGuire, had traveled all over the Americas as a missionary for the Anglican Church. Morgan originally left his home island of Jamaica in the late 1870s when streams of his fellow countrymen were immigrating to other nations of the circum-Caribbean and Central America.[30] He was appointed to church work in both Panama and Honduras, where a growing number of Black British Jamaicans and Barbadians had also flocked in search of work.[31] Unlike McGuire, Morgan was given an official charge by the Anglican Church to serve the growing British West Indian community in Panama, even though he was not recognized as a priest during this period. The Society for the Propagation of the Gospel in Foreign Parts recognized "the spiritual conditions of the labourers on the Panama Canal," believing that these communities lacked morality and spirituality. In response, they developed Anglican missions expressly for Jamaican laborers working in Panama.[32] Morgan served at one of these British missionary churches.

George Westerman, an important chronicler of British West Indian life in Panama, wrote about these missions. He confirmed that thirteen Anglican churches designated for British West Indians existed in Panama during this period. In fact, it was the most established denomination among this population.[33] In other words, the Anglican Church had managed to transport the ecclesiastical institution alongside its adherents when it abandoned the British Caribbean. According to Westerman, this gave West Indian laborers a much-needed reprieve from harsh working conditions. More specifically, the Anglican Church provided "escape and consolation to those tropical 'ditch diggers.'"[34] The church rose in importance, Westerman argued, simply because there was little else to maintain the spirits of common laborers. Westerman captured the multiplicities and ambiguities of Blackness these Caribbean immigrants highlighted in a place such as Panama, where they were relegated to a distinct form of working-class Black people. Walker's theorization that Blackness operates as a "site of thinking" about the theological is important for understanding the ways British immigrants distinguished themselves through church while also making it a community resource where they were bereft of so much.[35]

These workers drew on their experiences of Blackness as a force field to create a church that not only operated as a space for respite for their souls but also articulated "a strategy to meet the political and theoretical challenges" Black people faced in multiple settings.[36] Westerman reported that the British West Indians imagined and created churches that had multiple functions for the community, "provid[ing] an effective organization of the group, an approved place for social activities, a forum for expression on many issues, and an outlet for emotional expression" for people who were overworked, underpaid, and unfairly taxed.[37] English-speaking Black people's reimagining of the spiritual was also an indication of the kind of experience that shaped church leaders such as Morgan. Morgan's work developing this important hub of religious activity for British Caribbean immigrants was the kind of work that was envisioned and executed by not just an ordinary priest but also a leader who sat higher in the church structure. Yet, in the compromised lives of "overworked, underpaid, and unfairly taxed" West Indians, priests of all ranks took on the work of institution building. This unique professional experience in the Caribbean, as well as experience of a particular form of racism, inspired Morgan to not simply do the groundwork but also study for his holy orders as a way to validate his experience.[38]

As Morgan continued his mission work in Germany, England, and Sierra Leone, his journey reflected his wide-ranging experiences but also the breadth of the Anglican communion. After working briefly with the AME Church, he pursued his formal education in England, where he finally received his holy orders from the Anglican Church.[39] Morgan was ordained a deacon in June 1895 by Bishop Leighton Coleman of the Episcopal Church.[40] In fact, Coleman confirmed George McGuire in the same year, although there is no record of McGuire and Morgan meeting at this point. After being ordained, Morgan set sail for the United States to begin his clerical profession, a position the church likely recruited him for to develop another hub of activity among the Caribbean immigrants in the United States. Morgan's vocational history is similar to McGuire's journey. They both arrived in North America with extensive training and experience.[41] Yet, much of this training remained unacknowledged by their white peers because the experiences were not housed formally under their supervision and within their institutions. Despite their experience and credentials, both struggled to secure the respect and authority they deserved in a predominantly white denomination. An examination of McGuire's and Morgan's stories are histories that show us how West Indian religious labor, leadership, and Black diasporic migration remade the Episcopalian Church well beyond McGuire's Antigua and Morgan's Jamaica.

Despite Black clergy's creativity in growing the Episcopalian denomination, racism still abounded, sometimes with McGuire on the receiving end. By depending on a migratory stream of Caribbean-educated and -trained Black priests, the white church governance thought it avoided a certain kind of Black leadership, one rooted in the African American community. Furthermore, while white church leaders sometimes praised Caribbean priests (and the experiences they brought with them), they simultaneously invalidated and undermined their training by requiring them to be formally educated under their auspices. In other words, several pernicious strands of racism were operative that hindered a seamless integration into the US church. The first is that aspiring African American priests were overlooked for other Black migrants, which created a climate that bred infighting; make no mistake, this was a common tactic used by oppressors to maintain hegemonic power and order. The second is that Caribbean priests' gifts, talents, and training were being exploited, almost certainly in exchange for subsidizing the cost of migration in hopes that white Christians might avoid confronting the scourge of American racism. And the last is that they insisted on an unnecessary and cumbersome educational vetting process that required additional schooling, which essentially limited the possibility for Caribbean priests to easily climb the ranks of governance within the church.

Some of this racism described above was embedded in and articulated through the workings of the church, while other experiences were simply a result of being a Black man living and working in the American South at that time. This was the kind of racism that surely undergirded Reverend McGuire's charge to destroy all white religious iconography; it is a charge articulated in an organization full of African Americans intimately experiencing racism. The racism McGuire experienced was multilayered and went well beyond racial undermining. It was the kind that refused to fully recognize his ethnic heritage and geographic and cultural ties to spaces outside North America. In fact, his experiences often erased McGuire's ethnic identity without consideration of the critical and material differences that accompany expansive definitions of Blackness. This manner of prejudice reflected the deep-seated racism that comprised the practice of Christianity, and it warranted a response: a liberating rebellion from the established church. Morgan and McGuire, both fired up with righteous indignation, began to fully consider, promote, and integrate racial uplift as a central part of their Christian experience.

Morgan and McGuire crossed paths several times once they reached the United States. While Morgan awaited his appointment to an Episcopal Church, he began working as a public school teacher in Wilmington, Delaware. After about a year (between 1896 and 1897), he was named the deacon at St. Matthew's Episcopal Church in Delaware.[42] No records exist of his time at St. Matthew's, but it is clear that Morgan did not remain in this position for long. Soon after he began working at St. Matthew's, the Episcopal Church transferred him several times to South Carolina, West Virginia, and finally Virginia. McGuire's and Morgan's journeys and time lines intersect clearly in Richmond, Virginia, where Morgan took a post as the rector of St. Phillip's Episcopal Church in 1905.[43] Around the same time, the records of St. Phillip's indicate that McGuire was also working at the parish.[44] Historians such as Gavin White have long assumed that Morgan and McGuire knew each other, but scholars have not made evident where the two actually made each other's acquaintance. Through my piecing together of biographical details, I found the tie to be vocational training and migration.[45] McGuire had a long-standing relationship with the Episcopal Church through his family of origin despite having been trained as Moravian. McGuire's father was raised as an Anglican.

Further, both McGuire and Morgan followed the path of most Caribbean migrants, finding work and moving from island to island until they met each other in the United States. Their journey both vocationally and geographically was similar. However, they only came to know each other personally in the American South, which seems a curious place to meet another West Indian immigrant because northeastern cities such as New York served as the center of Caribbean life in the United States. Perhaps their meeting in the South is of critical importance largely because the scarcity of Black immigrants might have bound them even more profoundly together. Their meeting was one that joined together much more than church leaders. It was a connection built on the hardship of migration, an experience mapped onto their bodies and cemented by accents that allowed them to recognize themselves in each other. The meeting likely served to remind them that they were not alone and could perhaps envision a kind of solidarity stitched together by virtue of similar callings, vocations, and migrations. Furthermore, these two men would continue to encounter one another beyond their time in Richmond. For example, their paths crossed again in Philadelphia, where both McGuire and Morgan were appointed to work in the heart of the city at the Church of the Crucifixion. McGuire remained at this post for four years before being transferred to Cincinnati.[46] From Cincinnati, McGuire returned to Philadelphia with a promotion as rector of St. Thomas Episcopal Church.

It was not unusual for West Indian immigrants such as McGuire to lead Episcopalian churches in North America. In fact, West Indian clergy contributed immensely to Black leadership within the church in the early twentieth century.[47] In New York City, the hub of West Indian migration, there were many Caribbean-led churches that catered to all classes of West Indians. For instance, St. Cyprian Episcopal Church, which was located in San Juan Hill, primarily served working-class people from the Caribbean. St. Martin Episcopal Church, on the other hand, was composed of the Caribbean middle class, which included a host of professionals.[48] These leaders served their communities and used the church to preserve island culture and tradition. McGuire and Morgan had actively re-created a religious space of familiarity for immigrants, but they also imagined these institutions to reflect the multiplicities of Black religious expression.[49] However, when McGuire and Morgan lived and worked in Richmond and Philadelphia, they experienced a period of deep spiritual introspection during which both reconsidered their affiliations with the Episcopal Church. Eventually, each decided to break away from the Episcopalian denomination, albeit for different reasons.

In 1908 the bishop of Asheville suspended Morgan from the Episcopalian Church, charging him with abandoning his ministry.[50] The author of the 1915 Who's Who of the Colored Race claimed that Morgan "maintained serious doubts concerning the teachings of the whole Anglican Communion."[51] During his suspension, he continued his migrations. He engaged in a three-year study and evaluation of Anglicanism, Roman Catholicism, and orthodoxy. He visited Russia, Turkey, Cyprus, and the Holy Land, all in an effort to gain some clarity about his theological orientation.[52] This was yet another moment marked by migration that served as a profound moment in Morgan's spiritual growth. It is unclear why he left the Episcopalian Church after having dedicated so much time and effort to the denomination; however, sometime during this period he actively searched for an ecclesiastical alternative to Anglicanism. In the end, Morgan wrote, "I feel now firmer and stronger spiritually than I did before I came."[53] His strength, he determined, would best be harnessed in the Orthodox Church.

Morgan eventually joined the clergy of the Holy Greek Orthodox Catholic and Apostolic Church. His choice of the Greek Orthodox Church rather than the Russian Orthodox Church was very likely due to free-dom. By this I mean that he likely valued the Greek Orthodox churches in North America because they were autonomous. In fact, at the turn of the century, the Greeks were decades away from appointing North American bishops. Church historian Mathew Namee notes that "the Greeks in America were quite disorganized. There were no bishops, no seminaries, no real national structure of any kind." Namee found it curious that Morgan joined the Greek Orthodox Church rather than the much more organized Russian Orthodox Church and describes the contrast between the two churches. "They had a bishop, St. Tikhon, who was well-known among the Anglicans," Namee states.[54] And "right around this time . . . the Russians established their first seminary, in Minneapolis." He concludes that the Russians, with their organization and even their connections to the Anglicans, seemed like the obvious choice. However, Morgan's history of iterant work with the Anglican communion throughout the world and even his short break to the Black independent AME Church suggest that his experience working in and for the church was highly racialized.

It is very likely that, like McGuire, Morgan felt the ramifications of a racial order and color scheme. This order that was embedded in Anglican communion extended to the Russian Orthodox Church. Further-more, during Morgan's spiritual exploration there was no evidence of Black priests working in the Russian Orthodox Church in America. The Greek Orthodox Church's disorganization and autonomy was actually an advantage for Morgan; it was a place where he had the agency to build. He could escape racism within the church structure, and he could con-trol his own church without interruption. Namee recognizes him as the first Black Orthodox priest but does not always explain the impact of that within the church context. Namee's racialization of Morgan is important because he recognizes Morgan's religious work as part of the church's iconic leadership. Yet, Namee does not fully reckon with the ways Morgan might have actually navigated being Black within the Anglican and Epis-copal Churches. While the AME Church might seem to deeply oppose this point, it is important to recognize the way that ethnic tensions have been at the center of AME governance certainly in Africa, where the AME Church did not allow self-governance within the continent for decades. In other words, both McGuire and Morgan seemed committed to Christianity as evinced by their investment in various congregations and denominations. However, they strategically sought autonomy to build their own churches where they might escape the racism and xenophobia that plagued other churches. As spiritual migrants they kept moving, looking for a church home until they found good ground from which to lead.

MCGUIRE LEAVES THE ANGLICAN COMMUNION

Racism rather than theological change was McGuire's impetus for leaving the Episcopalian Church. After McGuire had served in Richmond, where he met Morgan, and in Philadelphia at the esteemed St. Thomas Episcopal Church in 1905, McGuire accepted a position titled "archdeacon in convocation for colored work" in the diocese of Arkansas.[55] He worked under the guidance of the Right Reverend William Montgomery Brown, the diocesan bishop. Brown, who was nicknamed the "bad bishop," was a white man who began his career as a priest in Grace Episcopal Church and was later named the bishop of Arkansas between 1899 and 1912. The Episcopalian Church eventually deposed of Brown for heretical teachings.[56] When McGuire arrived in Arkansas, Brown was determined to implement the "Arkansas Plan," which encouraged racial separation within the Episcopalian Church. With it, Black Episcopalians would be relegated to their own designated chapels and worship spaces. As a longtime advocate of racial segregation in the church, Brown disparaged the topic of integration in his book *The Catholic Church and the Color Line*: "I pass this nauseating theory . . . as ruinously wrong. . . . [I]t is wrong for different races even to try to get along with one ecclesiastical Chapel."[57] Brown believed that "a God-implanted race prejudice makes it impossible, absolutely so, that Afro-Americans and Anglo-Americans should ever occupy the same footing in a dual racial Church," a sentiment shared by so many given that Sunday mornings are still the most segregated time in the United States.[58]

Additionally, Brown relied on these theorizations to argue for the creation of a separate denomination for Black Episcopalians. His Arkansas Plan was to construct a Negro episcopate, a church hierarchy similar to the Episcopal Church. Like the Episcopalian Church, it would have three orders of Black priests, deacons, and bishops. Rather than permit the Black bishops to have the same authority and power as white bishops, though, they would be consecrated as suffragan bishops, or assistant bishops. They would not attain the status of full bishop and thus would be denied a vote in the General Convention. Brown also opposed any possibility of having a Black man serve in the House of Bishops, a decision that would ultimately strip a bishop of any power. Brown's racism was difficult for any person of color to bear, but it must have proved incredibly difficult for McGuire, who was one of the brightest and best priests of his time. McGuire likely felt robbed of his rightful appointment given his training. His perseverance and patience throughout his experiences in the church was likely the product of prayer, one anchored in the model prayer that called forth God's kingdom to come and all things to fall into alignment.

Initially, McGuire protested Brown's proposal for a separate Negro episcopate. McGuire argued that it had not been necessary in the Caribbean. He pointed out that in the West Indies, "there has existed no need for special or racial Episcopal supervision."[59] He declared to George Bragg, editor of the *Church Advocate* and an African American, that Brown "failed to appreciate the necessity for this movement." Yet, it seems that some Episcopalians found the racial division necessary. In 1907, the General Convention instituted a plan to consecrate suffragan bishops. These assistants to the diocesan bishop would never vote in the House of Bishops, nor would they ever gain full status as diocesan bishops. Despite this plan's ratification, it did not come to fruition until ten years later.

McGuire spent only three years under Brown's tutelage before transferring to a new post in Boston. In Cambridge, McGuire took up ordinary church work, ministering over a flock of West Indian immigrants. This church was made up of West Indians who had defected from St. Peter's Episcopal Church and Christ Episcopal Church because white parishioners had not welcomed them.[60] McGuire established St. Bartholomew's Church, with close to seventy Episcopalians from all over the British and French West Indies. Although the congregation flourished under McGuire, it became clear to him that the church would never be granted full authority to operate independently. Once again, McGuire's hopes for expanding Black Episcopalians' domain within the larger North American communion were dashed. This was yet another example in which McGuire's talents and ambitions were not fully realized. As a result, he continued to search for a position within the Episcopalian Church in which his vocational worth might be acknowledged. He returned to an administrative position at the Episcopalian Church headquarters, perhaps as a means to better position himself within the church.

From 1911 to 1913, McGuire was the field secretary of the American Church Institute for Negroes in New York City. The institute was an arm of the Episcopalian Church that was created in 1906 as a response to educational disparities between African Americans and whites.[61] Its primary focus was on African American education particularly in the South, where educational resources were limited. While the institute's focus was on higher education, it also sought to promote religious instruction to African American students. Its strategy was to train African Americans to be successful tradesmen, entrepreneurs, educators, and clergymen in the hope that these professionals would funnel their shared educational benefits throughout their communities while also taking on leadership positions within the church.

The American Church Institute for Negroes supported schools in North Carolina, Georgia, Tennessee, Alabama, Mississippi, Louisiana, and South Carolina.[62] To receive support, a school had to be located in the area of its state with the highest concentration of African Americans. The first and largest schools supported by the American Church Institute for Negroes included, among others, St. Paul's Normal School in Lawrenceville, Virginia; St. Augustine's Normal School and Collegiate Institute in Raleigh, North Carolina; and Bishop Payne's Divinity School in Petersburg, Virginia. Later, Fort Valley High in Fort Valley, Georgia, and the Voorhees School and Junior College in Denmark, South Carolina, also received support from the church, both receiving the greatest financial support of any of the schools. As a representative for the organization, McGuire traveled all over the country speaking to Episcopalians and seeking funds for their programs. This work was somewhat rewarding for McGuire, but it dislocated him almost entirely from ecclesiastical work. He returned to ministerial work after three years of service at the American Church Institute for Negroes. This time, McGuire returned to Antigua. It remains unclear why he went home, but between 1913 and 1918 he resumed his ministerial calling as the rector of St. Paul's Episcopal Church in Falmouth, Antigua.[63] After serving for five years in that parish, he returned to New York.

Upon his return McGuire withdrew his membership from the Episcopalian Church, in which he had spent close to fifteen years officially serving. His act of resignation, given all of his years dedicated to Anglicanism, signaled a shift in his lived theology. McGuire's resignation was an act of refusal to accept the God of oppression that the Anglican communion meted through its racism and discrimination. This "theology of refusal," as South African theologian Allan A. Boesak labeled it, insisted on a God of liberation that McGuire could only reach by leaving the Anglican communion.[64] His abandonment of mainline Protestant leadership met some of his own spiritual needs by liberating him from a stifling and racist Episcopalian structure. Humbling himself to serve a decade and a half in a position that both undermined and underemployed him also gave him the training and knowledge about how the denomination's infrastructure and operations functioned. He was armed with seminary training, professional experience, and wisdom from hardship when he left the Episcopalian Church. The continued waves of Black clergy, whether in the United States or South Africa, leaving white-controlled churches was not just circumstantial, opportunistic, or an individual consequence of a professional course. McGuire's leaving was political and theologically grounded too.

McGuire joined the Garvey movement and by 1919 had established his own Independent Episcopal Church in New York called the Church of the Good Shepherd. McGuire was one of many clergymen who created his own church during this period. According to African American author, critic, songwriter, and politician James Weldon Johnson, churches were the fastest-growing institution in Harlem, which had more than 130 churches by 1930.[65] Exactly 93 percent of these were not considered traditional mainline Protestant churches, which meant that only 7 percent were.[66] West Indian poet Claude McKay writes that Harlem was home to a "legion of mystics and medicine men" who called themselves "prophets and priests, shepherds, bishops confessors and even sons of god."[67] McKay asserted that religious diversity came in the form of "Pentecostal Pilgrims, Orthodox Ethiopians, Moorish Science Templars, Black Jews, and many others, Christian and non-Christian," all of whom created a new form of religious pluralism.

McGuire led the Independent Episcopal Church for less than a year before establishing the AOC. He claimed that the impetus for the church was "an awakened Negro consciousness to the humiliating racial barriers existing in white Episcopal churches."[68] The priests and laity who comprised the Independent Episcopal Church defected from the Episcopal Church because of their experiences with racism. They "desire[d] to cast off white dominance and desired their own as leaders in the Ecclesiastical world."[69] Their twofold mission of combating racial hierarchy and seeking racial empowerment attracted a host of malcontent priests and church leaders. On September 2, 1921, McGuire gathered a multitude of clergy at the Church of the Good Shepherd. There, he held the first synod of the Independent Episcopal Church. At this gathering, McGuire and these clergy members decided they would follow Episcopalian governance and policy while maintaining their autonomy.

McGuire's bold move to create a reformed Episcopalian denomination reflected his own experiences of racism, first as the archdeacon of colored work in Arkansas and again when he was unable to gain full congregational status for St. Bartholomew's in Massachusetts. McGuire was dissatisfied with his limited leadership opportunities, but he insisted that "the new church was neither schismatic nor heretical." Instead, he asserted, the new church was "an expression of the spirit of racial leadership in ecclesiastical matters."[70] The idea of religious freedom was a salient part of the sentiments circulating in the Independent Episcopal Church. At first examination, McGuire's Independent Episcopal Church seemed like an amended version of Brown's Arkansas Plan of racial separation. The difference between McGuire's Independent Episcopal Church and Brown's Arkansas Plan was that McGuire's priests believed that the greatest form of spiritual freedom was to have Black bishops preside over their governing body.

The Independent Episcopal Church amassed a transnational following stretching from Manhattan, Brooklyn, and Pittsburgh to Nova Scotia, Cuba, the Dominican Republic, Bermuda, and elsewhere in the West Indies and Latin America.[71] McGuire and his leadership team sought ecclesiastical respect through a historic episcopate and apostolic succession. To this end, the leaders of the Independent Episcopal Church used their synod meetings to organize their new denomination. The first such synod was an intense organizing meeting. McGuire and a small cadre of Episcopalian priests gathered to discuss and write a declaration of faith, the constitution and canons, the liturgy, and a hymnal and to establish their own theological seminary. They adopted "African Orthodox Church" as the name of the ecclesiastical body. They also elected George McGuire as a presiding officer and named him bishop-elect. The most important concern for this new church and its bishop-elect was to secure McGuire's consecration. They believed that with episcopacy, their church would fully be legitimate. Although they reached out to the Episcopal Church, the Roman Catholic Church, and the Russian Orthodox Church for ecclesiastical recognition, all of those churches declined to grant the episcopacy and the apostolic succession to McGuire, very likely because he was Black.[72] McGuire's inquiries might have also been unsuccessful because he had no intention of making the AOC an addendum to any white denomination. The AOC is one of the only Black denominations to this day with a "valid, though some might add irregular episcopacy."[73]

Reverend Joseph René Vilatte, the exarch and metropolitan of the American Catholic Church, finally agreed to bestow McGuire with the episcopacy. To be granted episcopacy, the members of the newly formed AOC had to produce a letter of request along with the credentials and papers from its first general synod, which listed its officers, membership, and procedures.[74] Before gaining approval, McGuire and the synod's secretary, William E. Robertson, had to present themselves to Vilatte in Chicago. McGuire and Robertson spent eight days petitioning for episcopacy at the American Catholic Consistory. In the process, the consistory heavily scrutinized the AOC's declaration of faith, constitution and canons, and purposes and aims. The American Catholic Consistory approved McGuire for the episcopacy but also required that he join the Conclave of Bishops of the American Catholic Church. Under this agreement, McGuire could consecrate bishops only with the permission of the Conclave of Bishops. McGuire and his colleagues underwent this laborious process to ensure that their church was officially and ecclesiastically recognized.

Reverend McGuire's commitment to earning episcopacy was very likely a reflection of the religious milieu among African American churches. Religious beliefs and practices ran the gamut during the American interwar years. During this period, a proliferation of churches redefined the contours of African American denominations, especially for University of Chicago scholars such as E. Franklin Frazier, St. Clair Drake, Horace Cayton, and Charles S. Johnson. Storefront churches were the primary focus of their criticism. These churches dotted the urban landscape of cities such as New York, where southern migrants settled and created their own spiritual homes. These scholars had rigid ideas and typologies about what constituted an African American church. According to Wallace Best, scholars such as Frazier, Drake, Cayton, and Johnson did not fully understand storefront churches' unique position as a product of both southern folkways and urban progress because they represented a sort of "religious Diaspora."[75] Most of these storefront churches—many of which were Baptist and others of which were called Pentecostal, Holiness, or Spiritualist churches—did not maintain any relationship with a governing head. Rather, they condemned them, calling them anachronistic and backward.

In many cases, these churches represented an ontological shift in the Black church. As Best has shown, this ecclesiastical mode captured southern migrants' identity.[76] These storefront churches stood in sharp contrast to the more traditional denominations—namely Episcopalian, Congregationalist, and Presbyterian—that many established northerners attended. The proliferation of these churches and countless small sectarian movements ignited controversy among not only distinguished African American scholars but also ordinary northerners. Northerners were concerned with the distinct church culture and ritual that emerged from these Pentecostal, Holiness, and Apostolic churches. They departed from the

High Church atmosphere that characterized worship in the mainline Protestant churches. As a result of this concern and criticism, groups such as the AOC very much sought to distinguish themselves from many of the storefront churches that emerged at the same time. McGuire believed that episcopacy, among other features of the highly ritualized AOC, would accomplish this distinction.

On Sunday, September 25, 1921, McGuire and his deputation received conditional baptism, confirmation, and the minor orders from the American Catholic Church.[77] The following day McGuire was also admitted as a deacon, and on the day after that he was made a priest. All of these services took place at the Church of Our Lady of Good Death in Chicago. In New York, Reverend Dr. George Alexander McGuire was given a service of enthronement in his own Cathedral Chapel of the Good Shepherd. Many of McGuire's former colleagues from the Episcopalian Church came to honor him at his enthronement service. After this arduous process, McGuire and the other priests of the church were proud of their new church and especially proud of having earned episcopacy, no matter how irregular it might have seemed to others. The episcopacy gave them ecclesiastical authority by connecting them to the first apostles, a divine connection to those who first organized Christianity.

In his new church, McGuire recruited in a fashion that reflected his own history and ministry of migration. He selected delegates from across the globe, including America, Canada, and Cuba. He worked vigorously to build his movement and encouraged and envisioned church formation in a variety of countries and on a global scale. He welcomed a host of clergy who had abandoned their posts. McGuire started by building his denomination among Caribbean-headed churches, such as one congregation led by a Barbadian priest named Reverend Reginald Grant Barrow and a man named James G. Mythen.[78] Mythen had once been a deacon at a parish in Sante Fe, New Mexico.[79] Mythen left the Episcopalian Church and eventually affiliated himself with the Russian Orthodox Church, becoming Archimandrite Patrick. McGuire tried to use his contact with Patrick and another priest, Father Anthony, to gain episcopacy through the Eastern churches. He had expressed interest in receiving "consideration" from the Eastern churches and eventual "union with the ancient and apostolic Abyssinian Church of glorious heritage, sacrifice, and continuity."[80] This ecclesiastical connection never came to fruition. It is very likely that McGuire was not able to link himself with the Russian Orthodox Church because the church insisted on a level of supervision over him and his following; in essence, he valued his freedom. Heavy supervision undermined his reasons for leaving the Episcopalian Church as he sought to gain agency and come out from under the grip of white church leaders. Furthermore, McGuire was not celibate, and subsequently this would mean he could not have been consecrated by the Russians even if they did grant him autonomy. McGuire would continue to secure the AOC's episcopacy.

McGuire would also lean on Morgan to secure a meeting with the chancellor of the American Catholic Church. However, they waited to receive a reply from the church because they sought to evade control by white church leaders. They wanted to be granted episcopacy and also have complete autonomy. Finally, the American Catholic Church granted them episcopacy in 1921. McGuire was consecrated as archbishop and primate of the AOC and was placed on the consistory body. Fathers Joseph René Vilatte and Carl Nybladh, two white former Episcopalian priests, consecrated McGuire. Vilatte had welcomed McGuire's old colleague and friend Morgan to the American Catholic Church years earlier. It is likely that McGuire was actually granted the episcopacy because of his friendship with Morgan. This mentorship among two former priests of the Anglican communion was paramount to McGuire's success in establishing the AOC. It is also very likely that when McGuire heard of a priest in South Africa by the name of Daniel William Alexander seeking entrance into the church, he remembered his arduous attempt to gain religious autonomy.

FIVE

Garvey's God

Racial Uplift and the Creation
of the African Orthodox Church

Meetings of the Universal Negro Improvement Association (UNIA) always began with officers of the Black Cross Nurses, the African Legion, and members of any auxiliaries clothed in full regalia singing the hymn "Shine Eternal." The processional ended with a prayer before turning to business. This order of the meeting, much like a call to worship, reflected the ways religious leaders such as Reverend George McGuire and Rabbi Arnold Ford set the atmosphere for worship and spiritual impartation. McGuire and Ford's attempt to standardize UNIA chapter meetings worldwide reflected the religious creativity at the center of the association and was also a product of the migratory period in African American history called the Great Migration. UNIA leaders relied on their experiences of migration, race, politics, and a complex engagement with Christian theology to institutionalize religion within their organization in the 1920s. Garvey's genius was that he welcomed these religious leaders who held various theologies, interpretations, and ecclesiastic configurations under the UNIA. Garveyism created a space for religious possibility and new paradigms far beyond what the Black church had long established. The UNIA functioned as sanctuary for those in search of their political, economic, and spiritual freedom where no current church configuration existed. In this chapter, I examine and contextualize the religious infrastructure of the UNIA to ask questions about who made it, how they imagined it, and how the religious ethos continually referenced their religious past but also pointed to their fraught diasporic longing for Africa(ns).

The UNIA was the largest Black mass movement; it sought both economic and political strategies of self-sufficiency to uplift Blacks worldwide. Marcus Garvey originally established the UNIA in his home island of Jamaica in 1914.[1] The UNIA has been described as a "social, humanitarian, charitable, educational, institutional, constructive, and expansive society . . . founded by persons, desiring the utmost, to work for the general uplift of the Negro peoples of the world."[2] When Garvey and his associates moved the UNIA headquarters to New York City, it had broader objectives steeped in Black nationalism. Garvey's vision of a particular form of Black brotherhood was expressly declared in the UNIA's "Constitution of 1914" and then rearticulated more expansively in the powerful "Declaration of the Rights of the Negro Peoples of the World," which he wrote and issued in 1920.[3] The UNIA's objectives were

> To establish a universal confraternity among the race; to promote the spirit of race pride and love; to reclaim the fallen of the race, to administer to and help the needy; to assist in civilizing the backwards races of Africa; to establish Commissaries in the principal countries of the world for the protection and representation of all Negroes, irrespective of Nationality; to strengthen the imperialism of Liberia, Basutoland, etc.; to establish a conscientious Christian worship among the tribes of Africa, the fatherland; to establish and support universities[,] colleges, and secondary schools for the further education and culture for our boys and girls, etc., etc.[4]

Garvey's vision of liberation, particularly his desire to offer "universal [Black] confraternity" and his promotion of "the spirit of race pride and love," reflected his desire for a new world order that freed Black people from socioeconomic, political, and cultural oppression.

Among the societies and fraternities of Garvey's time, the UNIA was distinct.[5] And yet, his vision was also vexed and fraught with discourses of African barbarism and Western civility that animated his charge to "reclaim the fallen of the race" and "assist in civilizing the backwards races of Africa." Some of the UNIA aims articulated from the West and extended to the continent echoed the commitment to God's kingdom come, while others simply reified a form of Western imperialism that shaped much of Christian culture at the time. The UNIA's vision, albeit it vexed and fraught by cultural and religious imperialism, was still popular among Africans who had long fought for their own liberation from mounting forms of colonialism. Overall, Garvey and his followers were quite successful in some of their proposed endeavors. The association's initial aim had been to proselytize to "the backwards and primitive races of Africa."[6] Its early founders sought to establish missionary work in either Liberia, Ethiopia, Cameroon, or South Africa because they believed that their missionary efforts would serve a dual purpose. The first purpose was to allow Garveyites to evangelize and convert Africans to Christianity. In the midst of conversion, Garveyites sought to transform Africans into a seemingly more sophisticated and civilized Christian people. The second purpose was to use Christian conversion to secure Africa for remigration, a scheme that had been debated for many decades.[7] In the end, the organization was not able to embark on any mission work in Africa.

Instead, the UNIA was much more successful as a religious forum for its own followers. The closest the UNIA came to Christian evangelism might have been through the circulation of *Negro World*, the organization's newspaper and mouthpiece. The newspaper was the "greatest missionary in building up divisions and making converts."[8] The divisional minutes, speeches, and sermons printed in the newspaper achieved the proselytizing work that Garvey and his colleagues had originally hoped to pursue.[9] Garveyites in South Africa heard about the UNIA, the church, and the movement through *Negro World*. It was "Garvey's most effective promoter[,] with a circulation of 20,000" at its zenith.[10] The newspaper connected members in disparate locations to an "imagined community" that Garvey hoped and believed would become a Black nation.[11]

And in the case of West Indian immigrants, they used it to navigate an entirely new society altogether. The UNIA provided a structure under which its members both processed and came to understand their lives—politically, economically, and spiritually—as they endured living in racist societies. Black nationalism was the philosophical and political heart of the UNIA. Narrowly conceived, Black nationalism has the primary objective of establishing a nation designated solely for people of African descent. More broadly understood, Black nationalism promotes much more than nationhood, but it also highlights a form of racial solidarity that is not neatly mapped onto a nation-state. UNIA chapters demonstrated these complexities well. Even though the organization was global, the New York base (and its surrounding areas) was largely composed of West Indian leadership, with many African Americans as rank-and-file members.[12] However, African Americans led most UNIA chapters outside of New York, Philadelphia, and other large northeastern cities, such as chapters in the rural South.

Claudrena N. Harold's book *The Rise and Fall of the Garvey Movement in the Urban South, 1918–1942*, points to the US South as the backbone of Black organizing. Her scholarship offers a complicated understanding of the South, where working-class African Americans and West Indians in places such as New Orleans, Miami, and Hampton Roads, Virginia were just as common even though previous scholarship has focused on northern cities.[13] Harold shows us that grand visions of Black freedom cannot simply be attributed to Black northerners or even solely to seemingly radical West Indians and that working-class Black southerners' political imaginary was broad and cosmopolitan in nature. Indeed, descriptions of the working-class Blacks who gravitated toward Garveyism abounded. The *Baltimore Observer* described Garveyites as "cooks, porters, hod-carriers, and washerwomen, scullions, and day laborers."[14] These working-class people sought important features of the UNIA such as friendship, fraternity, benevolence, and a new expression of Christianity, all aspects of the power North American society often denied them. Overall, the UNIA functioned as much more than the mutual aids of the day; it stood for the uplift of Black people and was a form of kingdom building.[15] Garvey set in motion these economic and political plans for self-sufficiency through projects such as the well-known shipping company the Black Star Line and a coterie of other businesses and factories aimed at reframing Black experiences around the Black nation-state.

Garvey's vision moved beyond nationhood. He wanted to build a Black empire through "the absorption and transformation of the entire African continent to the political ideology and economy of the UNIA."[16] His work followed the tradition of earlier Pan-Africanists such as Martin Delany, Edward Wilmot Blyden, and David Walker. Like Delany, Garvey called for remigration to Africa, known as the Back to Africa movement. The purpose of remigration was to establish Black nationhood, but until nationhood seemed possible, Garveyites actively promoted race pride, charity, and established Black institutions, where Garvey modeled a new vision of "conscientious Christian worship" that wasn't simply about evangelizing African people but also developing their own spirituality. Sylvester

Johnson, a scholar of Black religion, describes it this way: Garveyism fore-grounded "Blackness as a diasporic formation and [it was] stridently as-serting a Black theology . . . that enabled the flourishing of Black ethnic religion."[17] Johnson's conclusion that Garveyism was a religious incubator is captured in the growing historiography on religion during this period.

The scholarship of Randall K. Burkett, Richard S. Newman, Barbara Bair, Warren C. Platt, Gavin White, Byron Rushing, Morris R. Johnson, and Beryl Satter is foundational to understanding the place of religion in the UNIA.[18] Together, they created archives and analyzed some of the first materials that readily engaged with religion. Burkett's scholarship was among the first to distill the importance of religion in Garveyism, particu-larly the contributions of Black clergy to sustaining the movement. While Burkett defined Garveyism as a "civil religion," with religious symbols and rituals, much of its leadership were dedicated clergy committed to far more than a nominal Christianity.[19] Indeed, local UNIA leadership largely con-sisted of Black clergy who imbued it with a milieu of faith. After leaving the Anglican Church like Alexander, Reverend McGuire found solace in a community of Black people who shared his quest for freedom through a practice of religion. In this chapter, I examine the ways McGuire leveraged both his leadership within the UNIA and the movement's own religious fluidity to create the African Orthodox Church (AOC), even though it was not officially tied to the UNIA.

While Garvey worked to promote race pride and economic stability—two factors paramount to Black nationalism—the organization never em-barked on mission work in Africa. The UNIA was much more successful in using the organization as a religious forum for its own followers. The closest the UNIA came to Christian evangelism was through the establish-ment and growth of the AOC. Reverend McGuire's work introducing Afri-can people to the denomination and the terms under which he framed its growth in South Africa illuminate the way that he too internalized racist ideas about African people who, obviously, had long participated in and established Christian churches. Those South Africans such as Daniel Wil-liam Alexande, who led the AOC on the continent, were doing the work, spiritually and religiously, that Garvey never achieved.

The AOC grew more vigorously on African soil because its theological impulses mirrored clergyman Mangena Mokone's Ethiopian movement and furthered the work he started. Likewise, South African Christians used the AOC to circumvent the 1924 state mandate for white supervision over Black congregations. Due to the loophole about US nationality, South

Africa accepted the AOC's Black leadership as the authority and supervisor over African clergy. South African Christians established the AOC with hopes of self-governance and the expulsion of racist authority, and they longed for support without overbearing supervision. Reverend McGuire had shared these commitments when he first founded the AOC to reimagine church life beyond the racism he experienced in the Anglican Church. On both sides of the Atlantic, the AOC existed as a space of spiritual liberation and refuge from racism. The conception of the church was partially a response to persistent forms of prejudice and racism that West Indian priests and laity, in particular, experienced in North America within mainline Protestant denominations. The AOC functioned as an extension of the Ethiopian movement on both sides of the Atlantic. As the chaplain-general, McGuire did not control the eclectic forms of religious expression among the divisions, but he—along with other religious leaders at the executive level—fomented religious structures that clergy enacted and adapted for those under their spiritual covering. Taking note of religious symbols and rituals, Burkett placed Garvey at the helm of the movement, even dubbing him the "unordained theologian."[20]

Barbara Bair and Beryl Satter extended this scholarship by considering the impact of gender on political forms of redemption. Bair offers a critical analysis of the UNIA, suggesting that it was "built on the social foundation of the Black church."[21] Despite "Garvey's claim that 'Liberty Halls [UNIA meeting places] were not to be used as churches'" and that the UNIA "'did not organize as any church,'" Bair has explained her thinking further by liking the creation of new UNIA chapters as a similar process of "digging out" new churches.[22] If anyone took on the digging, Bair and Satter determined, it was Black women.[23] Scholars such as Gayraud S. Wilmore, Richard Newman, and Morris Rodney Johnson pick up on Bair's finding about the UNIA operating as a church by demonstrating the crucial ways Garveyism helped Black people reimagine Christianity. Garveyism pushed the notion that white Christians obscured ideas of God, Christ, and humanity.[24] Indeed, an ethos of Black nationalism set the tone for a religious logic in which "an all-black world demanded a black God."[25] This rhetoric and its accompanying ideas mirror much of what South African church leaders declared in the nineteenth-century Ethiopian movement, making it appealing to African clergy already committed to its tenets.

More recent scholarship has continued this line of thinking but has suggested that Garveyism moved beyond Christianity and cultivated a myriad of religious traditions.[26] This scholarship has offered new insight about other forms of religious practice stemming from Black nationalist circles such as Ula Taylor's work on the Nation of Islam, Jacob Dorman's scholarship on Noble Drew Ali's Moorish Science Temple, and Judith Weisenfeld's book that also covers the Moorish Science Temple of Noble, the Nation of Islam, the International Peace Mission movement, and congregations of Ethiopian Jews, among others.[27] To be sure, what I wish to assert in this chapter is that Garveyism was ecumenical, with a network extending to Christianity, Judaism, and Islam. This ecumenical spirit cultivated a different climate from that of other organizations of its time. Religion became a critical philosophical foundation for understanding the world.[28] This new work offers much-needed insight, yet in my search to understand how Christians imagined a racial project of freedom, I seek to return to Barbara Bair and Gayraud Wilmore's early theorizations on Garvey because they speak directly to church work. This scholarship collectively points to the UNIA's function as a church as well as an alternative form of radicalism to the conventional Christianity, which attracted preachers such as Reverend McGuire who had been searching for the kind of "conscientious Christian worship" that they had cultivated amid migration; these ministers of migration yearned for spiritual freedom. What ostensibly may have appeared as a political gathering under the auspices of Black nationalism was in fact the formation and practice of "conscientious worship," a missional call for spiritual freedom beyond McGuire's vision.

BENEVOLENT PARTNERSHIPS AND OVERLAPPING RELIGIOUS MIGRATIONS

Between 1900 and 1930, streams of immigrants from the Caribbean met millions of African Americans relocating from the US South northward. Two and a half million African Americans left the Jim Crow South for opportunities in northeastern, midwestern, and western cities such as New York, Philadelphia, Detroit, Chicago, Pittsburgh, Los Angeles, Portland, and Seattle. Southern migrants exchanged unfair wages, racial violence, and general hardship for cities they referred to as "the Land of Hope" and "the Promised Land," where they might grasp more fully the promises of citizenship through socioeconomic and political equality. West Indians, having witnessed the fall of sugar and tired from colonialism, traveled through the circum-Caribbean to the United States also searching for access to social, economic, and political possibility. The influx of these US southerners and West Indians was most evident in the northeastern corridor, where both groups radically transformed these cities. If African Americans and West Indians were building a new Black world in the 1920s, then scholar Wallace D. Best was perceptive in declaring that they set "a new sacred order" too.[29] While Best was referring to the ways that migration inspired different ritual and institutional expression in Chicago, similar insight applies for West Indians who were also tending to the "exigencies of [post-migratory] life."[30]

Immigrants from the Caribbean represented an 80 percent increase of Black foreigners in America—from 20,000 in 1900 to 100,000 in 1930—and while these numbers do not compare to the millions of migrants that arrived from the South, historian Winston James suggests that this "wave of Black humanity that washed up at Ellis Island was small. . . . But its impact . . . was much larger than its size might suggest."[31] Like southern migrants, these immigrants had traveled from small towns and cities throughout the Caribbean, parts of Latin America, and circum-Caribbean, carrying with them experiences and cultures that only found full sacred expression in settlement.

West Indian immigrants such as Reverend McGuire, who had traveled this path firsthand, brought with them spiritual insight. In seeking refuge through complex connections in the United States, these newcomers served as critical conduits for new religious paradigms that disrupted an old established Black northern order that had sometimes conformed to white control. Yet, Caribbean influence on religious institutions in this period—much like the histories of African American storefront churches before they were documented in the work of Milton Sernett, Wallace D. Best,[32] and Deidre Helen Crumbley—have not been fully historicized or contextualized.[33] As Cheryl Townsend Gilkes professed, "the multitude of denominations that opened up storefront churches during the Great Migration were not just Pentecostal, but were Holiness, Pentecostal Apostolic, and Deliverance churches."[34] In one of the most significant contributions of the Great Migration, Garveyism afforded an opportunity to examine other sites of religious formation beyond the storefront. The UNIA's malleability was rooted in how Garvey had initially conceived of the UNIA as a "place of conscientious worship." To be sure, Christian theology seemed a part, at least nominally, of a number of organizations that emerged around the same time.

By 1919 when the UNIA relocated its headquarters—moving within the same block of West 135th Street in Harlem—African American organizations such as the National Urban League, the NAACP, A. Philip Randolph's Brotherhood of Sleeping Car Porters, the Black Women's Club movements, and many benevolent societies emerged. For West Indians, benevolent associations functioned as an important safety net especially during the Great Migration. Mutual aid societies were voluntary organizations in which people worked together to develop strategies and resources in times of financial hardship, death, illness, and natural disasters. In the reductive sense, these associations might also be understood as rotating credit associations.[35] West Indian immigrants established a number of mutual aid societies such as the Grenada Mutual Benevolent Association, the Sons and Daughters of Barbados, the Bermuda Benevolent Association, the Trinidad Benevolent Association, the Montserrat Progressive Society, the West Indian Ladies Aid Society, and the British Jamaican Benevolent Association, among others. West Indians and African Americans relied on mutual aid societies, lodges, and social clubs to navigate their new northern surroundings. But the UNIA loomed large among all of these organizations—political, cultural, and otherwise—because of both its size and political influence. By the 1920s, the Garvey movement amounted to seven hundred members in thirty-eight states. And further, its overall membership of six million followers in forty different countries gave it greater acclaim than any other benevolent society of its time. The UNIA, unlike many of the other organizations, functioned as a multimodal organization that inspired new forms of Black politics and secured Blacks socioeconomically while also providing them with spiritual refuge, an organizational prototype for kingdom come.

"CONSCIENTIOUS CHRISTIAN WORSHIP" IN THE UNIA

Although George McGuire dubbed Marcus Garvey the "unordained theologian," McGuire was the driving force behind the religious milieu of the UNIA. Reverend McGuire was elected the "titular Archbishop of Ethiopia," the chaplain-general of the High Executive Council of the UNIA. What I wish to emphasize here is that, through McGuire's influence, the UNIA more formally began to articulate itself through the performative grammar of Christian religious worship. His dedication to Christianity influenced the organization's spiritual ethos as he presided over all chaplain-generals in the UNIA. Yet, even with this great authority, most members came to know McGuire from many of his fiery sermons printed in *Negro World*.

McGuire's words drove home the various ways UNIA leaders sought to change Black life, including their religious practice. If Garvey's movement indeed broke new theological ground, then McGuire was the one to institute many of these ideas within the organization and beyond. Despite his charismatic plea, McGuire's call to erase white iconography never came to bear. Members did exchange much of their religious and political iconography in their homes and, when possible, in their churches with photographs of Garvey and High Executive Council leaders of the UNIA. While Garvey did cultivate some political zealots of the movement, many of these changes reflected their allegiance to the UNIA rather than their worship of its leaders.

Reverend McGuire called for a change in the ways that Black people envisioned God. By the 1924 convention, McGuire demanded bolder changes in Black religious thought. This time he used his platform to make clear to the delegates that God, in every form, looked like them. He deified Jesus Christ as the "Black Man of Sorrows" and he canonized the Virgin Mary as the "Black Madonna."[36] McGuire's Christological perspective captured the hearts and souls of UNIA members because he argued that a Black Jesus understood the trials of Black people living in a racist society. If Jesus Christ lived among them, McGuire exclaimed, "he could not live on Riverside Drive on account of his color, but he would have to live in Harlem." As a scenic thoroughfare running across Manhattan, Riverside Drive had been designated for wealthy white New Yorkers, while Blacks of all classes called Harlem home. McGuire made clear that this socioeconomic division in New York organized by race—more specifically, white supremacy in the form of residential segregation—was not of God. McGuire argued that Jesus's claim to support the persecuted meant that he would not only live in Harlem but also, most importantly, would find communion with Black people. For emphasis and clarity, McGuire stated that "the white man [not God] was responsible for the color scheme in religion." In other words, the racism in the church was a reflection not of God but rather of racism in the church. McGuire's point was that white religious iconography was a pernicious form of racism that undermined Black Christians' relationship with God. And while McGuire respected the idea that the Holy Spirit had no human form and was neither Black nor white, he wanted Black Christians to know that they were created in the image and likeness of God.[37] This concept, also referred to as the Imago Dei, can be described as the metaphysical expression of God within humanity found in the Genesis story of creation. The Imago Dei reflects the symbolic connection between God and humanity. In emphasizing this connectivity, McGuire insisted that nothing could separate them from the love of God. McGuire's use of racially cognizant contextual theology evoked Garvey's larger mission of racial uplift, but McGuire placed a greater emphasis on Christianity.

McGuire's influence was much more profound than his charismatic addresses. He created religious structure within the UNIA. Eight months after his appointment as the titular archbishop of Ethiopia, McGuire outlined the role of all UNIA chaplain-generals. Relying on the UNIA's newspaper, *Negro World*, to disseminate this information, he called all priests and laity to provide spiritual guidance, order, and borders for each of their UNIA chapters. McGuire used his seminary training to write and create the *Universal Negro Ritual* and *Universal Negro Catechism* in his first year of chaplaincy. Both texts drew heavily from the *Common Book of Prayer*, a mainstay in the Anglican tradition. He used them to define, legitimize, and standardize the role of religion in the UNIA while also planning the theological foundations of the African Orthodox Church. McGuire wanted all chaplains to be prominent agents of religion and to "conduct Divine Service according to the *Universal Negro Ritual* on Sunday morning or afternoon."[38] The chaplain-general was supposed to rely on the *Universal Negro Ritual* to lead all mass gatherings and members' meetings. Additionally, he was given the task of ensuring that each member purchas a copy of the *Universal Negro Ritual* and the *Universal Negro Catechism*. McGuire's encouragement for each member to own these religious manuals demonstrated his desire to organize and legitimize the use of religion in the UNIA. The revenues were great incentives for local chapters, not to mention their wish to be like other divisions. Within his chapter, the chaplain-general was given the responsibility of enacting racial uplift. The chaplain-general was charged to "instruct the members of the Juvenile Branch"[39] in order "to visit the sick and afflicted members of his Division and report to the proper officers any case needing charity."[40] Finally and perhaps most importantly, each chaplain-general was instructed to lead his "life and conversation in such a manner as may prove him worthy to be a moral and spiritual guide to his fellow members."

Reverend McGuire also published qualifications for chaplain-generals. First and foremost, he insisted that all chaplain-generals be ordained ministers, further infusing Christianity into the ethos of the UNIA.[41] He amended the *Constitution and Book of Laws* to state that "all chaplain-generals must be ordained but in the case that they were not ordained, he as the head of the chaplaincy would examine and license the clergy-man/evangelist himself." McGuire emphasized that with this provision for ordination there could be "no excuse for lack of qualification." In other words, McGuire wanted each chaplain-general to have legitimate priestly authority while acting for the organization. McGuire worked to formalize as much as he could, given his authority. Much to his chagrin, the organization never fully institutionalized his standards for chaplain-generals. In fact, these standards generated conflict. McGuire's push to make Christianity foundational to the UNIA undermined Garvey's move toward ecumenicalism for the purposes of religious inclusivity.[42] A large part of the conflict involved McGuire's implementation of Episcopalian practices despite the organization's religious diversity. McGuire used his position in the UNIA for what he deemed a larger calling: creating a unified Black church. Under the aegis of the UNIA, he hoped that the African Orthodox Church would be the denomination to attract Black people to Christianity worldwide.[43]

LITURGY FOR BLACK NATIONHOOD

Most UNIA meetings followed a "carefully ritualized pattern" described in the *Universal Negro Ritual*.[44] This book contained an order of service that structured all Garvey chapters. This subsection includes the structure of these meetings to highlight the ways McGuire and other religious leaders infused the organization with spirituality. As mentioned, all meetings began with the processional of rank-and-file members of the Black Cross Nurses, the Royal Engineering Corps, the Royal Medical Corps, the Universal African Legion, and all other UNIA auxiliaries as they sang the hymn "Shine on, Eternal Light."[45] They marched into Liberty Hall in full regalia carrying the red, green, and black UNIA flag. The songs and accompanied music in particular occupied a deep ecumenicalism tied to the Old Testament scriptures, which served an important role among Christians and Jews alike. To that end, McGuire and a colleague, Rabbi Arnold Josiah Ford, the musical director and bandmaster of the UNIA, chose and sometimes composed the selected music. McGuire and Ford's work, particularly in music, signaled the important ways the Old Testament figured in how Black people imagined freedom on a spiritual level. After the processional hymn, "the customary religious congregational singing the anthem and prayer" followed.[46] Ford had composed the opening hymns such as the UNIA anthem "Ethiopia Land of Our Fathers,"[47] which was often paired with the well-known Anglican missionary hymn "From Greenland's Icy Mountains."

Rabbi Arnold Josiah Ford was a formally trained and accomplished musician, having studied music theory at Edmestone Barnes of London in 1899 and later serving in the musical corps of the British Royal Navy. His work was a substantial contribution to the Universal Ethiopian Hymnal.[48] Ford, who was from Barbados, was one of the first Black rabbis in North America.[49] He represented a small group of active Jews in the Garvey movement who were interested in shaping the religious direction of the UNIA. Outside of the UNIA, Ford led the Beth B'nai Abraham congregation of Manhattan's Black Jews.[50] Jewish presence grew in the UNIA when Ford's protégé, Matthew Wentworth, took an active role.[51] Ford's vocational calling as a rabbi directly influenced the songs he produced for the UNIA. Hymns such as "Shine on, Eternal Light" were certainly cloaked in the rhetoric of African redemption, but his music had a particularly "strong Hebraic character."[52] His music, like Garvey's convictions about Black nationalism, were an extension of his own Black nationalist project among New York's Black Jews. Indeed, Ford and McGuire competed as they worked to influence Garveyites. Yet, with a large Christian base, UNIA members gravitated more readily to McGuire.

McGuire's musical selections, particularly the popular "From Greenland's Icy Mountains," had a different mission. The hymn itself was written by the Church of England's bishop of Calcutta, Reginald Heber, after his father-in-law, William Shipley, dean of St. Asaph and the vicar of Wrexham, commissioned it.[53] Heber's reflections on writing the hymn reveal that it came to mean much more than a gesture to please his powerful father-in-law when Shipley needed a hymn to highlight his sermon on missionary work. Instead, Heber's own sacrificial calling to serve in India pointed to the ways this hymn prophetically echoed his own journey of faith. Likewise, McGuire's and his West Indian colleagues' migration to North America and the profound ways they built a new mission field through Garveyism also seem spiritually tied to some of the words in hymn.

"From Greenland's Icy Mountains" originally appeared in a hymnal published by the Society of the Propagation of the Gospel, a missionary arm of the Church of England.[54] Heber's hymn is a staple Protestant hymn, written at the height of British evangelicalism. It chronicles Heber's experiences as a missionary in India but also extends itself to a discussion of Christian obligations to people in Africa. West Indian Episcopalian priests very likely introduced the hymn to the UNIA. It was a conscientious or perhaps strategic choice on the part of the UNIA to adopt the hymn, because it speaks directly to the UNIA's stated mission of African evangelism. A section of the hymn reads "to deliver their [African] land from error's chain . . . [t]il each remotest nation has learn'd Messiah's name."[55] The hymn might have resonated among Garveyites because Heber's persuasive reference to African freedom was in concert with the UNIA's efforts to gain spiritual and political emancipation for all Blacks, although Heber subscribed to a form of racial paternalism.

Prayers were always recited intermittently between the singing of hymns. McGuire had painstakingly included numerous prayers in the *Universal Negro Ritual*, much like the lectionaries of daily prayer that are used in the Anglican tradition. The foundational role of Anglicanism was true for a number of other prayers included in *The Universal Negro Ritual*. In many ways, the book was an expression of McGuire's Anglican training and expression of faith. For instance, the first commonly used prayer was a prayer for guidance, which had been included verbatim from *The Book of Common Prayer*.[56] The UNIA "Prayer for Missions"[57] was actually taken directly from a prayer titled "A Collect for Guidance," also in *The Book of Common Prayer*.[58] It is not clear whether other UNIA leaders or even members of other denominations fully perceived the overbearing presence of Anglicanism. UNIA members might not have recognized the overlapping similarities. It also is unclear whether there was any opposition to these prayers or any Anglican elements McGuire had included in UNIA meetings, rituals, or ceremonies. However, it must be noted that because not all Garveyites had access to or even used the *United Negro Ritual* consistently, clergymen were able to use extemporaneous prayers that were more in line with denominational traditions within a UNIA chapter.[59] From the Christian tradition, these were likely prayers of supplication, intercession, agreement, thanksgiving, and praise, depending on divisional needs. McGuire also included his own special prayers for the Black Star Line, prayers for divisional conflict, and a prayer for the annual UNIA convention, perhaps at the behest of Garvey or because of McGuire's own attention to UNIA chapter heads. Some of McGuire's most notable contributions were prayers that focused on the uplifting of the race and the redemption in Africa.[60] One such prayer petitioned by saying "Almighty God, we beseech thee to assist us . . . in bringing peace, justice, liberty, and happiness to our race." Another asked for favor while "this race [is] still struggling beneath the cross of injustice, oppression, and wrong."[61]

Scripture also was integral to the UNIA meetings, despite a lack of evidence detailing a specific time set aside for scripture readings. Perhaps the informality in the order of service concerning scriptural readings reflected the cautious use of Christian references, especially in those UNIA branches with great religious diversity. But notes from UNIA meetings suggest that scripture was often referenced. Psalms seemed to emerge the most. Psalm 23 was recited in one UNIA meeting,[62] while in another meeting Psalm 17 was quoted.[63] Another more commonly used psalm in the UNIA was Psalm 68:31, the same psalm that was evoked during the nineteenth-century Ethiopian movement in South Africa. This psalm in particular had a special meaning to the UNIA; its meaning signaled God's promise to make "Africa for Africans." Psalm 68 would resurface and gain currency again in the 1930s during the Second Italo-Ethiopian War, when pro-Ethiopian sentiments engulfed many African American communities. This scriptural reference was used to express and justify the political, cultural, and spiritual aspirations of UNIA members. But perhaps more importantly, Psalm 68 affirmed the vision and work Garvey and his followers had for their life on Earth. These words were a spiritual confirmation that the UNIA's initiatives were a manifestation of God's promises.

In many UNIA meetings, psalms were used as scriptural readings incorporated into the sermon, homily, or speech given by a UNIA member. Yet, the use of psalms occupies a formal place in the Episcopalian/Anglican, Eastern Orthodox, Catholic, Presbyterian, and Lutheran traditions. In the Anglican tradition in particular, the recitation of psalms bore a special integrity that was preserved by reading them separately from sermonic scripture.[64] A psalm is typically thought of as a liturgical response to the word of God. It is a prayer in its own right. The psalms that appear in the UNIA record, and particularly Psalm 68, all seem to reinforce the overwhelming discourse that Black people outside the continent were burdened with civilizing it through Christian salvation. The use and positioning of the psalm in the UNIA reflects its Episcopalian/Anglican tradition.

After the hymns, prayers, and psalms, the Liberty Choir and the Black Star Band took center stage. They often showcased a detailed and well-rehearsed musical program that transitioned into the message. The message was given as either a speech or a sermon, depending on who delivered it. It was often a word of encouragement, an update on their political mission, and a religious charge. In New York, this was Garvey's moment to shine. Outside the city, a chaplain-general or invited guest speaker gave the homily. With a strong clerical presence, the majority of UNIA branches used their pastors and church leaders as their speakers, which is why some UNIA chapters were made up of whole congregations.[65] Many of these speeches, especially Garvey's, were printed verbatim in *Negro World* for all members who could not attend meetings at Liberty Hall. After these invigorating speeches, the meeting transitioned to an official business meeting. A great number of Garvey business ventures—from laundries to restaurants—were planned and discussed in the business meeting. The entire meeting ended with a fundraising collection, a final hymn, and a benediction. This portion of the weekly meetings was similar to meetings of benevolent societies, to which many Garveyites already belonged. In fact, the UNIA was modeled almost entirely after benevolent associations. From rotating credit systems to religious ceremonies, the UNIA offered cultural, social, and economic support that newly arrived southern Blacks and West Indian immigrants desperately relied on to survive.[66]

What is of interest here is that McGuire did not just use Christianity to understand Black people's current state of oppression; rather, he relied on Christianity to combat their current condition. McGuire and Garvey both promoted the idea that Black people should not have to wait to relieve their political, economic, and social situation. This theological orientation permeated all their prayers. Despite any variations in the use of the prescribed prayers, all branches typically ended the reciting of prayers with the UNIA motto: One Aim! One God! One Destiny![67] Prayer served a very real purpose for Garveyites. It focused their energies on the power of God to implement change. The prayers, especially those that reflected the race consciousness of the organization, demonstrated the very real ways McGuire (and those who fervently believed them) not only believed that God could lift from them the yoke of racial oppression and discrimination but also that God had a preordained future for them, an early iteration of Black liberation theology that undergirded meetings.[68]

In essence, though the UNIA is remembered as a fraternal organization centered on racial pride, its strength was solidified through Christian expressive practices, especially a pronounced liturgy that circulated through the executive council of the UNIA's expectations for chapter divisions worldwide. Garveyism allowed for new theological expressions, but so many of the organizational meetings were expected to engage important elements of Christian theology. Meetings were structured like Protestant prayer meetings, with strong Christian references, and on special occasions the UNIA administered baptisms and celebrated burials with a special liturgy.[69] Because of the structure of UNIA meetings, they could easily be disguised as church worship services in places such as South Africa, where government surveillance did not permit subversive organizations such as the UNIA.[70] It seems likely that UNIA divisions in South Africa might have housed displaced elements of Ethiopianism that were more radicalized and unable to operate under the strict political scrutiny that these churches faced. More broadly, there were seldom any neat divisions between UNIA meetings and worship services, especially if Garveyites were largely made up of congregations; often their worship made manifest God's kingdom even if only in UNIA meetings. Like McGuire, most chaplain-generals in local UNIA chapters were ordained ministers whose work in the organization also compelled their members to join.

Sometimes entire congregations would join a UNIA chapter as often seen in *Negro World*, which provided chapter announcements and reports. These overlapping groups of congregants and UNIA members made it possible to offer important religious experiences. Black Jews, Muslims, and Christians made up the UNIA; however, the African Orthodox Church was the most well-known religious organization underpinning the movement. Yet, Garvey remained unwilling to formalize the UNIA's relationship with the African Orthodox Church, and it never became the group's official church. Due to the ways Christian religious practices unambiguously infused so many aspects of the UNIA, though, it is no wonder that African American critics of the UNIA—such as James Weldon Johnson, W. E. B. Du Bois, and E. Franklin Frazier—saw Garvey as the ill-conceived messiah of the movement. It remains crucial for us to understand the role and function of leading figures such as McGuire and other clergymen in UNIA, because they actively and openly incorporated religion into the organization's daily practice and embedded in it their vocational calling as clergy. Black empire and religion was a kind of lattice work that was resourceful to Marcus Garvey, Garveysim, and, more broadly, imagining freedom.

SIX

"We See on the Horizon the Sun of African Orthodoxy"

Church Growth in Southern Africa

In 1930, James Poyah wrote Archbishop Daniel Alexander of the African Orthodox Church (AOC) in South Africa to request the Canons and Constitution, the Declaration of Faith, the Divine Liturgy, and the church's periodical, the *Negro Churchman*, for his followers in Bulwayo.[1] Poyah, who had recently assembled a congregation, needed these documents to align his gatherings with the tenants of the AOC. After two years of seeking affiliation, the young leader hoped that this gesture would secure his congregation's entrance into the AOC. From 1924 until 1944, the denomination expanded to South Africa (1924), Zimbabwe and Uganda (1928), and Kenya (1935) and into the West African countries of Ghana and Nigeria (1944). After the AOC had secured fifteen churches and five thousand members in North America, it was now gaining a following on the African continent.[2] This growth was the result of African efforts to make this transnational church part of their local religious landscape. Richard S. Newman,

Stephen T. Hayes, Michael O. West, and Ciprian Burlacioiu are among the first scholars to chart the impact of the AOC beyond its North American roots; their respective work provides critical context about the growth of the church in southern Africa.

In this chapter, I extend previous scholarship by tracing the contributions of African leaders in building the AOC. African leaders relied on the Universal Negro Improvement Association's (UNIA) *Negro World* to contact the AOC's American-based founders whose conceptions of Africa(ns) obscured their willingness to welcome them into the denomination. Unfortunately, when South Africans took charge, they imposed colonial ideas of racial and class identity onto other Africans seeking AOC affiliation. Despite their differences in identity, training, and experience, many African church leaders remained steadfast in obtaining both spiritual autonomy and ecclesiastical legitimacy through the AOC.

The plight of Daniel Alexander, who would become the South African archbishop and primate, best illustrates the power dynamics and ethnic tensions that framed the church's establishment on the African continent. Alexander is arguably the most well-known clergy of the AOC outside of Reverend George McGuire. Alexander's recognition comes from the numerous congregations he brought into the denomination under his leadership. Yet, like so many other African ministers, evangelists, and laity who sought refuge in this church, Alexander struggled to win approval from the church's leadership in the United States. Once he became archbishop and primate of the African branch of the AOC, moreover, he became a denominational gatekeeper on the other side of the Atlantic for those Africans trying to affiliate with the church. Indeed, the transnational nature of the church—even within the borders of the African continent—made it an unusually attractive site for people of African descent to find human dignity and spiritual agency outside white-dominated church institutions. Looking beyond the rising currents of European empire building, these Black Christians not only flocked to the new Black churches of the AOC but also used them to imagine the possibility of a global Black community of Christians free at least in worship.

Like Marcus Garvey's dreams for a Black empire, which were animated by an uncompromising commitment to Black governance as well as an ecumenical Christian theology, the aspirations of Alexander and his AOC united faith and placed Coloured experiences of colonialism within a larger anticolonial narrative. Alexander's power was cemented by the number of church leaders who read about the AOC through the pages of the

UNIA's *Negro World*.[3] With the UNIA's encouragement and printed contact information in *Negro World*, hundreds of people wrote to Liberty Hall in New York City to learn more about Garveyism, including those attracted to the overwhelming influence of the AOC within the organization. Scholars such as Burlacioiu are right to center *Negro World*'s importance as a tool of evangelism. Garvey's *Negro World*, along with the AOC's periodical *The Negro Churchman*, delivered these dreams to a global Black community. Throughout the era, local postal workers as well as West Indian and African sailors and soldiers distributed these publications far and wide.[4] *Negro World* was disseminated to readers and nonreaders alike. They asserted that those interested "would gather around a reader of Garvey's newspaper, *The Negro World*, and listen to an article two or three times. Then they would run in various ways through the forest, carefully to repeat the whole which they memorized."[5]

These reading practices are reflective of Africans' investment, at least in sharing philosophies, politics, and perhaps even theologies inspired by Black nationalism in ways that cut across educational attainment, class, and geography. In South Africa, African postal workers ensured the newspaper's delivery and distribution. For instance, Josiah Semouse and Joseph Masogha[6]—postal workers and UNIA members near Beaconsfield, where Alexander lived—are likely the ones who helped Alexander make contact with Reverend McGuire and other leaders of the AOC in North America.[7] *Negro World* was a hub of attraction, dissemination, and perhaps even evangelism, as its writers noted, but it was no missionary enterprise in and of itself.[8]

If there were an actual missionary arm of the AOC it was Archbishop Alexander, who not only led his own congregation in Kimberly but also mentored new denominational leaders throughout Africa. Like the leaders he would shepherd, Alexander first made contact with the church by writing the UNIA. He very likely felt confident that his Anglican training, political consciousness, and West Indian roots would cement his connection with the church's leaders in New York City. That was not to be. Unfortunately, Reverend McGuire did not immediately recognize or embrace Alexander as part of his pious community of West Indian Christians, raising various questions: How did McGuire define West Indian identity? Did he exclude Africa as a site of migratory promise? Did he struggle to imagine Africans as part of or even leading the charge for racial and spiritual uplift? Many of these questions surfaced subtly throughout McGuire's relationship with Alexander as he tried to join the AOC.

Alexander's identity as a South African–born West Indian spoke to the discursive histories of circum-Atlantic exchanges connected to the British Empire, all of which seemed unusual to McGuire, whose journey from the Caribbean to North America was more commonplace. Had McGuire looked closely, Alexander's identity as a Coloured South African—more accurately described as being of Caribbean heritage—was like his own migratory response to networks of opportunity that Alexander's parents had detected as they considered their own colonial subjectivity. McGuire's lack of recognition was a rejection of sorts and perhaps was even another example of Alexander's experience of unbelonging that mirrored his ethnic dislocation as he was categorized as Coloured on African soil. Caree A. Banton describes these migratory Caribbean patterns back to Africa as "provocative relationships between freedom, nation-building and citizenship across different segments of the diaspora and Africa" that she concludes "affected conceptions of blackness."[9] Even before Garveyites espoused the slogan "Africa for Africans," some West Indians, especially those living within the British Empire, had actualized the claim and made the African continent their home. In appealing to McGuire, Alexander understood their paths as parallel to each other, making it deeply ironic that McGuire didn't initially find common cause with an African clergy man who made the same proclamations as he did in the AOC pulpit and at the UNIA lectern. In fact, McGuire's misconceptions about Africa and its people obscured his ability to maintain a steady connection with Alexander, whether as a fellow West Indian or a colleague. Their connection was apparently opportunistic, given that Alexander seemed useful to McGuire only after McGuire became aware of the church's exponential growth. Upon recognizing Alexander's natural ability to draw a following and organize institution-building efforts, McGuire felt conflicted to acknowledge Alexander's request for affiliation. When McGuire welcomed Alexander into the AOC fold, the latter brought with him new growth opportunities.

THE QUESTION OF AFRICA AS SPIRITUAL HOMELAND

The AOC had its greatest number of followers by the 1930s, when pockets of AOC members began to gather in South Africa, Southern Rhodesia (Zimbabwe), Uganda, Kenya, and eventually the Gold Coast (Ghana) and Nigeria. The continental hub was South Africa at Alexander's seminary St. Augustine of Hippo; it became a second headquarters for the AOC denomination even when McGuire would not acknowledge it. With Alexander's church at the center of African orthodoxy, he became known among African clergy as the head of the church, though McGuire never anticipated this possibility. In the end, the South African minister's ability to organize ten thousand followers and more than fifty ministers and his purchases of acres of property throughout the continent made his transition to being the official archbishop and primate of the African branch through the denomination logical.[10] The AOC expansion occurred in the middle of a larger and all-encompassing growth of Christianity between the early 1920s and mid-1930s. In 1921, 32 percent of rural Black South Africans called themselves Christians. Fifteen years later, the number of independent Christians had grown 1,500 percent to well over one million official members.[11] The rise of independent churches accounted for most of this growth. Most of these independent churches had Pentecostal and Zionist origins. The Christian Catholic Apostolic Church in Zion, the Apostolic Faith Mission, and the Apostolic Faith Church, among others, drew wide attention among African Christians because they allowed for spiritual freedom.[12] Alexander's followers—a continuation of the Ethiopianist tradition— were among those Christians in these growing African-initiated institutions, but Ethiopianist churches were splintering and in steady decline. It is hard to see the establishment of the AOC as anything but being moved by Alexander's charismatic personality and his administrative prowess.

Alexander's success at assembling multiple congregations whom he claimed celebrated the Anglican tradition did not keep McGuire from testing his knowledge of it. The Anglican tradition was critically important to McGuire. He had positioned the denomination as the Black arm of Anglicanism, a move that might have resonated with South Africans because they had seen similar transitions take place among Black Methodists when they established the African Methodist Episcopal (AME) Church in South Africa. Alexander's Anglican training mattered to McGuire, who was deeply wedded to Anglicanism. In fact, McGuire made his expectations transparent in a letter dated October 24, 1924, questioning Alexander's last affiliation with the Ethiopian Catholic Church in Zion, a growing independent denomination in southern Africa whose ministers had broken ties with the European-led Anglican Church. McGuire questioned not only the organization's legitimacy but also Alexander's leadership and use of the title vicar-general of Bertrams, a suburb of Johannesburg where he had once ministered.[13]

Alexander's vocational biography pointed to his long search for doctrinal belonging, but this journey was not evident to McGuire. Instead, churches initiated by Africans, such as the Ethiopian Catholic Church in Zion, likely generated more questions about whether Alexander's history and practices were respectable enough for the high church. He did not understand that when Alexander abandoned the Anglican Church, he had taken his Anglican beliefs, practices, and training to the Ethiopian Catholic Church in Zion. Perhaps McGuire was willing to entertain Alexander's request for affiliation simply because McGuire hoped that it reflected a modicum of Alexander's commitment to Anglicanism, since the position of vicar-general was held among Anglican Church leaders. It had not fully dawned on McGuire that Alexander and his mentor, Samuel Brander (mentioned in chapter 2) had been part of a grand effort to establish a Black Anglican Church in South Africa and a spiritual homeland for Anglican Blacks.

Brander and Alexander had previously served and received training from the Church of the Province in South Africa. The Church of the Province, much like the American Episcopalian Church where McGuire had once worked, emerged out of the Church of England. Anglican communion included the Church of the Province in South Africa and the American Episcopal Church; subsequently, both maintained an Anglican tradition. This was important for McGuire's commitment to keep Anglican doctrine central in the AOC. McGuire searched for signs of Alexander's commitment to Anglicanism when he wrote, "I am wondering if you are connected with the Ethiopian Movement within the Anglican Church, some time ago."[14] His seemingly pithy question served two purposes. First, it enabled McGuire to test Alexander's support for Ethiopianism while illustrating McGuire's localized knowledge of South African church politics. Its undercurrents speak to McGuire's desire to link Ethiopianists in South Africa to a global movement for Black governance that McGuire relied on his church to lead. Second, Alexander's answer might reveal his age and knowledge and the extent to which his experience of being a part of churches was undergirded by the Ethiopian movement. To that end, McGuire shared his own experience of racism within the Anglican Church. "It may help you to know that I was formerly an Anglican Priest and Archdeacon myself," wrote McGuire, pointing to his affiliation with and departure from the Anglican Church as well as his vocational experience again.

Alexander did not abandon the vetting process that had both offended and wounded him once he was appointed archbishop. Like McGuire, Alexander scrutinized all candidates for the ministry even if they had served in other denominations before they approached the AOC for affiliation.

For instance, in 1930 he questioned John Mansell Mphamba, a Nyasaland minister, who wrote to him requesting AOC materials and also hoping that he could tie his flock in Bulawayo to the AOC. Even though the two men corresponded regularly, it was clear that Alexander distrusted Mphamba's training because he was not willing to discuss theology, doctrine, or even practice with Mphamba like McGuire had done with him. No records between the men suggest that Alexander relied on correspondence to gain a sense of their theological or doctrinal understanding.

Instead, Alexander wanted Mphamba to prove his clerical knowledge through study. He requested that Mphamba leave Southern Rhodesia for South Africa to study the Anglican tradition at the institution Alexander created.[15] Alexander said that "by attending the Seminary the Spirit to serve God in the beauty of Holiness[] will be aroused," as the Anglican tradition was cemented in each of the ministers' spiritual practice.[16] We have no evidence as to Mphamba or Poyah's reaction to Alexander's daunting expectation for them to move to South Africa. However, letters do show that Mphamba was willing to acquiesce to Alexander's demands and that he had even formulated a working plan to maintain his growing congregation while he was gone. Writing through their attorney, Mphamba and his colleague, James Poyah, had decided that in order for one of them to continue preaching and serving their congregation, they would alternate when they would leave to study under Alexander.

Michael O. West, who suggested that the religious practices of African elites also defined their socioeconomic status in unique ways, described Mphamba and his associates as "colorful individuals . . . [who] played such a prominent role in the circulation of unorthodox political, social and religious ideas throughout southern Africa."[17] West's conclusion about Mphamba, Poyah, and others was right. These men had used their oratorical skills to assemble a powerful congregation despite the barriers they faced that kept them from being fully recognized. Mphamba and Poyah, just like Alexander, had a robust following but did not have a denominational home. For the Nysaland ministers, the AOC would likely grant them colonial recognition, an operational necessity for their congregation's existence. Poyah described this hardship to Alexander in a letter he penned with the help of their attorney: "we are holding our service outside the Bulawayo Location" away from and inaccessible to African residents. He ended his letter saying "we have great trouble"; this trouble was largely because the colony had put their church—one with neither buildings nor headquarters—on the margins even as they amassed a large following deemed illegitimate by colonial powers.[18] The Nyasaland leadership knew that connecting with the AOC would give them legitimacy, authority, and resources they desperately needed as migrants from Nyasaland.

Alexander had felt the same desperation when he called upon McGuire for refuge in the AOC. Even as he articulated a particular commitment to Alexander, in which McGuire claimed him as "son" and invited him to refer to him as "father," McGuire remained uncertain at first about a sustained future together. What was curious about McGuire's suspicion was that Alexander was as committed to the Anglican tradition as McGuire. Even with a shared denominational history and path of ecclesiastical autonomy, the American founder wanted to be clear with Alexander about the church's mission and tenets. McGuire explained that he envisioned a unified Black church "big enough for all Negroes to enter, retaining their own worship as Methodists, Baptists, Episcopalians, etc."[19] His dream for unity required ending Black people's commitment to all denominational practices except for Anglicanism. What McGuire meant when he described a unified Black church was that he would welcome other denominations into the fold of Anglicanism, not truly build an ecumenical body. His description of the AOC reflected this strong commitment to Anglicanism when he insisted on the place of High Church worship style embedded in an Anglican ethos.[20] Alexander would have found familiarity in these religious customs as well as the concomitant push for racial uplift. In fact, historian Alan Gregor Cobley has noted that by 1921 in Johannesburg, African Christians were having serious conversations about the consequences of denominationalism among Blacks. He writes that the "spectre of religious division," or denominationalism, "had been an inevitable consequence of the efforts of a wide range of competing varieties of mission societies active by 1900."[21]

African ministers had long concluded before Alexander made contact with McGuire that Black Christians needed to reassess their investment in European-run churches and the denominations they introduced in general, but the AOC connection inspired a rearticulation of these ideals shared in Africa and the diaspora. African Christians in the 1920s might have differed slightly in their discussions of the possibility of a Black church. A comment made by R. V. Selope Thema, an African leader who went to Britain and Versailles to advocate for better compensation for African veterans of World War I, best illustrates the African distinctions: "we can be Christianised without being Europeanised. And it is essential that it would be so; for we have qualities that are indispensible to the human progress."[22] Thema's point was that the "Christian religion has come to Africa [not] to abrogate

Bantu traditions and customs but to give them their completion." Thema insisted that Christianity can and should be practiced across cultures; his thoughts were indeed an extension of the nineteenth-century Ethiopian movement that had already occurred in South Africa. This context brings into sharper relief the ways McGuire's AOC was simply an option—one that was already established and viable—that rearticulated a socioreligious politics many African clergy held in the face of colonialism. The AOC spoke to many African Christians' need for an autonomous church beyond missionary and colonial control during the rise of the independent church movement in South Africa.

Early on Reverend McGuire stressed the importance of church autonomy, an autonomy that extended beyond white leadership; he wanted his South African colleagues to run the AOC. McGuire made this clear through a series of letters to Alexander. The American archbishop wrote, "We are very young but are zealous. . . . We are not believers in *Foreign Missionary Work.* The A.O.C. is the Black man's church for Africans in Africa and abroad."[23] In other words, while McGuire welcomed Alexander into the denomination, he asserted that his mission was not to extend time, energy, and resources to South Africans in the form of mission work. McGuire might have meant several things. The American founder might have sought to differentiate himself from the missionaries who had once stifled Alexander's ministry in the Church of the Province, or McGuire might have earnestly wanted South Africans to benefit from creating their own governance structures on their own terms. Or quite possibly McGuire aimed to be upfront about the limited resources that he had available for his South African counterpart, marking this affiliation as different from the AME expansion to South Africa.

The AME Church had been one of the first African American churches to support independent Christians. As mentioned in chapter 3, the process of consolidating the Ethiopian Church and the AME Church did not fulfill all the AME's promises to the South Africans, and some leaders were left wanting more agency given the limited ways North Americans supported South Africans. But the point was that McGuire's focus was on strengthening his congregations in the West. The US branch was not able to extend its work into other territories, but it was willing to support local church planting internationally. McGuire emphasized this point: "The African Orthodox Church is for the entire Race, and as its Primate I stand ready to aid our brethren in South and West Africa to secure the Episcopate and to erect independent and self-maintaining branches of the African Orthodox

Church which shall be autonomous parts of a great communion such as various sections of the Church of England are within the Anglican Communion."[24] McGuire's intentions were evident: he would assist South Africans in securing their own ecclesiastical autonomy but would make no promises to engage in the heavy lifting of establishing the church in South Africa. As McGuire adamantly declared, "self-support is the keynote, [so] you in Africa must be Independent of outside support, control, and supremacy." Such emphasis on (financial) self-support did not dissuade Alexander from affiliating. Alexander ultimately sought self-governance over his flock, and McGuire's arrangement would grant him the ecclesiastical freedom he so desperately desired.

As Alexander grew the church outside of South Africa, he relayed much of what McGuire had shared with him. When Mphamba and Poyah requested their affiliation in 1930, Alexander also insisted on their ability to maintain their own affairs in Southern Rhodesia. In one letter Alexander said to them, "you are the people to whom I am looking to assist in building up the work."[25] He stresses the newness of the church and its fragility: "what I want you to understand is that the work here is still young and I have to struggle to get the thing I need, [because] even in America, every congregation is busy building churches." His emphasis here was that all church recruiting, organizing, and assembling would be in their hands. He added further that "we have no rich people in our churches. Therefore each and everyone of us must do his part to work toward the upbuilding of the church." His point was one that McGuire had made when he joined. Alexander was not willing to offer financial support even though the entire African division fell under his branch of the denomination. Alexander offered the Nysaland ministers what McGuire had given him years prior: a template for structural organization.

After Reverend McGuire accepted Alexander's flock into the AOC in 1925, he made sure to enclose some critical documents that explained the Anglican faith as the AOC practiced it. The documents included the "Canons and Constitution," "the Declaration of Faith," "the Divine Liturgy," and the church's periodical the *Negro Churchman*, all the documents that African clergy eventually requested from Alexander in the 1930s. It was a bit more complicated to ensure that the African ministers implemented Anglicanism in their services, though. McGuire had anticipated this difficulty in 1925 when he wrote, "If our Rituals and Canons cannot be adopted in entirely [sic], adjust them to your conditions."[26] He concluded his letter empathetically: "As a former British subject I know the system in the

Colonies. . . . I also know the prejudice and suspicion of the government in Africa to Western Negroes." McGuire's recognition of the hardship that Alexander and others faced was a nod to his understanding of the looming scrutiny of the missionaries and, even more broadly, British rule in every measure of life. Therefore, it makes sense that while McGuire spoke of racial uplift, he knew better than to mention or link the church to Marcus Garvey, which might generate intense scrutiny. McGuire was willing to give Alexander a slight reprieve from church law if it interfered with his congregation's safety and well-being under colonialism.

Giving him tentative approval to self-govern, McGuire went on to advise Alexander that "instead of being a Department of the A.O.C. to be governed by the West, my advice is to call your priests and laity together and organize the South African Orthodox Church."[27] This reiterated his earlier assertion that the AOC in the West would not take any responsibility for the South African division and further that the denomination would function like the Anglican communion worldwide. This meant that Alexander would have the complete responsibility of preparing the church administratively, financially, and spiritually. The weight of this responsibility was enormous, and McGuire warned him that "we are making bricks without straw and the truth is that my brain and pocket have been the only resource of the A.O.C. . . . but we are like the Apostles who went into the world without Silver or Gold, but with Divine Commission and Authority." McGuire indicated that while he had actively worked to bring his church to fruition without any funding except his own, he had prevailed only by the grace of God. Alexander would have to do the same if he wanted to witness progress. Furthermore, McGuire believed that Africans themselves were destined to have their own religious freedom. He closed the letter by stating that "Ethiopia is coming into her own, and princes of the Church shall come out of Africa as did St. Hippo and others. . . . We desire you to organize as an equal branch of the A.O.C. not as a subject and my relations would only be like that of Canterbury, a directing & advisory one rather than Administrative." McGuire's vision for African autonomy left Alexander open to engage the discursive impulses of Ethiopianism and forge a new vision emerging out of Africa at this time.

McGuire's use of Ethiopianist rhetoric positioned the American and South African branches in concert with each other and the shared precepts of Ethiopianism. Indeed, McGuire seized on the same spirit of self-governance and self-sufficiency in establishing the AOC that had once guided the Ethiopian movement and encouraged Alexander to take on this spirit when building his own church in South Africa. McGuire was so committed to the tenet of self-determination that he even forfeited his potential leadership in a global church. In essence, the success of the church rested solely on Alexander's efforts. The future ecclesiastical arrangement McGuire described gave Alexander much-needed respect and authority as the leader of the African division. It allowed South African clergymen to govern their own affairs. This unique situation not only left power in the hands of local leadership but also bestowed South African leaders with apostolic succession. African Americans freely offered it to Alexander, McGuire said. "I have gone to my brethren dispersed in the New World, and though Silver or Gold I have none, the Apostolic Succession which I possess is for all of us black men."[28] Alexander knew how priceless this gift was, because by the time he had requested to affiliate with the AOC, he had already associated with a variety of denominations and leaders from the Anglican Church, the Ethiopian Church, the AME Church, and the Ethiopian Catholic Church in Zion. In each church, a strict hierarchy had stifled Alexander's own ministry. For Alexander, establishing a branch of the AOC in South Africa represented the possibility of genuine ecclesiastical freedom and leadership for African Christians.

These promises of self-governance, along with the direct apostolic connection, convinced Alexander to join forces with the US-based church. On December 8, 1924, after officially affiliating with the AOC as a probationary congregation, Alexander offered this enthusiastic proclamation: "We here are so proud . . . [that] all congregations and friends have come to congratulate us in our affiliation with our brethren in America and that we will also be the inheritors of that great Apostolic heritage."[29] Alexander asserted that God had bestowed them with a heritage that they "must safeguard." McGuire agreed and requested that Alexander begin the necessary preparations for episcopacy. The instructions that followed spoke to a greater mission than simply a route to Alexander's consecration; it also provided Alexander with a framework to move forward with developing. McGuire told Alexander to prepare his canons, declare their intention to be in communion with the AOC, and make plans to hold his church's first synod, where it would create its own constitution, a moment that standardized the denomination but also made its existence on African ground both official and sacred.

Looking further ahead, McGuire suggested that Alexander rely on the second synod to elect a bishop who would serve under him; the goal would be for Alexander to petition for the bishop's consecration at the general synod in Boston, Massachusetts, the following year.[30] The process seemed simple enough for Alexander, who a few years prior had helped establish the African Church before he had left the Ethiopian Catholic Church in Zion by writing church documents that would be scrutinized by the government. This pragmatically beautiful plan was much more difficult to implement than Alexander might have imagined. The greatest obstacle to establishing the AOC in South Africa continued to be McGuire rather than the European church leaders or even the South African state. The process to expand the AOC onto African soil was challenging, a reflection of the broken reality of the myths as well as misconceptions Blacks in the diaspora grafted onto Africa(ns) as they ironically declared New York, Africa for the Africans.

MARKING OURSELVES SACRED

While McGuire ostensibly gave Alexander his personal blessing and institutional support, he was not ready to grant Alexander full autonomy over the new South African church project. At the start, McGuire placed Alexander and his congregants under a two-year probationary period before Alexander's congregation could gain full status with the AOC in North America. In 1925 American leadership appointed Isaiah Palmerston Samuels, McGuire's brother-in-law who was stationed in Cape Town, to supervise the probationary period.[31] The problem was that Samuels had no training or authority; he was simply a piano teacher who had moved to Cape Town in search of economic mobility from the waning economy in the Caribbean. To Alexander's further dismay, Samuels, who had no training or allegiance to Anglicanism, soon became a Congregationalist minister to a small West Indian immigrant community nestled within a state-designated Coloured neighborhood.[32]

As McGuire explained to Samuels, he wanted to ensure that Alexander was a man of his word with a sufficient doctrine, a qualified ministerial staff, and a substantial following. The distance did not allow McGuire to take on this task himself. During those two probationary years, on McGuire's instructions, Samuels investigated all the ministers, evangelists, and laity as well as congregations and reported his findings to the American headquarters privately.[33] As Samuels intimated to his brother, head of the AOC back in the United States, "We shall deal justly with our brethren in Africa but they do not understand our Christian project of racial uplift."[34] For that reason, he continued, "we must think prayerfully and carefully before entrusting these natives with the precious gift they seek." Despite McGuire's early zealousness about accepting African Christians in the church, his correspondence with Samuels suggests that he continued to distance himself from Africans even though they shared his West Indian heritage. McGuire was uncomfortable with turning over complete power to these Christians, despite his grand promises of autonomy and equality to Alexander. The strong ties of race and religion alone did not eliminate the existence of a cultural hierarchy, one that would taint their relationship. A twisted form of paternalism surfaced inside as Alexander considered Mphamba and Poyah's Bulwayo branch for AOC inclusion.

The records do not provide enough information to substantiate this claim. However, a synod welcome address shows that it took Alexander twenty years to approve the establishment of the Southern Rhodesia branch, evidence of how mired he and so many others became in colonial ideologies of race. Alexander shared with the entire synod that the "Mashonaland Province was established in 1950."[35] Given the length of time it took for him to approve the branch, it is easy to imagine that his reservations reached beyond whether church leaders could run a congregation. It is plausible that Alexander remained committed to their study under his instruction, their full embracing of Anglicanism, and perhaps even their ability to acquire land from which to build an actual church. None of this is obvious based on the archival material at hand. However, currents of my own suspicions that Alexander's cultural bias and classism influenced African operations of the AOC resurfaced in later discussions of the church in East Africa. What is devastating, though, is that Alexander had experienced this same scrutiny from his US peers when they placed him on probation at the start of his AOC ministry.

Samuels, Alexander's supervisor, was not the only one who stood in the way of Alexander's consecration into church leadership. Reverend Edwin Urban Lewis, who had once been a member of the AOC, hoped to check the growth of the AOC, and his object of focus unintentionally became Alexander. Even though Reverend Lewis had recently been dismissed from the church for conspiring with the British Consul-General in New York City against Garvey's leadership, he still aired his grievances. Lewis said that McGuire had offered episcopacy to Alexander only in the hopes that Alexander might ensure Garvey's entrance into South Africa. Garvey had been in search of an African country from which to center his racial uplift work and activism. Lewis believed that the relationship between

McGuire and Alexander was transactional at best. For Lewis, Alexander gave McGuire access to and confirmation of an idealized or utopic Africa from which to launch a radical project of liberation. Lewis's sensitivity to the growing—and in his mind threatening—focus on Black freedom brought attention to various manifestations of Garveyism. In fact, it seems probable that the British Consul-General knew so much about Alexander because Lewis had made them aware of the connection.[36] And somehow, the British Consul-General believed that McGuire's effort to consecrate clergy such as Alexander from South Africa was part of a larger project to agitate Blacks throughout the British Empire.[37]

Other than the shared reflection on colonialism and rhetoric of racial uplift, there was no explicit sign of political discussion between the two priests. However, the church leaders did notice that some of their letters were being delayed, inspected, and on one occasion confiscated by the postmaster. It seems that with time, they were careful to distance themselves from Garveyism in official correspondence. In one of these letters that connected the denomination to Garvey, the target of much scrutiny across multiple borders, McGuire declared the following: "We are not officially connected to the U.N.I.A. but all of us are individual members of the Organisation as we are one sentiment, political, and religious."[38] Perhaps this connection was enough to make British intelligence wary, and it certainly complicated McGuire's effort to get Alexander to the United States. Ideas about Garvey, his politics, and the policing that came with it affected McGuire as the chaplain-general of the UNIA, the AOC, and anyone associated with this type of political activity. Alexander suffered accordingly. In this case, the British Consul-General concluded that the spread of the AOC to South Africa jeopardized the existence of the Anglican Church in South Africa. The British Consul-General was correct in its assumption that the end goal was the dismantling of the Anglican Church, yet McGuire and Alexander's hope was that the doctrine could survive in another form accessible to Black leadership.

Despite the evidence waged against the AOC, McGuire and Alexander must have been discreet in establishing the church officially. Alexander urged his colleagues in Southern Rhodesia to exercise the same caution, perhaps because he understood the cost of colonial scrutiny. At the sixth synod, Alexander charged all leaders connected to the church not to be "ministers who neglect their work for politics."[39] Alexander went to even greater lengths by insisting that it be an official mandate of the church. In the synod proceedings, Alexander hoped to make it official legislation.

Stating in the primate's charge, Alexander said, "You will be asked to pass legislation for those Ministers who would be politicians, to the determent of the church, and their spiritual calling." Alexander echoed this concern in personal correspondence when he wrote to his colleagues in Southern Rhodesia in 1930. The archbishop told Poyah that "there is one thing that I want to warn you against, and that is to keep clear of Politics, for you cannot serve two Masters, for you will either love the one and hate the other, and we who are doing the work of the Master must keep clear of these things."[40]

While some historians have evaluated these grand pronouncements at face value, suggesting that independent churches such as the AOC were deeply conservative, these analyses have missed the opportunity to read against the grain. Ogbu Kalu was more accurate and evenhanded in his assessment: "the conservative ones [African independent churches] were often regarded as useful for controlling the natives, while those influenced by African Americans, such as the African Orthodox Church in Zimbabwe, were viewed as subversive, to be hounded out of the religious space."[41] Kalu is careful to note that the political engagement of African independent churches varied but that the political activism of the AOC stood out. AOC church leaders' own politics often determined how individual congregations responded to the sociopolitical climate of their country.

Alexander is always a formidable example, but historian Michael O. West suggests that Alexander's positioning as a consummate race man is critical to the discussion.[42] Alexander was a member of multiple organizations that he believed advanced the struggle for African freedom. Beyond the UNIA, Alexander also belonged to the African People's Organization, a political association for those classified as Coloured in South Africa; the Non-European Unity Movement; and even adjoining movements that hit far-reaching issues such as temperance. His political activity suggests the opposite of his pleas to steer clear of politics. Instead, it seems that he is calling for caution from jeopardizing government support of the AOC because of its perceived threat to the colony. Indeed, Alexander was at once political but also earned the financial support of both the Oppenheimer and DeBeers families to fund AOC ventures. Alexander offers an exemplary model for the ways he stealthily navigated his involvement in subversive politics while receiving the acclaim of those invested in the colonial state. Perhaps his example even complicates how quickly we as historians call independent churches apolitical. What is certain, however, is that all government entities worked to deny Garvey entrance into South

Africa. In fact, it was the intense scrutiny generated from people such as Lewis that kept Garvey from ever setting foot on the continent.

On the ground, Alexander faced his own suffering at the hands of the American leadership. The greatest scrutiny came from Samuels in South Africa, fueled by McGuire. Yet, this painful reality was no different from the ways European missionaries or even African American clergy, particularly those representing the AME, led their missions in South Africa. This level of paternalism permeated the leadership between McGuire and Alexander. Alexander genuflected to McGuire to gain apostolic succession. This power dynamic was evident in the correspondence and church reports Samuels submitted to New York about Alexander. In response, Alexander resented Samuels because he wasn't even a clergyman.[43] Further, Alexander also lacked the very commitment to Anglicanism that McGuire questioned even though the South African priest remained steadfast in his desire for his affiliation. Alexander wrote to him that "the truth is powerful and we will ultimately prevail."[44] In this, Alexander implied that his flock would still be successful in establishing the AOC even as they faced Samuels's suspicion. Alexander's firm belief in his perseverance was actually a prophetic word declaring the realization of his ministry.

Alexander's instincts about Samuels were well founded. In a matter of months, Samuels left his post and became a minister in the Congregational Church, a decision that would torment Alexander even after he was consecrated as the archbishop and primate of the AOC in South Africa. It was apparent to Alexander that Samuels took church leadership in Africa lightly while simultaneously barring well-trained and committed clergy such as himself to lead their own flock. During his consecration ceremony, Alexander openly explained that when Samuels was appointed commissary, "We resented the selection of the gentleman as not being a proper person for this point, nevertheless we were obedient, and set ourselves to the task of proving ourselves worthy to appear before the Seventh General Synod."[45] Such bitterness, it seems, came from what Alexander saw as Samuels's inattention to his duties and likely Alexander's own prolonged and rigorous probationary period. To Alexander, his own twenty years of ministry made him deserving of the episcopacy. After two years of probation, in a ceremony in New York City McGuire approved Alexander for the episcopacy. The South Africans had finally earned the authority for Alexander's consecration, a process that would set him apart as sacred.

In September 1927 Alexander traveled by train from the interior to Cape Town, South Africa's "mother city," on his way to the AOC's headquarters in New York. In Cape Town, he climbed aboard RMS *Balmora*, which stopped in Madeira and then made its way to its final destination in Southampton, England.[46] It took Alexander seventeen "monotonous" days to travel from South Africa to England. He was the only "black person on board," but he was "well treated by officers and passengers."[47] Alexander believed he was "treated with great courtesy as a minister and ambassador of the Great King [Jesus Christ]."[48] Upon disembarking, however, immigration officers were "inquisitive, to my way of thinking." This was very likely primed by the British Consul-General's earlier concerns about Alexander's correspondence with a UNIA leader and the fact that he had used a French rather than a South African passport to leave the country.[49] The British Consul did question Alexander upon his return, so much so that the French revoked his passport.[50] When Alexander finally landed in England, he went ashore to connect with his long-lost cousin, who had been living in London for some years.[51] In the city's center, Alexander booked his ticket for New York with the White Star Steamship Line.[52] After a few days, he made his way to New York City. Alexander had been well positioned for the journey. His ancestral heritage and ties to the Caribbean and his socioeconomic status as an educated African veteran gave him the unique positionality to be able to travel outside of South Africa.

Although he was traveling for his consecration, Alexander served as a representative for his entire congregation, who longed for a freedom unattainable to Africans living in segregationist South Africa. In fact, Africans' commitment to the establishment of the AOC raised funds for his travel to North America before he left, and as others joined the church they continued to cover the debt for his passage many years after. The long voyage reflected multiple diasporas of the Caribbean and Africa, all of which were made to institutionalize the AOC. Alexander's experiences in London and New York, two different registers of race relations in the West, gave him new context from which to imagine his own freedom. He "discover[ed] that color is no bar in public places in England as it is in South Africa and the United States of America."[53] His experience in England might have had more to do with the fact that he was usually the only Black person in these settings. Racism might have still permeated Britain but appeared less apparent in certain parts of England that lacked racial diversity. Class dynamics informed these sites, and his education and profession might have protected him from a much more egregious form of racism inextricably bound to class. Alexander's exposure to what he believed was racial equality was further reinforced during his train ride, city travels, and hotel stay, all of which made him feel fully integrated in British society without regard to race.

As was the case with Garvey, the metropole was an important site of personal transformation in Alexander's imaginings of race relations. Alexander actually believed that British subjects could find a place of belonging, as he declared that "the Greatest City in the World is London."[54] He continued to extol his pride in the British, stating that "there is no individual born in any overseas possession of the British Empire—West Indies, South and West Africa—or elsewhere, who does not experience a feeling of achievement when he reaches London and visits the various ecclesiastical edifices and historical buildings of which he had read so much."

London occupied an important space in Alexander's own identity as a British subject, in part because his color had not prohibited him from experiencing the city. Alexander had been most impressed with the historic and sacred churches he visited, such as the Church of St. Clement Danes, St. Paul's Cathedral, and Westminster Abbey. For him, the uniqueness of the experience had to do with entering "Houses of Prayer for all People."[55] Apart from this transformative racial experience, Alexander also was markedly impressed with the construction of London's buildings. The city's architecture had such an impact on him that he would recall the structure and beauty of various buildings when his congregation drew up plans for its own cathedral in Kimberley. These welcoming "Houses of Prayer for all People" functioned as a model for his churches on the continent if he could just elude state scrutiny.

Alexander's counterparts in Southern Rhodesia had also hoped to travel to be consecrated as leaders of their churches in Southern Rhodesia. Their destination was South Africa, the functional headquarters of the church for them. Unlike Alexander, though, they were never approved to travel to South Africa. There is a series of letters between Alexander and the Coghlan, the AOC attorney for the Nysaland ministers, to the commissioner of immigration and Asiatic affairs in Pretoria. The correspondence routinely asked the commissioner to give passports to the Nysaland ministers. In one passionate plea Alexander wrote, "I am again making bold to ask you that you consider the matter, and if it [is] impossible to grant a passport to both." He made a case for their church, asserting that "it seems very hard on us who are trying to teach our own people after we have received instructions from the Europeans and are trying to do our bit towards the upliftment of our African Race" without access to travel.[56] In another letter when the Nysaland ministers' spoke for themselves, they declared, "may

God and Bishop help the young Africans who try to help themselves."[57] Pointing to his education and training, Alexander appealed to colonial paternalism for his colleagues' access to travel. He implied that the work of the AOC, or perhaps of kingdom building more broadly, was in line with colonial aspirations for African Christians. The ministers in Southern Rhodesia eventually gained recognition in the eyes of Alexander, but perhaps their political outspokenness barred them from entering South Africa even if it was for church work. Alexander was fortunate because he not only was appointed in a leadership position but also experienced a sacred ceremony of consecration. These experiences, particularly of his treatment and worship experience, indelibly shaped Alexander. In America, he found spiritual transformation.

THE ONE SET APART BY GOD

In March 1927, the *Negro Churchman* announced Alexander's consecration. Somehow between the time Alexander contacted McGuire and the publication of the article, Alexander had earned the title vicar apostolic and bishop-elect of the South African branch of the AOC. This announcement didn't seem particularly noteworthy, but upon closer inspection it pointed to a reversed religious migration route. Alexander traveled from Africa to the West. Records from his trip suggest that his consecration, which made him a high official within the denomination, did not keep him from teaching, preaching, and ministering to his Western counterparts. Alexander's ministry undermined the American notions of African dependency for religious instruction, an objective even the racially aware UNIA espoused. His trip expanded the very definition of the missionary enterprise, accounting for the efficacy of Black church leaders in their own communities. The *Negro Churchman*'s announcement signaled this shift. In it, the author declares that the consecration of Alexander would "add a new chapter in the religious life of Western Negroes, in that it will be the first time that a Native African has been consecrated in the Western Hemisphere for service in his homeland."[58]

This new chapter was an incredible breakthrough for independent Black churches, giving Africans the agency to conduct their own church work. The AOC bestowed Alexander with the authority to lead African church affairs, unlike their more established counterparts of the AME Church. The AME Church, as mentioned before, did not allow Africans to become bishops until 2004. The announcement in the *Negro Churchman* ended this declaration by stating that Alexander's consecration linked "together a scattered Race."[59] Perhaps the episcopacy did much more. Alexander's consecration as the archbishop and primate of the AOC in South Africa gave him the power and authority to lead in a local context while operating in a religious organization that was cognizant of the ways oppression had dispersed people of African descent to different parts of the world.

The enthusiastic article in the *Negro Churchman* also described the efforts by Alexander to expand the church in South Africa, stating that he had been "recently visiting Johannesburg, Germiston, and Witbank [*sic*] in the Transvaal, where he received into the African Orthodox Church several ministers and congregations who desired to be members of the One Holy Catholic and Apostolic Church."[60] It was during this intense period of evangelism that Alexander gained favor among AOC leadership. It was one of the first times that the denomination's leadership recognized his ability to grow the church. And indeed, Alexander traveled through a variety of cities, leaning on a network of clergy to build up a flock nationwide. He was also strategic in reporting his work to the *Negro Churchman*: "Let me then toil on that I may be accounted worthy, in the near future to sit with you in the approaching General Synod of the A.O.C., and share in your deliberations."[61] Never obtuse, Alexander made clear to his American counterparts that his work was meant to enable him to gain ecclesiastic authority in South Africa. When he did finally receive the esteemed apostolic succession, he continued to work tirelessly to proselytize and recruit many African Christians into the folds of this transnational church body.

Alexander envisioned the AOC as stretching well beyond South Africa. During the interwar years, a radicalized group of African Christians surfaced, with some seeking membership in autonomous churches such as the AOC. Black radicals including George Wellington Kampara, Clement Kadalie, and James Thaele were among these Christians even though their religious identity is often de-emphasized. Each of these leaders represented a different strand of religiosity. Kampara left his home country of Nyasaland for ministry in Southern Rhodesia through the Gazaland Zimbabwe Ethiopian Church.[62] Kadalie and Thaele were dedicated Presbyterians, although Thaele eventually joined an African-led church that maintained Calvinist doctrine. Yet, Kampara, Kadalie, and Thaele's Christian backgrounds are often eclipsed by their political work. These political leaders conceptualized, coordinated, and galvanized new African organizations and ignited new strategies in old associations, including the first African trade union, called the Industrial and Commercial Workers Union, and the oldest political organization in Africa, the South African Native National Congress (later called the African National Congress [ANC]). They also established the UNIA in South Africa. Many of their goals with the UNIA worked to change immigrant experiences, especially their own. These leaders relied on their work in the UNIA, the ICU, and the ANC, much of which was undergirded by their Christian tenets to implement change. Kampara, Kadalie, and Thaele's political organizing makes evident the importance of African immigrants in South Africans, radicalism.

Michael O. West argues that highly scrutinized activists transferred their political agendas into institutions, such as the AOC, that appeared safe from government attention. In his book *The Rise of an African Middle Class in Colonial Zimbabwe*, West shows that transnational organizations survived colonial scrutiny only because their leaders relied on organizational name changes to shield them. In the case of southern Africa, West makes note of the interchangeable ways organizations joined forces. He explains that members of the ANC worked with their comrades in the UNIA as well as Africans committed to labor politics and issues waged through the ICU.[63] West claims that "the proto-national moment became something of a pan-African moment as well."[64] He goes on to state "the local branches of all three organizations, which collectively formed his frame of political reference, had been fused into one broad movement under the leadership of the same person, James Thaele, a United States–educated activist and the leading Garveyite in South Africa."[65]

Robert Trent Vinson's insight is also useful in this discussion, as he notes that Thaele's transnational print culture illustrated the cross-organizational work when he cited and exchanged news between the UNIA's *Negro World* and the ANC's *African World*, a newspaper founded and edited by Thaele from 1925 to 1926. This exchange is plausible because Thaele also contributed directly to *Negro World* and *African World* alongside Kadalie's ICU newspaper, the *Workers' Herald*. Judith Byfield also makes this claim. She states that "Thaele's construction of the 'modern Negro' did not draw exclusively from Garvey's pan-African politics; he also was in a swell of international social movements," including the ANC.[66] Kampara did the same. While Kampara envisioned a place for Garveyism, he worked to bring the organization to South Africa with the support of local ministers in Evaton.[67] Other African leaders such as Frank Mothiba, Benjamin Majafi, and S. M. Bennet Ncwana spread their work across many organizations while citing their connection to Garveyism.[68] As a member of the ANC, Mothiba sent a letter of encouragement to the UNIA that urged "strike a blow brothers, we have nothing to fear . . . til Africa, the land of our fathers[,] is redeemed."[69] Majafi, who served as the Evaton secretary of the UNIA, confirmed that many politically active South Africans found solidarity with the UNIA as they learned about the organization through its newspaper.[70]

Ncwana established the newspaper *Black Man*, which fought for African liberation and also championed Garveyism in its articles. In fact, Garvey said the *Black Man* was the *Negro World* of South Africa.[71] Mothiba, Majafi, and Ncwana, like Thaele, Kampara, and Kadalie, saw the utility in relying on organizations to advance their convictions that "Africa was for Africans." The reclamation of Africa's land and resources was central to all of these political organizers, even the Garveyites who desperately sought an African homeland from which to launch their Black nation. Mothiba said it best: the liberatory project had much to do with gaining control over African land. The UNIA's global expression of Black nationalism centered on Africa overlapped with local organizations such as the ICU's and ANC's mission to enact African freedom. Africans relied on this model of political activism to bring about change through multiple political institutions.

Many politically active Africans worked across and in concert with multiple organizations, relying in some form on churches to function as alternative political forums. African Christians in Zimbabwe, Uganda, and Kenya believed that the AOC and its transnational politics provided a new hub for anticolonial politics. However, many Africans complained that they never got information about the church when they contacted *Negro World*. A number of them contacted Alexander instead, and he connected Africans directly with the AOC in North America. For instance, Dick Dube and John Mansell Mphamba in Bulawayo, Zimbabwe, tirelessly requested information from the UNIA in New York, but neither the organization nor the church replied. Eventually the two activists made contact with Alexander. Dube and Mphamba's interest was in "studying [the] problem of race" through correspondence classes, but they eventually started their own congregations in Bulwayo.[72] Interestingly, Mphamba, like Kampara and Kadalie, had immigrated from Malawi to Zimbabwe, representing yet another instance in which migration informed southern African politics. In fact, Mphamba eventually faced deportation for openly rebuking the connection between white supremacy and Christianity.[73] This inquiry, along with many others during the period, points to the ways that the creation of the AOC recenters the UNIA's Black nationalist politics on the African continent led by Africans such as Alexander.

Alexander's appointment to lead the AOC excited African Americans who desired a respectable connection to Africa. They, like Garvey, had a vested interest in being connected to the motherland, which North Americans thought legitimized their cry for "Africa for Africans." In other words, Alexander and his leadership in the AOC served as the bridge between anticolonial Christians and North American Black nationalists. A writer in the *Negro Churchman* made this connection evident when he suggested that Alexander's new position as the archbishop of the African province of the AOC would be "the beginning of a New History in the ecclesiastical life of the Natives of South Africa."[74] Alexander's leadership brought to fruition Garvey's long-standing desire to create a nation (including Black-led churches) predicated on Black governance.

Eventually Alexander's new ecclesiastical position did signal a great change in South Africa. It would be the first time South Africans represented their own churches in self-governance while holding the apostolic succession, something entirely unique to independent churches. This point was unambiguous when the writer posited that "South Africa awaits eagerly this Consecration. At least two Negro Methodist Churches have labored in South and West Africa, but they have always sent American Negroes as Bishops."[75] The author's critique of the AME Church was particularly relevant with a great number of African clergy who had defected from European-run mission churches, only to be further subjected to an empathetic but disconnected African American leadership. The denomination's American leadership acknowledged this disjuncture, saying that "the Africans have never been satisfied with this [appointment of foreign bishops], and the forward policy of the African Orthodox Church, in consecrating a Native as first bishop among his people, will win large accessions into our fold."[76] The way the AOC operated was the ultimate embodiment of self-governance, because even its bishop would be drawn from its own local leadership.

Leaders of the American-based church believed that consecrating Alexander was a great opportunity to empower South African Christians; they believed local leadership was ordained by God. They wrote, "We verily believe that we are divinely guided when we chose our name as 'The AFRICAN Orthodox Church.'"[77] The sentiments were mutual. Alexander and his flock wrote in a letter to the editor that since their affiliation with the church, when they spoke of beloved Primate and Lady McGuire, they felt the Holy Spirit in their midst. They wanted to return the favor in part by bringing McGuire home to Africa. In another entry to the editor,

Alexander wrote, "May the day arrive when His Grace and Lady McGuire shall visit us to see their African children and the beauties of their Motherland. GOD Bless AFRICA."[78] The desire to have McGuire visit was also echoed in the African provinces' formal report to the American synod. Alexander also reiterated this in his remarks at his own consecration.[79]

Alexander was consecrated in September 1927 at St. Michael's Church in Boston.[80] Church members and leaders from all over the nation packed the church, including His Eminence George Alexander McGuire, patriarch of the AOC; His Lordship William Ernest Robertson, bishop of the Jurisdiction of the South; and His Lordship Arthur Stanley Trotman, auxiliary bishop of the Jurisdiction of the North. The presence of these denominational leaders from across the nation indicated the true intent of officially turning over sacred power to Alexander. Robertson and Troutman, each representing a region of the United States, assisted McGuire in the ceremony. Symbolically, the two bishops signaled full denominational support for Alexander. Venerable Archdeacon R. A. Valentine officially introduced and presented Alexander as the bishop-elect to all who gathered that day in Boston. Valentine was followed by the Right Worshipful Louis Alexander Jeppe, who read a "Testimonial of Alexander's Character," a patriarchal mandate for consecration as well as some assurance to those clergy and members just getting acclimated with Alexander.

After these formalities Alexander took the Oath of Obedience, during which he knelt before the patriarch and his assistants.[81] Alexander pledged his obedience to "the Holy African Orthodox Church, and our Eminent Father Alexander Patriarch, and His Successors canonical elected."[82] While the act of taking the oath reflected the denomination's desire for church leadership to submit themselves to God, the church, and its tenets, in many ways for Alexander it was still symbolic of the hold that the American patriarch had over him. The pledge of allegiance stated, "I shall take care to preserve, to defend, increase and promote the rights, honors, and privileges and authority of the African Orthodox Church." Alexander also promised to attend the synod when summoned and to offer a report of his pastoral duties, the state of his congregations, the discipline of the clergy, and the people. Alexander took this Oath of Obedience seriously even though it still kept him tethered to American authority after he assumed his role as the archbishop and primate of the African province.

The Oath of Obedience was followed by the Litany of Saints, a sacred prayer of invocation to God coupled with prayers for the intercession of

Mary, the angels, martyrs, and saints. This portion of the ceremony mirrored routine aspects of the High Church services of the AOC; here, its old Catholic roots are truly reflected in the veneration of Mary among other entities. This routine portion of the service familiar to the congregation recognized Alexander's submission to not only God but also the high principalities falling beneath him: Mary, archangels, angels, martyrs, and saints, among many others. It suggested that church leaders such as Alexander acted as the bridge between the people, the heavenly realms where Mary and others rest, and finally God. No matter how high in the church he rose, his authority was submitted to all in the heavenly realms. Next, a special prayer known as the prostration of the bishop-elect cemented Alexander's proclamation of submission.

During this prayer, the clergy performed the "imposition of hands," or the laying on of hands, that ultimately led to the anointing of Alexander's head and hands. His anointing was a sacred act to set him apart from others, a dedication of both his mind and his body to divine work. The two assistants—Robertson and Trotman—"laid their hands upon the head of the Bishop Elect, and uttered the words 'Receive the Holy Ghost.'" The prayer, the laying of the hands, and this special dispensation of the Holy Spirit to Alexander were all signs of consecration. According to church devotees, upon Alexander's receiving of the Holy Spirit, congregants and clergy witnessed the unbroken chain of episcopacy that reached back to the apostle Peter. A divine sign of confirmation marked the moment. The *Negro Churchman* reported, "Nature seemed to join with men in the solemn act, for a peal of thunder instantly broke forth followed at once by a copious shower which, spectators state, fell in direct vertical sheets to the earth."[83] African people might have added in agreement that the sign of rain also demarcated this moment as divine. Next, Alexander joined the church patriarchs first in receiving and then dispensing the Eucharist to those present. He ended the ceremony by delivering his consecration address followed by a final blessing.

Alexander began his address by thanking McGuire, the clerical dignitaries, the first ladies, and respected laity. He also thanked God for his watchful eye over the great distance he traveled for his consecration in the United States. He specifically thanked the patriarch for his "broadmindedness . . . in outlining and defining our relationship, without any equivocation or reservation, which has stirred us to work as *free* men and collaborators in the Master's vineyard."[84] Although it had taken several years, McGuire had held fast to his promise of granting his African counterparts freedom under the denomination. Alexander remarked, "I stand before you to sing with David 'I will lift up mine eyes unto the Hills from whence cometh my help.'"[85] He was certain, he exclaimed, that without God's help he would not have successfully carried out his ministerial duties. Quoting scripture, he confidently asserted, "Yet I have dared to venture, not without misgiving, to take the Master at His word which says, 'All things that ye ask the Father in My Name, shall be given you.'" The episcopacy was Alexander's greatest request, and he believed that God had bestowed it to him with great ceremony. Alexander's consecration satisfied a legacy of petitions by South African clergymen to govern themselves. Indeed, Alexander believed that God had answered him even if it might have been generations later.

Alexander also took time in his address to offer a full account of his work in South Africa. In it, he gave a tour de force of his own faith, Christian development, training, and leadership, all of which he followed up with a report on the growth of the church in South Africa. The South African church leader showed North Americans just how much power the denomination wielded on the continent. Alexander began by explaining his early connections with the Anglican Church. He claimed to have severed his connection with the Anglican Church in 1914. Although he did not mention his time establishing the Ethiopian Catholic Church in Zion, this was his primary focus between 1914 and 1919 as described in chapter 2. Alexander noted that his exposure to McGuire had come in 1924 through *Negro World* and said that McGuire had organized locally to bring together "several of the Clergy and their congregations in the independent work in which we were engaged."[86] McGuire asked him "to call a meeting at which 450 persons [were] present, tired of being led by certain 'ignorant parties.' This group decided to organize under the African Orthodox Church in South Africa." Alexander described how congregants eventually elected him as a candidate for bishop of this new church and gave him the task of seeking consecration. After he communicated with Patriarch McGuire, he "discovered that the Black man had become a new factor in the Ecclesiastical world." From that time, he said, "the work has continued to grow."[87] The expansion of the church in South Africa was rapid, Alexander noted. His flock had grown from the humble beginnings of 450 people to quadruple that in less than four months. He also brought church leaders into the fold, from priests to deacons to readers. In a matter of months, Alexander established and supervised fifteen churches.

The church growth and development Alexander facilitated brought into sharp relief the tension and envy that North Americans had as their congregations waned in membership. Six months after his consecration, Alexander returned to South Africa.[88] His congregations throughout South Africa had paid the fare for his passage from South Africa to America with the promise that the Americans would pay for his return. After the consecration, however, Alexander was forced to conduct a lecture tour throughout the denomination to raise money for his travel. It took many months to gather the funds. Alexander complained that even when he preached at churches, he was allowed to receive funds only for his return voyage from the second offering, which usually didn't amount to much.[89] His inspiring preaching often benefited the individual congregations he visited. Even with these complaints, McGuire only nominally supported Alexander by sending announcements meant to rally support to get Alexander home.

Along with these announcements, McGuire encouraged congregations to join the effort by publishing the names of congregations that obediently contributed funds. Those that did not contribute, however, were shamed into giving. He tried to entice them by stating that "He [God] gives twice who gives quickly."[90] Despite the effort, Alexander remained in North America struggling to get his funds together. He set sail and returned home to South Africa almost six months after he had intended. The process of appointment for those leaders serving in Southern Rhodesia was much less ceremonial, at least as far as the documents show. After twenty long years attempting to gain recognition, Alexander established the Mashonaland Province in 1950 with one trained reader, one catechist, three elders, and one secretary along with twenty-five faithful members.[91] Although it did not carry the same ceremonial pomp and circumstance of Alexander's consecration, the clergy in Southern Rhodesia had somehow met the seemingly impossible standards of Alexander and the colony to begin their work officially. Together their work was advancing the kingdom through building formal institutions.

Alexander never returned to North America. Despite the denomination's stated obligation to attend synods, the cost was simply too great for any part of the church to bear especially during the Great Depression, when most of the North American arm of the church lost property and assets to debt. Nevertheless, Alexander maintained regular communication with the North American province via the articles he published in the *Negro Churchman*, some of which explained the origins of the separatist church movement and the status of these churches.[92] As these pieces illustrate, Alexander aimed to contextualize the separatist movement apart from the AOC and in doing so prove to North American leadership not only that Africans had imagined their own religious autonomy but also that Alexander was among the leaders capable of supporting that goal. Indeed, as Alexander said about the church's expansion throughout Africa, "We see in the Horizon the Sun of the African Orthodoxy in Africa."[93]

SEVEN

Seeds of Freedom

Growing Orthodoxy and Freedom
in East Africa

Shortly after his consecration in Boston, in 1928, Archbishop Daniel Alexander established the only African Orthodox Church (AOC) seminary outside of the United States.[1] By the time the seminary was functional, the archbishop had cultivated a formidable group of clergy in both the Transvaal and the Cape to support his work in the African province of the AOC.[2] He had also purchased land, cultivated financial partnerships with people from the highest colonial ranks, and organized primary and secondary schools all while maintaining the church's Anglican ethos and reporting it all to *Negro World* and the *Negro Churchman*. Alexander even pledged to build the denomination's first cathedral, a site that symbolized religious permanence and that few African leaders imagined possible without the support of European missionaries.[3] Alexander and his colleagues had generated such a productive ministry that members of the North American province started to declare that "it may not only be necessary to stop sending missionaries from Chicago to the 'Dark Continent,' the Dark Continent may have to send some of its missionaries to darkest Chicago."[4]

Alexander's vision and establishment of the AOC challenged Western colleagues' perceptions that Africans could not govern their own affairs, a belief that likely guided George McGuire's treatment of Alexander early on.

Additionally, McGuire's admission of Alexander's success in Africa was a powerful geopolitical and ideological reversal that centered an African-led faith envisioning liberation on Earth and in the afterlife. Figures such as Alexander had won, at least on the surface, a long-standing battle against paternalistic perceptions that Black people in the diaspora sometimes appropriated from European missionaries. North American clergy quickly recognized the advantage to having African Christians lead their own congregations while they claimed victory in the denomination's growth and the scriptural promises they had spoken for decades: "'Ethiopia may one day stretch forth her hands unto God' and bring true Christian Civilization to America."[5] The AOC's successful growth was a testament to the way church building could enact kingdom come, which also muddied any vision for people who had only understood Africans as needing white saviors to uplift them.

Placing the AOC, African clergy, and African Christians at the center of growth and possibility signaled that Black freedom and futurity were in Africa(ns). This chapter's focus on the AOC's development in Africa points to a new phase of institution building that made Africans' focus on education, the seedbed for liberation. The chapter turns to East Africa as a remaining site for African Christians to define freedom for themselves through ministerial training, a reclamation of ancestral land, the creation of political auxiliaries, and even a campaign to control what Africans ought not do with their own carnal bodies. Scholarship by Morris R. Johnson, Francis Githieya, Elekiah Andago Kihali, Joseph William, and Adam Ewing contribute to burgeoning discussions of the AOC in Africa in different ways. As Johnson, Githieya, Kihali, and William focus on church history, they rely on diverse disciplinary methodologies to historicize the church and distinguish regional church developments, particularly in Kenya.

I engage these important overviews on AOC development; however, in this chapter I specifically contend with Johnson, Kihali, William, and Ewing's discussion of education as a way to institutionalize and elevate the denomination to the public in both the western and southern hemispheres. Among the scholars, Ewing's focus on Garveyism captures portions of the churches' history, but he is committed to relying on the church to highlight how Garvey's politics worked in concert with African nationalism. William details Ewing's findings by pointing to the Kikuyu's history of Christianity, land alienation, and the religious independency that fostered AOC members' involvement in anticolonialism. Johnson's and Kihali's wrestling with the rise and fall of the church allows us to consider more rigorously the place of education within African independent churches.

Johnson's and Kihali's competing analyses of education offers insight about the importance of creating training institutions for Alexander. Johnson suggests that Alexander searched for clergy who were already educated and trained, although he argued that it was all a means to control clergy conduct.[6] Kihali extends this same thinking but with a different motivation of improving the current church. Kihali is diligent in pointing to the ways this movement was led by politically conscious Africans who believed that education would render them higher socioeconomic status and might also support their campaign to reclaim their ancestral lands. Ultimately, this chapter seeks to make clear that East Africa is the only place where Garvey's dream for political freedom came to fruition, and it all came to pass through the church; the faithful declared this freedom—which they had worked for and built—as kingdom come on Earth.

ESTABLISHING THE SEMINARY

As early as 1928, Alexander established educational institutions for AOC leadership that reflected a form of respectability politics that he insisted AOC leadership absorb, standards that to some extent harbored an internalization of colonialism. Alexander had conceived of these training grounds as sites to impart tools for survival in an inequitable colonial economy. Yet, he knew that the seminary could be so much more; it was an incubator to imagine freedom outside of colonial rule and a pathway for church leaders to enter the priesthood and imagine self-determination. Alexander had not accounted for just how expansively his followers envisioned the freedom that could come with education. His plan for a denomination connected to educational institutions reflected the missionary pragmaticism he had been exposed to as a South African Christian whereby missionaries built a critical mass of schools for Christian converts early on. Missionaries established thriving educational centers such as the Presbyterians' Lovedale Missionary Institute and the Methodists' Healdtown, among many others that produced a set of African elites that claimed these spaces as political training grounds for anticolonial efforts.[7]

The same was true outside of South Africa. Kihali makes a similar claim for mission schools beyond South Africa when he states that "the mission church had helped towards the education of Africans; therefore, these intellectuals were first and foremost, Christian intellectuals."[8] Kihali declared that Julius Nyerere of Tanzania, Kwame Nkrumah of Ghana, Namdi Azikiwe of Nigeria, (Jomo) Mzee Kenyatta of Kenya, and Patrice Lumumba of Congo need to be understood in tandem with the AOC church leaders Alexander groomed through his seminary. Kihali's argument is that historians, particularly Western ones, have dissected these freedom fighters' faith from their politics when, in fact, they cultivated both their faith and politics simultaneously at mission schools. This brings to bear the greater importance of Alexander's work as a leader of an African-led initiative that cleared the space to consider the moral stakes of anticolonialism that missionaries' complicity with colonialism disallowed. Alexander's correspondence with church leaders in Southern Rhodesia was simple; he told those who first sought training that he wanted to create a seminary for clergy and laity training. He had to keep his letters simple and covert because both his African identity and his politics made him subject to the scrutiny of the state. Alexander never positioned the AOC or its seminary explicitly as political struggle because to do so would be dangerous, but the people he eventually trained, just as Kihali's theorizations have shown, need to be understood as part of religious and political movements.

Initially the archbishop had centered his efforts on the seminary's curriculum, hoping that the institution would develop and flourish in time. Alexander relied on his trained clergy to pool theological and doctrinal knowledge of a number of priests from the surrounding area to create a prospectus of courses, the backbone of the institution.[9] The church leader showcased the prospectus not only to prepare for the seminary but also to help fundraisers imagine the seminary as a site of contemplation, evolution, and practical training for the AOC.[10] It also marked a shift in AOC growth in that Alexander both conceptualized and directed the establishment of this learning center. This additional form of institutionalization was also an idea that came directly from African Christians. It seems especially appropriate that Alexander named the seminary St. Augustine of Hippo in honor of the African division's mother church and the African philosopher.[11] St. Augustine of Hippo was a North African whose major contributions—defining original sin and the trinity—still have a lasting impact on Christian theology. Alexander's naming of the mother church and the only AOC seminary after Augustine centers Africa(ns) as a site of significant theological, institutional, and administrative contributions to the AOC. Furthermore, because Augustine has been traditionally revered especially by the Anglicans, it also positioned the denomination as respectable if not at least legitimate. Even if Alexander's motivation in creating this seminary concretized the church's doctrinal dissemination and transmission in ways that went beyond individual parishes, he also was driven by his desire to formalize ministerial needs for education and training.

Creating the Seminary of St. Augustine of Hippo was an incredible milestone in the AOC. Modeled after Endich Seminary, the American counterpart, St. Augustine was one of the only religious institutions established by Ethiopianists in South Africa. It was a pivotal contribution to independent Christians because few had the resources to even imagine creating their own institutions on their own terms. Perhaps Alexander may have also been aware of or motivated by Ethiopianists' early attempts to establish an African Methodist Episcopal Church seminary through James Dwane around 1908. Historian Stephen Angel explains that this endeavor failed in part because of limited funds but also because Americans felt that it gave South Africans too much autonomy.[12]

Although a great many of them had been educated at some of the most prestigious institutions in the region, they had not planned for the education and training of the next generation of clergy. This made St. Augustine particularly important to the continuation of the Ethiopian movement. Its primary focus was to educate and train clergy and evangelists working in the church, but it also solidified some of the burgeoning tenets and precepts of the church itself as these ideas were taught to the new ministers. Unlike other African-initiated churches, such as the Ethiopian Catholic Church in Zion, the AOC documented almost every aspect of its church practices out of pedagogical necessity. This documentation proved to be an important site of knowledge for the church.

Alexander's objective was for all aspiring readers, licentiates, deacons, and priests in the denomination to have access to rigorous training. He articulated this need clearly and plainly. The aim of the seminary was to "train men for the Priesthood of the Church under the constitution of the Seminary."[13] Underpinning this practical need was Alexander's hope that education would ensure moral leadership among his own clergy. His quest for the seminary did more than replicate missionary ideologies for African education. Lovedale, like Alexander's St. Hippo, pledged to produce "native teachers, preachers and ordained ministers."[14] But more importantly, Lovedale claimed, "Christian character is the end of missionary education. . . . We do not educate unless our work here produces both stability and resources in [the] individual, moral and mental, and a sense of responsibility to his fellow-countrymen."[15] Caroline Elkins explains that missionaries played an instrumental role in "Britain's civilizing mission in Kenya, as they did throughout most of the empire. Missionaries were determined to convert the African not only to Christianity but to an entire western way of life."[16]

Alexander shared these aims, but central to them was also his desire that they be taught and led by Africans for their own clergy. To this end, Archbishop Alexander, Venerable Archdeacon Ice Mbina, Dr. Christian Van Haght, and Father James Mdatyuluwadi taught these courses throughout the years.[17] This was a new model for ministerial education not just in South Africa, where Christian schooling was saturated, but also for other parts of Africa that had not received as much attention from various Christian denominations.

The AOC seminary's curriculum was traditional, even though its African faculty made it an anomaly among institutions even in South Africa. All prospective students who applied to seminary had to be recommended by their denomination and deemed morally suitable for the ministry.[18] Beyond this localized screening process, Alexander also required that all candidates for priesthood reach at least Standard VII, the equivalent of ninth grade in the US education system.[19] Students chose from a range of courses, including pastoral theology, church history, the Reformation, and moral theology as well as more practical studies of Christian worship, liturgies of the AOC, and the theory and practice of the sacrament of penance.[20] Through the years, Alexander was responsible for teaching liturgy, church history, and philosophy. Mbina taught courses on the Old and New Testaments, Van Haght focused on Afrikaans and philosophy, and Mdatyuluwadi taught English, church history, and homiletics.

In the first year of study, candidates for ministry enrolled in courses on both the Old Testament and New Testament. They engaged in these teachings while also reading the worship books of the AOC, which served to forge connections between the ways students might imagine a specific set of worship practices with scriptural teachings. The seminary designated students' second year for Christian ethics and dogmatics. Seminary faculty defined ethics as "dealing with the positive ideals and standards of Christian life." While the definition might seem overly simplistic, Alexander's approach in both attracting and teaching ministerial candidates was to elevate ordinary church leaders in their doctrinal understanding. Dogmatics, on the other hand, was defined as "the doctrine of God, the doctrine of the trinity, the creation, angels, man and his fall." Following these classes, third-year students studied "ecclesiastical polity, the Canon and Constitution of the African Orthodox Church, the reformation, Liturgics of the Church."[21] The latter portion of the year was spent on moral theology and the theory and practice of logic and the sacrament of penance. In the fourth and final year, students attended classes on ethics, logic, psychology, physiology, sociology, political economy, and the Koran. Together, these topics moved beyond routine seminary courses even for European missionaries who were afforded the opportunity for clerical study.

This fourth year culminated their study and allowed them to consider a myriad of psychosocial as well as religious influences shaping African society. Alexander had always hoped that the seminary provided education to his ministerial leadership through its curriculum, but he also believed that it could live up to the meaning of the word "seminary": seed plot. He had envisioned the AOC seminary as a field where the church might sow, grow, cultivate, transplant, and deposit the students' faith not only within themselves and each other but also among the larger African community. He ensured this possibility of planting churches through these students by having students recite and sign the "Oath of Canonical Obedience" in which they promised to be faithful to their duties and their alma mater. The oath also called them "to live an honest and faithful life, striving always to uphold the dignity of the said alma mater, so that others may be encouraged to come and help us in carrying the objects of the African Orthodox Church."[22] In writing, Alexander declared that these courses worked to legitimize AOC leadership and also functioned as a cloak of respectability that few African independent churches were afforded. In actuality, however, this seminary and others like it were subversive places where saints conspired. Alexander sowed a vision through this seminary that served as a seedbed where anticolonial ideas could be cultivated as part of a doctorate in divinity.

Alexander took further steps to support the seminary as a living institution and ensure its legacy. For instance, he had no interest in a static course of study; to that end, in 1941 and again in 1951 he and his staff reevaluated the curriculum for coherency and relevance.[23] Meanwhile, the seminary not only awarded both a bachelor of divinity and a doctorate of divinity but also gave certificates of licentiate, deacon, and reader, three key leadership positions in the church. To complete these courses of study, all candidates, irrespective of the degrees, engaged in several years of study, part of which included "the lecture-tutorial, seminar, or fieldwork method."

This meant that Alexander was developing not just clergy but also a very educated laity with the malleability to work as well as function in different vocational registers. These consecrated skills also allowed them to engage in different sacramental practices when clergy were limited and granted clergy the chance to work for wages while still serving in a spiritual capacity. This flexible thinking transported to a seminary setting meant that a key seminary mandate—that all students be in residency for at least eight months before pursuing educational correspondence—allotted a new institutional space for African clergy in independent churches. With the exception of the African Methodist Episcopal Church, no Black denominations had developed such rigorous institutions for nonmainline Protestant churches. As Alexander had envisioned, the curriculum was meant to equip clergy to serve in their localized context whether in South Africa, Southern Rhodesia, or elsewhere.[24] To ensure that students were best equipped to develop churches attuned to their local situation but were also aware of larger transnational struggles, faculty customized the remaining coursework for each student to take up during correspondence learning from home.

Creating the Seminary of St. Augustine of Hippo was an incredible milestone in the AOC. Modeled after Endich Seminary, the American counterpart, St. Augustine was one of the only religious institutions established by Ethiopianists in South Africa. It was a pivotal contribution to independent Christians. Although a great many of them had been educated at some of the most prestigious institutions in the region, they had not planned for the education and training of the next generation of clergy. This made St. Augustine particularly important to the continuation of the Ethiopian movement. Its primary focus was to educate and train clergy and evangelists working in the church, but it also solidified some of the burgeoning tenets and precepts of the church itself as these ideas were taught to the new ministers. Unlike other African-initiated churches, such as the Ethiopian Catholic Church in Zion, the AOC documented almost every aspect of its church practices out of pedagogical necessity; this is how Alexander institutionalized by leaving a discursive trace.

Alexander had invested a great deal of energy in education. His efforts ran parallel to those of McGuire, who was maintaining his own much smaller seminary in New York. Both clergymen recognized the advantage of education for their people, whether in the United States or on the African continent. In fact, the church leaders relied on education to sharpen their leadership and even to address their congregants, largely because they believed that a solid education positioned them well among the growing cacophony of independent churches. Alexander formalized the place of education within the denomination and produced a dynamic, wide-ranging, and relevant curriculum for St. Augustine students. For instance, while McGuire's Endich Seminary focused on providing theology students with the practical skills to administer their duties, Alexander strove to also enhance their worldviews. Therefore, he felt it necessary to include some courses on other religions, such as Islam, and he even included politics and sociology in the studies. The logic behind offering these courses very likely spoke to Alexander's desire for ministers to think about both the religious and political milieus they were working in. To bolster their learning, he also insisted that part of their studies should take place in their home churches, giving them the critical vantage point to consider their congregations' most pressing needs. These experiences didn't just build ministers; they built church leaders who could guide their congregations, districts, and communities autonomously.

For the AOC, education became a critical tool. Its innovative form of relevant and specialized education for church and community leaders attracted a number of politically conscious Africans throughout southern Africa and later East Africa who could mold and use the church for pressing and more localized concerns. Alexander's seminary was a successful site from which to meet the needs of the local clergy community. In fact, Alexander focused so much energy on the seminary because he used it as an entry point from which to grow his leadership beyond South Africa and into other countries, making the AOC a transnational church. The American branch of the AOC only spread west to San Francisco and to select places in Canada in the late twentieth century. This was not the case for the church on the African continent. Through Alexander's determination, the church grew across various regions in Africa. Autonomy and self-sufficiency, the same key words McGuire had once stressed to him, became the guiding principles of a new movement to educate African Christians.

TO LEARN OF SOME OTHER FAITH: EAST AFRICA
AND THE AOC CHURCH

It did not take long before African Christians were reading about Alexander's work, especially his focus on clergy training and education. Three former Anglican clergy established the AOC in East Africa with the help of

Alexander: Reuben S. S. Mukasa and Obadiah Basajakitalo in Uganda and Arthur Gathuna in Kenya. Like so many others, church leaders in Uganda had been instructed to contact Alexander after reading about the church in the pages of *Negro World*. To be sure, Kikuyu Christians might more readily attribute their chance meeting with Alexander at the Mombasa port after his Uganda trip as God's provision after their divine petitions for a church that understood their anticolonial posture. Despite their different trajectories, the congregations in East Africa, much like those in South Africa and Southern Rhodesia, had found common cause in the Universal Negro Improvement Association's (UNIA) ability to hold both faith and politics as a guide to their British colonial societies. At the forefront of these stories always seemed to be male church leaders who had defected from missionary-run churches, especially the Anglican Church.

In 1924, Mukasa (better known as Spartas because of his Herculean strength and athleticism) heard about the newly established AOC while reading *Negro World*. Spartas and his friend (and soon-to-be brother-in-law) Obadiah Basajakitalo had recently abandoned their seminary studies within the Anglican Church.[25] These two men are central to Ugandan Christians' connections to orthodoxy. In fact, Basajakitalo's legacy and commitment to orthodoxy allowed his grandson, Jonah Lwanga, to become the metropolitan of Kampala and all of Uganda of the Eastern Orthodox Church of Alexandria. Both Spartas's and Basajakitalo's experiences of racism within the church ignited their quest to find a church that they believed truly reflected the original tenets of Christianity. Like leaders such as Mphamba, Poyah, and Dube in Southern Rhodesia, after Spartas read McGuire's UNIA address at the 1924 conference in *Negro World*, he couldn't help but contact the UNIA. In Spartas's passionate letter to the UNIA, he vowed "to go to hell, jail, or die for the redemption of Africa."[26] Spartas's statement indicated the measures he might be forced to take, given the violent nature of colonialism, to ensure African freedom. Four years later through his connection to Alexander, Spartas formally affiliated with the AOC as an avenue of spiritual agency and anticolonial change he had vowed to bring to Uganda. American Garveyites directed him to Alexander in South Africa, just as they had instructed church leaders in Southern Rhodesia.

Spartas, like Alexander in South Africa as well as Mphamba and Poyah in Southern Rhodesia, through the help of a South Africa–born attorney, relied on writing as a means to enact local change and connect global movements. Epistolary writing, a residual of Victorian era Ethiopianists, became a medium not simply for Native petitions to the colony or metropole; over time, church leaders in the interwar period relied on epistolary writing to communicate and organize across regions to organize and build a church that demanded the same rights as African delegates to the metropole on behalf of their people. As a result, a new phase of the Ethiopian tradition grew and connected people transnationally. Leaders such as Spartas helped precipitate these connections. Four years after Spartas wrote to the UNIA, he also wrote to the *Negro Churchman* to convince the AOC that "if every Church has its Patriarch where they unanimously want him to dwell, I think I am not wrong nor am I mistaken to say that Our Patriarch of the African Orthodox Church should dwell and reside in Africa."[27] Spartas's challenge to North American clergy not only positioned Africa as the place for the church patriarch but also signaled the importance of Africa to the denomination (and, by extension, to orthodoxy).

Spartas also wrote, "There are many good healthy, splendid places in this continent fit for any dweller. And as a scientist once said, 'The Paradise is within AFRICA, especially in Uganda.'"[28] Spartas concluded that "if there be some fear as to which is the best healthiest place where we may build a palace for our Patriarch, think of Uganda first which is the central country in Africa." Spartas might have started the church in Uganda had Alexander not contacted McGuire first. Making my point clearer, many of the African Christians who contacted the UNIA and later joined the AOC understood the denomination as the realization of the faith and politics they already espoused. When Spartas did finally get hold of McGuire to ask him about expanding the church to the African continent, Alexander had already established the church in South Africa. The American church leader directed Spartas to Alexander, his South African counterpart in Kimberly. Yet, as Kihali has importantly noted, Spartas did not have the same resources to help him grow the church in Uganda. Kihali explained that even though Spartas "possessed the zeal, the stamina, and determination," he "lacked organized human resources" and had "no educated and skilled personnel to help him run the mission, had no financial income whatsoever."[29]

The difference between Spartas and Alexander might have actually been the already established transnational faith work undergirded by the Ethiopian movement. McGuire's fiery sermons had inspired Spartas, but Alexander's pragmaticism in providing the much younger Ugandan priest with an opportunity to complete his Anglican-based studies crystalized his commitment to the AOC. To add, through a surprise visit from the archbishop of Canterbury, the Anglican Church that Spartas had left acknowledged the AOC as a legitimate church, true encouragement to a young African minister who had trained under these Anglican Church leaders.[30] Soon, Alexander expanded the church to Uganda through Spartas's ministry. Alexander was able to extend the work in Uganda only because it resonated with his own calling to train, educate, and set a moral tone for clergy, more so than he had been able to do in Southern Rhodesia.

In 1930, Alexander traveled to Uganda to meet Spartas, Basajakitalo, and others who were dedicated to establishing the AOC in Uganda. According to Alexander, Spartas's and Basajakitalo's lack of education was the only obstacle in launching the church. Kihali actually shows us through his oral histories that Spartas was not only a priest but had also had a political career in his own right. If we read at face value a report by the Central Intelligence Department in Uganda, it corroborates Alexander's conclusion that Spartas was uneducated and plead to uplift and educate Ugandan clergy.[31] It is important to recognize that while Spartas might not have been formally educated, his efficacy in organizing his own political party in the face of staunch colonialism reflects his intelligence and ability to organize and navigate great obstacles. Interestingly enough, Kihali's oral histories suggest that Ugandan leaders were unimpressed with Alexander's striking poverty, which they viewed as a marker of his intelligence.[32] Alexander's training might have been intellectually instructive, but it could have also worked to standardize church practice as well.

Either way, Alexander insisted that Ugandan leaders had to complete their theological training before they could be recognized in the AOC. Spartas's and Basajakitalo's experience in the Anglican Church made their transition to the AOC simple because many of the denomination's tenets were rooted in Anglicanism. In fact, the Anglican communion connected Spartas and Alexander. Spartas proudly declared that Alexander had left the Anglican Church and established "the African Orthodox Church—a church established for all right-thinking Africans, men who wish to be *free* in their own house, not always being thought of as being boys."[33]

Spartas's correspondence with Alexander sounded eerily similar to the correspondence Alexander had shared with the American-founded denomination years before. Just like Alexander, Spartas was drawn to the AOC because of its similarities to Anglican structure and practices. Between 1931 and 1932 Alexander provided Spartas and Basajakitalo with theological training, drawing on his experience leading and teaching at the seminary St. Augustine of Hippo. During this period Alexander evangelized throughout Uganda, preaching widely and building a deep network of African Christians. He made it his mission to extend the hand of Christian discipleship and fellowship to all the people he met, and he baptized hundreds. Having built up a credible following, he welcomed them all, including converts, to the AOC. His trip was supposed to culminate in the ordination of Spartas and Basajakitalo, who would become the leaders for the church in Uganda. Even before his travels, Alexander endorsed Spartas and his colleague for potential ordination, stating in correspondence that "I hope that the Day will be a great Day for Africa, when an African in the heart of Africa will be ordained to the Priesthood by an African Bishop."[34] Spartas left the church before Alexander could ordain him.

One of Alexander's members had explained that the archbishop's practices did not reflect orthodoxy. Similarly, one of Alexander's members had noted the discrepancy in teachings when his daughter was baptized, citing that it didn't follow the normal protocol he had seen within the Greek Orthodox Church, whose practices he participated in when he lived in Tangyanyika through the leadership of Father Nicodemos Sarikas, an Orthodox priest there. This critique of Alexander's practices affronted his insecurity with the legitimacy of his denomination even though he had wanted to break away from European-led churches. I include Spartas in this history even though he left Alexander's AOC because their connection helped him build community with African Christians in East Africa. While Alexander did not find traction among the Ugandans, they did benefit from his vision to provide an alternative site of education that cultivated a transnational culture of anticolonialism among African Christians.

On his way back to South Africa from Uganda, Alexander stopped in Mombasa, Kenya, where he found fertile ground to grow the AOC even if Uganda had no interest in the denomination. In Mombasa he met James Beauttah, a leader of the Kikuyu Independent Schools Association (KISA), who became impressed with Alexander's work through the AOC. Beauttah was a postal clerk who, like many African radicals, relied on his transnational network and most likely the waves of traffic crossing through port cities such as Mombasa to learn and disseminate new anticolonial strategies among the Kikuyus. Alexander was one of many people Beauttah met while awaiting his ship back home to South Africa. Most impressive to Beauttah was Alexander's church, which operated independently from white mission control, an ecclesiastical freedom that grew increasingly appealing to the Kikuyus. At the time the Kikuyus hoped to affiliate with a denomination that would carry out important sacraments such as communion, baptism, confirmation, wedding ceremonies, and burial rites for faithful Christians. Likewise, Beauttah knew that for KISA and the Kikuyu Karing'a Educational Association (KKEA) to educate the next generation of Kikuyu learners, they needed a denomination that would support their breaking away from missionary leadership to establish their own schools and start their own churches. Their radical activism kept in mind their commitment to Christianity as well as their desire to maintain Kikuyu customs. Having broken away from the mission church leaders they summoned Alexander, whose Ethiopian tradition permeated throughout the transnational church as he worked across ethnicity.

OVERTURNING THE TABLES OF COLONIAL CARNALITY

Kenyan Christians in the central region of Kiambu established the AOC after enduring religious, social, and political upheaval during the interwar years. In large part, the heart of the AOC outside of southern Africa was established in Kenya during the interwar period. This period brought new meaning to the colonial question of "the Native problem," what Ugandan scholar Mahmood Mamdani describes as the ways "a tiny foreign minority rule over indigenous majority."[35] The British in Kenya, along with other colonial powers, transformed Africans into a population whose sole purpose was to develop and support the colonial project. The colonial project sought to control land to extend an empire's political and economic reach. The interwar period brought into sharp relief a new consequence of the colonialism in Africa: a spiritual crisis that ensued from Kikuyu landlessness. In Kiambu, the region largely occupied by the Kikuyus, African Christians latched onto the religious autonomy imbued in the AOC to create new ways of navigating an increasingly colonial society that demanded new skills beyond those used to maintain Kikuyu agrarianism. The Kikuyus long believed that being a faithful and learned British subject could secure socioeconomic stability, and while they sought to create those opportunities, they also worked to maintain their own sense of self.

Kenyan missionary work began with Portuguese Roman Catholics in the coastal towns of Mombasa and Lamu during the sixteenth century. A second wave of missionaries came in the nineteenth century under the Church Missionary Society. With time Sir William Mackinnon, the Scottish founder of the Imperial British East Africa Company, worked with a large network of missionaries. The chartered company supported the British government's plight to develop, control, and administer African trade across Kenya and Uganda, two areas controlled by the British government. Before World War I, several missions worked among the Kikuyu, Kamba, and Maasai peoples, including the Roman Catholics Consolata Fathers, the Holy Ghost Fathers, the Church Missionary Society, the Church of Scotland Mission, the African Inland Mission, the Evangelical Lutheran Mission of Leipzig, and the Gospel Missionary Society. MacKinnon, Alexander Low Bruce (the son-in-law of medical missionary David Livingston), Sir Fowell Buxton, Robert Unwin Moffat (grandson to world-renowned missionary Robert Moffat), John Linton, Thomas Watson, and Cornelius Rahman were all part of the private East African Scottish Mission in central Kenya. The East African Scottish Mission joined forces under the Church of Scotland Mission among the Kikuyus, some of whom eventually established the AOC in Kenya. These Scottish missionaries took over the East African Scottish Mission as they brought the Kambas, Maasais, and finally the Kikuyu to faith.

The Scottish missionaries' approach relied on practical needs of education, medicine, and industry/employment to introduce Western Christianity as a means of transforming African societies to mirror those in the West. Missionaries successfully relied on education to connect the Kikuyus to Christianity, but the Kikuyus became interested in education as tool to navigate colonial society rather than to simply assimilate to it. MacKinnon drew his approach from the schooling that the Scottish mission had established in southern Africa through such figures as James Stewart, the venerated Scottish founder and educator of the Lovedale Missionary Institute in the Cape.[36] MacKinnon hoped that Stewart might instill the same desire for education as he had heard that Stewart had done among the Xhosas.[37] Stewart, like MacKinnon, believed that the Kikuyus' growing commitment to education reflected a deeper promise of Christian conversion even though it seemed more of a litmus test of Africans' assimilation to Western cultural mores. Caroline Elkins writes that "missionaries were determined to convert the African not only to Christianity but to an entire western way of life."[38] The members of the East African Scottish Mission didn't consider that both the Xhosas and the Kikuyus, among other Africans, might be strategically invested in missionary education. As a merchant-imperialist, MacKinnon hoped that education would produce a class of Africans who would sustain the colonial economy. The East African Scottish Mission paved the path for more successful missionary work by the Church of Scotland Mission, which took over in 1901. Historian Robert Tignor describes this kind of religious work as "the civilizing and Christianizing influence of disciplined agriculture and handicraft."[39] The East African Scottish Mission and the Church of Scotland Mission subscribed to such a civilizing mission because their aim was societal transformation, albeit not always altruistic because it often benefited merchant-imperialists such as MacKinnon.

Colonialism, particularly land alienation, limited cash crop success, and increasing taxation pushed Africans off their ancestral land and into wage labor. Colonial administration reinforced socioeconomic segregation by introducing a poll tax and a hut tax for Africans that led to significant economic loss.[40] As labor demands grew, the British drew upon labor from women and even children, further entrenching the wage labor system within African society. These factors influenced the rise of migrant laborers, who often worked to further develop colonial city infrastructure. British railroads connected commodity-producing regions to facilitate economic projects. The British also sought to connect the larger network of colonies they ruled. In other instances, colonial administrators joined undeveloped regions because they became hubs for African labor supply. The railway system expanded to such places as Kiambu, which was meant to provide transportation to the cooler Kenyan highlands that the colonial administration deemed most suitable for white settlement. The whites who did settle in the highlands invested in expanding crop production, thereby escalating the labor crisis. The British had started building railroads in the 1890s, which white settlers benefited from by the time they made the central highlands their home. Many years later, the British continued to develop the railroad but this time as a means to secure exports during World War I. Whites settled into their new lives while pushing Kenyans off their land. Blacks, particularly those who served in World War I, felt even less connected to their homeland because they had lost their land even though they had pledged allegiance to the British.

White anxieties about Black men fighting in World War I made the British reluctant to turn to African soldiers for support. But World War I was both brutal and expensive. In the end, they relied on African, Indian, and Caribbean men of the British Empire to ensure a costly win. Kenyan men met the call of duty by serving under the British in World War I. Thousands of drafted African men fought on the side of the British against the Germans in Tanzania and in campaigns in Europe. African soldiers proved their worth; they acquired new skills as scouts, porters, and cooks and remained loyal. With millions gone, though, women and children fought to meet labor shortages at home and in the fields.[41] Each European soldier, whether British or German, had at least four "Native carriers" who gathered food supplies, arms, and artillery; cooked; scrubbed; and met all of their needs to the point that some carriers died from exhaustion, malnutrition, or disease. In fact, of the approximately 250,000 soldiers and 750,000 civilians who died among them, 45,000 were from Kenya. And because the war was also fought on African soil, at least 750,000 square miles of land was destroyed, a heavy blow to the already devastated British economy but perhaps even more so to the Kikuyus, whose long history had always tied them to the land. Those African soldiers who did return home safely had hoped that their support of the British would earn them the very rights and equality that ignited the war. Rather, the British used the victory to cultivate white settler morale by rewarding white soldiers with land in Kenya but left Black soldiers throughout the British commonwealth to fend for themselves.

With dashed hopes, Black soldiers had to find their own way in a broken economy. The cost of World War I—in pounds and bodies—turned Britain's attention away from saving African souls to feeding an insatiable British economy. Britain contended with rising interest payments, inflation, and the reluctant loss of Ireland as well as the unexpected costs of annexing the German colonies of Papua New Guinea, Namibia, and Tanzania as well as Ottoman territories in the Middle East, all of which caused real logistical nightmares. As Findlay and O'Rourke describe it, "World War I brought the liberal economic order of the late 19th century to an abrupt halt."[42] The war ended the reign of the German, Habsburg, Russian, and Ottoman empires, while Britain's imperial possessions seemed to stretch from Cape to Cairo, extending from the Suez Canal to Singapore, cementing colonialism throughout Africa. The war's consequences were identical for Africans. If they had not lost their lives or land, they became further entrenched in a system supported by missionaries, colonial agents, and a growing number of white settlers, particularly in the central highlands among the Kikuyus. Devastation permeated African society, especially among those whose military service had raised their expectations for British recognition, citizenship, and economic equity. World War I ensured British sovereignty and crystalized colonialism in ways that undermined African spirituality, customs, and livelihood by alienating Africans from their ancestral land. In a related way, female circumcision became the battleground from which the Kikuyus settled their losses centered on land.

Female circumcision among the Kikuyus brought to the fore an enormous spiritual crisis that African Christians faced as they converted to

Christianity while attempting to honor Kikuyu customs. This history has received ample scholarly attention, but female circumcision became representative of Africans' objection to missionaries' explicit rejection of Kikuyu culture and African culture more broadly as non-Christian.[43] Other contested issues included dowries and polyonymy. In other words, European missionaries were imposing new cultural mores without any reverence to African elders and their wisdom on how they might negotiate Christianity and cultural practice. African American politician Ralph Bunche's article on the rite of passage at Githiga Market in the Kiambu District helps unpack an implicit argument that some Kikuyus made that much more than the act of circumcision was at stake when the Kikuyus lobbied to maintain the practice in the 1920s and 1930s.

In fact, Kikuyu freedom fighter Jomo Kenyatta argued that "this operation is still regarded as the very essence of an institution which has enormous educational, social, moral and religious implications, quite apart from the operation itself."[44] Bunche also emphasizes this idea when he underscores the importance of "not merely the circumcision but the entire process of initiation and [gendered] teaching." Transgenerational transmission of gendered knowledge, which ties the young, the elders, and the ancestors in community, Bunche suggests, is critical to Kikuyu womanhood.[45] Overall, the initiation, not simply the circumcision, knitted these generations together. One Kikuyu woman explained one aspect of this experience when she said she had become karing'a (pure) and consequently learned to limit her interaction with men to avoid the possibility of premarital pregnancy. In the words of one Kikuyu woman, female circumcision means "to have earned the stage of maturity, when . . . one no longer moves about with those not circumcised," a demarcation of womanhood.[46]

Bunche's anthropological account directs us to the dialectical process between Kikuyu young women, living elders, and ancestors, all contingent on their access to ancestral land. He explains that this procedure required the gendered transmission of knowledge and could only occur on and within sacred space inhabited by the Kikuyus. Bunche writes, "The soil is sacred to them because their ancestors lie buried there."[47] The intimate connection to ancestral land allowed girls to grow into womanhood. When the Kikuyus conducted circumcision on the mission station, they did so to the chagrin of those missionaries who allowed them to conduct it or performed an abbreviated version of it in secret.[48] Over time campaigns against the practice generated an outpouring of opposition, making it nearly impossible for Kikuyus who had left their land to hold these rites of passage on the mission station. With no land from which to carry out circumcisions, this campaign alienated the Kikuyus for not only their land but also their ancestors.

Despite the sanctity of female initiation and its functional purpose of female purity, missionaries generally opposed the practice. Missionaries neither knew nor recognized circumcision as a respectable part of their Christian journey. Dr. John Arthur, a medical missionary of the Kiambu District from 1907 to 1937, led a formidable opposition against female circumcision. While a number of ethnic groups engaged in the practice, including the Massai, Samburu, Nandi, Kipsigis, Kuria, Gussi, Embu, Meru, Kamba, and Taita peoples as well as the Kikuyus, missionaries targeted their oppositional campaign efforts on the Kikuyus, Embus, and Merus, who had the larger Christian base. Missionaries had adopted and infused male initiation with Christianity, even going as far as allowing the circumcision process to take place in their hospitals, but they labeled the female version brutal and barbaric despite the fact that they relied on the procedure to tame female hysteria as well as masturbation.

Church leaders first sought to check the practice among their own members. This began by denying sacraments and services from African Christians. Initially, church leaders forced their baptized members to take an oath against female circumcision. The church leaders also denied communion to members who participated in the ritual.[49] With little success in curtailing the practice, missionaries kept Kikuyu families who supported the initiation process from sending their children to the mission school. More specifically, both the Methodist Church and the Scottish Presbyterian Church barred church-excommunicated families who allowed female initiation. Arthur took this strong stance, especially after one student was abducted and forced to be circumcised against her will. Historian Lynn Thomas suggests that missionaries such as Arthur saw African Christians' continued engagement with circumcision as "a direct challenge to their education efforts, as girl students routinely left the mission schools when their time for initiation approached."[50] Yet, this reading does not account for how Africans reconciled their actual commitment to Christianity itself. Kikuyus were actively engaging the same ideas South African church leader Maake Mangena Mokone had questioned: What does it mean to worship their own way when faith, cultural practice, and self-determination are taken seriously? This experience, alongside the mutilation and murder of a female missionary, moved Arthur and others to stand firm in their campaign.

By 1925, the church declared the entire initiation process a threat to all its mission work in education, health, and even the possibility of African salvation. In 1925 and 1927, the missionaries made official demands to the colonial government to control the process with the intent of eliminating the practice entirely. Kikuyus responded to the missionary campaign to stop female circumcision by withdrawing from missionary-controlled institutions, especially schools. By 1929, a substantial number of Kikuyu children left mission schools. Missionaries and colonial administrators blamed female circumcision for the shift in their mission work. Yet, female circumcision was one of many issues that undermined mission schooling. The controversy surrounding female circumcision made Kikuyu Christians reconsider the way they functioned within colonial institutions. While Kikuyu parents continued to pursue mission education for their children, they understood that their children received an inferior vocational trade education rather than classical education. In 1929, mission schools had 82,455 students enrolled, but they expended only 74,043 pounds on African and Arab education, as compared to the 49,993 pounds they spent on the 1,500 white settlers' education.[51] Kikuyu parents questioned these educational discrepancies even more when missionaries attacked Kikuyu traditional customs. Derek Peterson's scholarship shows that female circumcision was one of many concerns for Kikuyu parents, which also included concerns about the erasure of Kikuyu language. Local government wanted to make Kiswahili the lingua franca of the colony.

This move to manage Africans' facility with English undermines the original British goals of cultivating an elite class of Africans during this same period. The metropole's attempts to raise the Africans' character, while ensuring that only "a select group of Africans should be groomed for the training of those who are required to fill posts in administrative and technical services," was in line with many aspiring Kikuyus.[52] A government memorandum from 1925 suggested that "the first task of education is to raise the standard alike of character and efficiency of the bulk of the people." The document then asserted that a select group of Africans should be groomed for the training of those who are required to fill posts "in administrative and technical services," in line with many aspiring Kikuyus. The replacement of English with Kiswahili as the medium of instruction suggested to the Kikuyus that colonial powers were attempting to check social advancement, because sometimes Africans eclipsed the socioeconomic status and education of white settlers.

White settlers, who were more conservative in their notion of African paternalism, argued that the Kikuyus' ability to communicate in English served as a political tool in the hands of educated Africans. Ewart Grogan, a white settler best known for walking the length of Africa from Cape Town to Cairo several decades earlier, expressed his anxiety about the ways Africans might use their education.[53] Grogan forfeited his education and dishonored his family name and legacy when he left his studies at Cambridge University without a degree. Grogan feared that educated Africans would produce a respectable class that could threaten his business interests in the rice, coffee, and cattle industries as well as commercial logging. At the Settlers' Convention of Association, Grogan aired his frustrations with African education when he stated, "Imagine a more desperate happening than that we should introduce the language (English) to large numbers of people . . . whose proper education is in the fields."[54] Grogan's unsettling declaration illuminated his own insecurities but also pointed to the ways white settlers' racism curtailed African access to education for their own benefit. The Kenyan businessman's ideas about African education reflected white settlers' tenuous hold on a class status they deemed threatened by educated Africans.

In response to these colonial pressures, Kikuyus created an alternative educational space for their children. In 1922 well before Alexander arrived in Kenya, the Kikuyus envisioned and established a school in Gituamba. In 1929 Kikuyu parents petitioned the director of education, asking him to establish nonmission schools. These parents even offered to pay one-third of the teachers' salaries. The Church of Scotland, alongside other missions, resisted this proposal, arguing that the Colonial Office in London believed that all African schooling must be in the hands of the church even though they feared Kikuyu backlash.[55] Years later more and more schools cropped up, especially by the 1930s. Some missions even struggled to maintain control of their own school sites as Kikuyu schooling took over.[56] At the end of the 1920s, Kenyan Christians in the interior of the country founded two educational associations, the KKEA and the KISA. Members of these two organizations wanted to establish schools outside of the influence of missionary control. Eventually, both bodies strove to "further the interests of the Kikuyu and its members and to safeguard the homogeneity of such interests relating to their spiritual, economic, social, and educational upliftment."[57] These organizations extended themselves to meet the needs of "all natives of Kenya and negroes more generally," although the KKEA's influence was confined to the Kiambu District. The KISA was concentrated in Fort Hall and also stretched to the northern Kiambu and Nyeri Districts as well as Tanganika and the Rift Valley Province. The schools themselves fulfilled an educational purpose, but the colonial milieu also made it so that the schools marshalled a political authority, especially among those connected to the KKEA.

Every African organization—especially those focused on African education—that considered African social, political, and economic advancement within a colonial setting appeared political. The KISA and the KKEA, which created their own set of schools, provide such an example. However, the KISA appeared seemingly less political than its counterpart.[58] The KISA also had close ties with the Kikuyu Central Association (KCA), which had been established a few years earlier, in 1924, to confront the British government about lost African farmland. The KCA was created to replace the newly banned Young Kikuyu Association, which argued that the government contend with Kikuyu grievances, including low wages, prohibition of African coffee planters, and female circumcision. Young Kikuyu men pledged to retain their land even in the face of European hostility.[59] The Young Kikuyu Association, led by its inaugural president, Harry Thuku, laid the groundwork for collective Kikuyu political organizing. Thuku's radical agitating forced him into exile, bringing to bear a new political leader, Jomo Kenyatta. Kenyatta served as the general secretary of the KCA and would later become the first elected president of Kenya. The KCA had a general aim: "to make things easy so that when the Kikuyu want to say something to the Government they can tell it with one voice."[60]

Kenyatta also emphasized this point, writing that the KCA "worked hard to build up its organization and to strengthen the bond between its acknowledged members and the mass people."[61] He ends by asserting that "between the two World Wars, [it was the] leading political movement of the Young East Africans." Even with this overlapping history, when KCA and KISA members worked together, the KISA claimed to be apolitical, perhaps for multiple reasons. By 1929, the KCA had tense relations with the colonial government and missionaries, both of which had expressed support of KISA schools. It is less likely, albeit possible, that members of the KISA believed that the KCA's petitions functioned as a much clearer definition of political engagement than their education work. However, colonial officials continuously believed that the KCA dominated all independent school organizing; they were frustrated because Africans had enacted an intellectual agenda much greater than they even envisioned for Africans.

The KISA took its cues from past Kikuyu spirituality and prophecy. The organization honored Kikuyu eighteenth-century prophet and ancestor Mugo wa Kibiru, who had predicted white settlement and its demise on the Kikuyus. The KISA embraced his prophecy as a source of guidance. School officials encouraged students to acclimate themselves with European secrets to secure an autonomous Kikuyu society that was not undermined by white control. This magnificent history guided the Kikuyus, but so did the very missionary culture they had escaped. For instance, the KISA followed Christian respectability codes when it affiliated its independent schools with churches. In fact, the government subsidized many KISA schools, and some of their early aims aligned with missionaries' reformist movement, particularly around health, hygiene, and cleanliness. Some of those objectives included "the building of a dispensaries to provide medical service to Africans, the instruction of mothers in hygiene and morality, and the holding of quarterly teachers' conferences."[62] The KKEA, which eventually affiliated with the AOC under Alexander, was much more radical. Both schools, however, taught their pupils in English. In line with Black nationalist politics, the KKEA worked to uphold traditional customs without the support of the white settler population. The most pressing custom was female circumcision, which had become a symbol of anticolonialism and an affront to civilized European society. Those Kikuyus who adhered to their ethnic customs and fought missionary conservatism often did so by performing a song and dance called the muthirigu.

The muthirigu ridiculed missionaries and uncircumcised girls. More broadly, it stood in opposition to European control over African customs. Thomas explains that Kikuyus relied on the muthirigu to express their dismay with missionaries who wanted to eliminate female initiation practices but also with other Kikuyus who did not observe the female circumcision. She explores the muthirigu in detail, citing that in one verse the muthirigu mocked a Black clergy man who did not circumcise his daughter. Thomas writes that the Kikuyus believed that "girls who had reached puberty but were not initiated represented reproductive aberrations; they were physically able but not socially consecrated to conceive and give birth."[63] Young people, Thomas continues, "defended excision as a reproductive necessity." The verse itself states "Elder of the church, your uncircumcised daughter is pregnant and she will give birth to dogs." This collective expression of Kikuyu dissent made damning claims that banning cutting perverted customary markers of womanhood and seduced girls in an effort to steal land from the Kikuyus. Far from simply being a gesture of foreign opposition, colonial officials believed that it threatened political stability. To them, female initiation was also a clear articulation of Kikuyu nationalism, so much so that they eventually banned it and called those who performed it seditious.[64] If they found people performing it, the government fined them heavily and sentenced them to months in jail. Even with these consequences, the young people had made their point. Historians refer to this period between 1929 and 1931 as the muthirigu controversy, which was defined by anticolonial agitation.

African Christians set the agenda that undergirded Kenyan radical politics leading up to the Mau Mau Revolution waged decades later in the 1950s. The groundwork for the Mau Mau Revolution began among these Kikuyu Christians who had established the AOC in the 1930s. The establishment of this church—and, more specifically, Christian activism—put in stark relief Kikuyu's attempts to preserve traditional customs and simultaneously their demand for modern educational sites that ensured their children's ability to navigate a world predicated on Western colonialism. What is key to understand here is that the AOC was simply a vessel from which to enact Kikuyu demands. The decades-long battle over female initiation followed by the subsequent withdrawal of Kikuyu students from mission schools decentered Kikuyu politics from their most critical demand: land. Land, whether to carry out customs or to house institutions such as schools and churches, closely linked Kikuyus' past and future in ways that were often illegible. The AOC's commitment to racial uplift translated into honoring Kikuyu tradition. And yet, the idea of the church in and of itself was at least initially amenable to colonial Christian sensibilities. The Kikuyus followed the missionary model of affiliating the AOC with a school even if it was connected to the KKEA. These Christian activists focused on a mission to retain their power as Kenyan Natives indelibly connected to their homeland; they believed that an African-led church such as the AOC would give them this freedom.

Many Kikuyu leaders believed that Alexander, who led the AOC, might understand their mission to preserve Kikuyu customs and maintain ancestral land because of Alexander's own African identity. Alexander became aware of Kikuyu frustrations while he was in Uganda; Alexander's East African colleagues pointed to the far-reaching ways land alienation affected their own sense of self, livelihoods, and customs. Beauttah, the postal clerk that Alexander met in Mombasa, had shared with the KKEA and other activists the ways the AOC might be a forum from which to consider their concerns about land tenure, labor policies, and African education. Both the KKEA and the KISA recognized the advantages of working with and through their own self-governing church, because European scrutiny was seemingly ambivalent to Christian leaders. Unbeknownst to Alexander and the KKEA, colonial authorities grew suspicious of Alexander's connection with the Kikuyus. The colonial secret police in Kenya wrote to their counterparts in South Africa to provide information about Alexander's travel but also to ask for more information about Alexander's politics. Even with multiple lenses of scrutiny reaching from the United States, South Africa, and now Kenya, Alexander agreed to work with the KKEA to bring it into affiliation with the AOC.

Johana Kunyiha began corresponding with Alexander shortly after Beauttah shared with KISA members about his meeting with the archbishop. Kunyiha sought religious instruction and laity training from the South African church leader. In May 1935, Alexander agreed to return to Kenya following an invitation. Kunyiha wrote in response, "I was pleased to hear that you have decided to come to Kikuyu country and give our people spiritual uplift."[65] Kunyiha humbly noted that his people "are in the beginning of modern civilization, so it is our duty to educate them," but he also expressed his hope that Alexander's "work will be a nucleus in which [the] Negro Race will set an example to the world indicating what the race can do itself without external assistance." Much like his American mentor, McGuire shared the history, tenets, and rules of the church with the East Africans. He described the church as having a Catholic ethos but with its orders from the Eastern Orthodox Churches. Alexander also emphasized that the church attempted "to reach out to the millions of African descent in both hemispheres and declares itself to be perpetually autonomous and controlled by Negroes entirely."[66] This unifying charge of people of African descent was not new to the Kikuyus, as they had made similar pan-ethnic calls to anticolonialism.

Alexander arrived in the Muranga District of Kenya in 1935.[67] He requested that the KKEA and the KISA recommend and sponsor a cohort of theology students to work under his training. To that end, he specifically asked that all laity connected to independent and Karing'a churches raise money for the cost of his voyage, stay, and training in Kenya.[68] In the interim, Alexander traveled to as many congregations as possible to perform important sacraments such as baptism to the Kikuyus, who had long been awaiting the religious rites. Even his performances of these sacraments signaled to both Alexander and the religious community that the Kikuyus needed their own local church leadership. Alexander had made a distinct impact on the Kikuyus, and consequently KKEA members aligned themselves with him, while the KISA labeled him conservative and restrictive.[69] One of the candidates for ministry was Arthur Gathuna, whom Alexander described as "humble and uncovetous." Other candidates included Harrison Gacokia Kimanga, Nathan Ngure Munyiri, Daudi Maina Kiragu, Jason Muhungi Makara, Stefano Wachira Rugara, Philip Kiande Wamagu, and Nathaniel Miano Nelson, all of whom Alexander trained at Gituamba Seminary for eighteen months. Initially Alexander envisioned the theological study to last a total of fourteen years, largely because many of the candidates had not received any level of formal education. The courses he proposed included basic education, doctrinal study, and some practical theology via an internship at a local congregation.[70] His hope was, as always, that the students would have enough training to function with the integrity and morality he had always held as a high standard.

Yet, Alexander was forced to compromise his standards when KKEA and KISA leaders insisted on a cohort of ordained ministers to serve their community. Ultimately, he condensed the course of study he had initially planned for fourteen years to only eighteen months. Even though Alexander had spent an inordinate amount of time working on a curriculum for ministers, he relied on the Anglican book of prayer from nearby mission stations to teach after having spent a great deal of time attempting to work with translators to turn the Greek Orthodox liturgy from Greek to Kikuyu. He also used Divine Liturgy that honored the Anglican, Catholic, and Orthodox traditions but was developed by the denominational founder in the United States. More specifically, Alexander had the minor and major orders translated into Kikuyu during his time in Kenya for an accessible document for Kikuyu clergy as they served their communities. But still, the Kikuyus leaned heavily on the Anglican traditions, with many of their hymns taken from the Protestant hymnal *Nyimbo Cia Kunira Ngai*, created by an Anglican priest.

If Alexander's work there was largely successful, toward the conclusion of his time in Kenya tension developed between the KISA and the KKEA around the candidates for ordination. KISA questioned Alexander's ordination of Gathuna, a member of the KKEA, whom they claimed was an immoral drunkard. This strain reflected larger concerns between the two organizations around recruiting ministers through missions as far back as 1933. The KISA had wanted to draw from its pool of interested candidates, while the KKEA wanted to academically and morally cultivate a group of students for at least seven years' ordination. Alexander arrived two years later amid these tensions. When Gathuna was admitted to Alexander's makeshift seminary later than the other candidates, the KISA questioned whether he had received preferential treatment because it had not approved him for study. The two organizations underwent lively discussions about how they would proceed. According to Kenyan historian Francis Kimani Githieya, the KKEA agreed to work under the advisement and guidance of the KISA, conceded that all its candidates for ministry would be subject to KISA approval based on KISA interpretation of Christian tenets, and acknowledged that the KKEA would not sponsor any more candidates for theological training.[71] The KKEA, it seems, agreed to these terms only to ensure that Gathuna became ordained. Aside from these politics, Alexander had a mind of his own in that he wanted to ordain only those candidates he deemed well trained for the candidacy of minister. Gathuna very likely appeared suitable to Alexander, perhaps even over the others, because he was greatly proficient in English and was thereby able to articulate himself. Gathuna and Philip Kiande were the ones Alexander felt worthy of ordination, even though he ordained six other archdeacons on June 27, 1937, before returning to South Africa the following week.

Gathuna and Kiande were among the few to actually organize congregations under the AOC in Waithaka, near Nairobi. Between 1937 and 1945, Gathuna grew his own church to an estimated twenty thousand members; he even spread it beyond the Kikuyus to the Luhyis in Kiambu. Yet, even during this period of growth many among them questioned their orthodoxy. In fact, in 1938 Spartas contacted Gathuna to mention that the AOC rites did not align with those of the Greek Orthodox Church. The two East African priests also began to question the apostolic orders of Vilatte, who was excommunicated in 1938. Spartas and Gathuna wrote about their concerns to Patriarch Meletois II of the Greek Orthodox Patriarchate of Alexandria. Interestingly, Alexander had also pursued a relationship with the Greek Orthodox Church, suggesting that they ally with each other. Gathuna and Spartas's correspondence reflected their commitment to a church that practiced the Karing'a, or pure tenets of Christianity, one that went beyond undermining their culture.

Not even two decades later, in the eyes of the colonial administration, independent churches such as the AOC were marked as centers of anticolonial politics. Between 1952 and 1953, the Kenyan government placed its country under a state of emergency because of African resistance movements. The government responded to unrest and anticolonial agitation by arresting members of independent churches and schools. Gathuna and

Kiande, two of the candidates Alexander had ordained almost twenty years earlier, were jailed. During the height of the anticolonial movement in the 1950s, these two leaders, along with their congregations and others in Gathitu, Birithia, Kangure, Gachilka, and Giachiera, were monitored and eventually detained because of their involvement in the Mau Mau movement. Gathuna in particular was accused of taking the Mau Mau oath and subsequently sentenced to eight years in jail. Indeed, the AOC was such a political hub and site of leadership that once again the Kikuyus, who had been under the helm of the AOC, found themselves without leadership. To avoid colonial harassment once all independent churches had been banned, members of the AOC were forced to join the Presbyterian Church of East Africa, the mission church in the area. Alexander, it seems clear, had planted much more than a congregation; he had laid the groundwork for an anticolonial movement spearheaded by Black Christians and their institutions.

Epilogue

Thy Will Be Done

By 1935, Black Christians had not only imagined new churches but also built new ones that they dedicated to freedom work, a reflection of God's kingdom come in South Africa and throughout the diverse African diaspora. While the African Methodist Episcopal (AME) Church had developed beyond the United States to South Africa and West Africa, the African Orthodox Church (AOC) extended its mission to South Africa, Zimbabwe, Uganda, and Kenya as well as to those African branches of the church as far flung as New York, Nova Scotia, Cuba, and the Bahamas. In doing so, the AOC articulated a new globalized transnational expression of Black Christianity in which freedom from white supremacy was part of Black Christians' divine inheritance here on Earth. The church was not only a site of religious worship but also truly an incubator in which to imagine sovereignty and freedom. And while these stories tie directly back to the Black nationalist politics that emerged as a global phenomenon in the early twentieth century, most of these Christians believed that the foundations of Christianity insisted on freedom for all, white people included. Indeed, even as segregation hardened internationally, self-governance and self-determination remained critical components of civil society that Black

Christians aspired to bring to all parts of the globe. This transnational Black Christian network became a productive space from which to theorize and enact the possibilities of African religious agency, form Black transnational networks guided by spiritual and moral obligations, and dismantle and rewrite the colonial lexicons of race, anticolonialism, and African liberation.

Archbishop Desmond Tutu looms large in histories of South African religious activism. In these narratives, Tutu has come to metonymically stand in for religious activism in South Africa writ large, as if he alone not only carried that tradition out of the apartheid era but also created it. This book has shown otherwise, uncovering and reconstructing a longer and more pronounced tradition of political work by Christian religious leaders who sought to live out their faith in God's kingdom by working for liberation in their present political one. Likewise, Tutu's Nobel Peace Prize and his postapartheid appointment by his country's first democratically elected president, Nelson Mandela, positioned him as both a religious luminary and an extension of the postapartheid government. True, Tutu was integrated into the political fabric of Mandela's administration in ways that acknowledged the former archbishop's political work, perhaps best illustrated by Tutu's appointment as chair of the Truth and Reconciliation Committee, a court-like restorative justice body created to disclose and document the human rights atrocities perpetrated under apartheid. And yet, Tutu's political stature only came to bear because, as I have thus far shown, other leading clergy imagined and positioned the church as an integral part of South Africa's political agenda. In his seminal text *The Church Struggle in South Africa*, historian John W. de Gruchy suggests that clerical agitators such as Tutu played a "crucial leadership role in the absence of the recognized Black political leaders[,] many of whom were in prison or exiled."[1] In other words, it was church leaders who stepped in as the state incarcerated, exiled, and killed political activists. In fact, the church maintained the antiapartheid struggle in the absence of political leadership, politicizing and ushering congregants into the movement.

Kingdom Come shows the South Africa origins as well as the global reach of this religiously inspired resistance by turning to the stories of Black Christians who made the church into an engine and institution of change. Maake Mangena Mokone (the father of Ethiopianism), Charlotte and Katie Manye (organizers of the AME in South Africa), George McGuire (Universal Negro Improvement Association executive chaplain and founder of the AOC in the United States), Daniel William Alexander (founder of the AOC in South Africa), and numerous other African Christians organized their own branches of the church in Uganda and Kenya. These lives of faith and freedom striving showcase just how integral political freedom was to spiritual agency and point to the fact that self-radicalization within the church is nothing new. They insist that theological definitions and institutional organizing of and for freedom were localized phenomena not always informed by the West. Africans often recognized the similar ways Blacks in the West articulated their political desires. Instead, those African leaders living and working in places such as Kimberly, Harare, Nairobi, and even my hometown, Soweto, found resonance with other activists in cities as far away as London and Harlem. In this light, Africa can be understood for what it was in the nineteenth and early twentieth centuries: a crucial center and site of origin and a place of transmission, a starting point and centerpiece of religious and political ideas that circulated westward.

My own life story mirrors these critical circulations. In 1986, alone and at the tender age of six, I fled South Africa through a network of support that bridged radical Christians across South Africa, Zimbabwe, and America. While my own story is not one so acutely rooted in a history of Black nationalism, it is one that illuminates the networks of religious activism and social justice that so crucially link so many of us in diaspora who imagine a way forward on bridges forged by equal parts faith and a desire for freedom. Apartheid, a government-sanctioned system of racial hierarchy and oppression, defined life in South Africa from 1948 to 1994 and beyond. The nation was engulfed in violence. The president, P. W. Botha, declared the country to be under a state of emergency that lasted until 1989, when he resigned. South Africa seemed almost ungovernable, especially in Soweto where I lived. Soweto, a bastion of antiapartheid activity, was occupied by the military, whose repressive strategy targeted civilians. At six years old, I witnessed African people respond to state-sanctioned violence by imagining, defining, and fighting for a freedom they had never experienced. They collectively declared "the people shall govern," a political desire articulated in 1955 with *The Freedom Charter*, a joint coalition document that defined African demands for equality and equity, with self-governance as a central plea.[2]

My parents were among many ordinary people who joined the antiapartheid movement. They believed that their Christian convictions mandated that they respond to this political turmoil and oppression. Furthermore, my father's position as a Presbyterian minister and church leader emboldened him to use the church and his faith as platforms for action and change. My parents protested, organized political meetings, and participated in antiapartheid organizations, and both wrote and circulated what some called "subversive documents." By leveraging their positions within the Presbyterian Church and its global reach, my parents even helped endangered activists escape death by fleeing into exile. However, this need to fuse faith and politics was not a recent development in my parents' lives, one brought about by the apartheid state's actions in the 1970s and 1980s. No, my parents had been radicalized decades before. Their formal schooling at the Lovedale Missionary Institute, the University of Fort Hare, and the Federal Seminary alongside the informal learning they gleaned from old evangelists and community leaders had convinced them. African students headed newspapers, called for teach-ins outside of formal classrooms, and held conferences that debated strategies to counter the apartheid government, and African leaders, whether religious, political, or both, built coalitions. Such institutions had already educated many of the most prominent Black politicians throughout the African continent, including Nelson Mandela, Seretse Kama (the first president of Botswana), Julie Nyerere (the first president of Tanzania), Robert Mugabe (the first president of Zimbabwe), and Kenneth Kaunda (the first president of Zambia) as well as other leaders such as Desmond Tutu, the eventual archbishop emeritus of Cape Town. Like my parents, many of these leaders described their time at institutions such as Lovedale and Fort Hare as political training grounds where they knitted together a network of people to imagine and plan for the freedom to which they, like all people, were entitled.

My father, like Tutu, found his and our family's place in the church. By the mid-1980s, my parents had led several churches and returned home from graduate studies and training in Zimbabwe, Zambia, and the United States. Their time abroad introduced them to new forms of political consciousness. Their experiences make clear the notion of white supremacy as a global project that reached well beyond the borders of apartheid South Africa. My father's education outside of the country also made him a formidable candidate for an administrative position in the headquarters of the Presbyterian Church in southern Africa. Given my father's position and his political leanings, his passion always led him to liberation theology. Not surprisingly, the South African intelligence agency noticed. The agency described him as a "rebellious agitator" and a "terrorist against the state." In time, the intelligence agency deemed my parents' activity so threatening that we became key targets. The government of the late 1980s, facing new threats to its authority not only from within but also throughout the international community, attempted to silence political organizers by threatening their families. The state tapped our phone, followed us, and even broke into and bombed our home. This period was marked by intense scrutiny in the form of house arrests, incarceration, and the execution of resistance leaders. Others fled and pursued political work in exile. There were no limits to what the South African government was willing to do to stop political organizing. Even the church and its leadership were not immune. They became targets like the rest of the opposition, the surveillance and repression of clergymen seeming to undermine the very foundation of the Christian republic that white South African leaders claimed to uphold.

My parents' story of a politicized theology was no anomaly. If anything, they and their colleagues were able to embrace antiapartheid politics because of its deep roots. In this they continued a long-standing tradition of protest informed by their faith, reaching as far back as the late nineteenth century when African people not only conceived of liberation from white colonial domination but also relied on the church to bring it to fruition. Though many (both scholars and others) have associated this particular vein of politics to "outside" influences (especially for those South African figures who traveled), this book has argued that much of this religious ethos was not foreign-born but instead was a home-grown response to the global problem of white supremacy.[3] My father, whose political work started in the 1970s and continues into postapartheid South Africa, found his political footing within this larger history. Though his theological training might have exposed him to important ideas, he was not simply an extension of Howard Thurman, James Cone, and even Dietrich Bonhoeffer's political theology. Rather, my father's intellectual, political, and professional trajectories reflected a theological paradigm carved out by South Africans themselves. Even as a child, it was evident to me that "the struggle" became our life in ways that we could not fully fathom or imagine and was about collapsing the distance between Earth and heaven, and we returned to this mandate every time we recited the Lord's Prayer.

When my parents were able to escape from South Africa, they found refuge in Atlanta, Georgia, where we lived for several years during my parents' graduate school training in the late 1980s. Atlanta was a natural sanctuary for us not simply because it housed the Columbia Theological Seminary of the Presbyterian Church U.S.A.; it was also the home of important civil rights leaders such as Coretta Scott King, John Lewis, Andrew Young, Ralph David Abernathy, and Hosea Williams, among the many prominent leaders who galvanized local communities—especially students at the Atlanta University Center—to join the antiapartheid movement. Perhaps too simplistically, many historians position these activists and their politics as simply an extension of the civil rights movement. But it seems more appropriate to understand my family's work with them within a longer century-old history of religious activism, one that forged the terms of Black freedom in global terms across the African diaspora.

Within this vibrant Black Christian community in Atlanta, our family remained intimately connected to the antiapartheid struggle. Our position as exiled South Africans left us watching and organizing for the liberation of the nation outside of its borders. We followed all major news outlets, relied on an international community of exiled South Africans to share and exchange news, and corroborated everything with the snippets of information from activists who sent word to us. It was a different struggle but one that remained connected to the church as an institution of political change. When my parents returned to South Africa in 1992 at the dawn of a new democratic age, I remained in the United States to keep from disrupting my studies as they reimagined South African society. They went home to bring to fruition the South Africa that they and their ancestors had long envisioned. For my father, this vision was inextricably connected to Maake Mangena Mokone. Only after I completed my historical research for this book did I learn that my father and I are descendants of Mokone; indeed my scholarly research had curved toward my family's history in unexpected ways and reaffirms the notion that Black freedom struggles are comprised of deeply rooted, profound, and enduring networks that we have yet to fully understand.

My father, like Mokone, had at all times sought to worship in his own way. In the 1990s, he worked to ensure that spiritual liberation was indeed part of the new South Africa. My path was different. Though I became invested in working alongside my parents even at a young age, this distance complicated my interaction with my country and "the struggle." For the most part, that consisted of getting an education about a country with a complicated past and an even more complicated future. Books became not only a key form of connection to South Africa but also my solace. I have relied on them to maintain my relationship with my country of origin for more than thirty years.

Throughout my graduate studies, I found myself in a constant state of engagement with histories of sorrow and the long and treacherous treatment of people in the context of global Black oppression. It was depressing at best, but it also highlighted that Africa was at their center in some form. I found that most histories of Africa, albeit interesting, flowered out of colonial libraries that obscured the true African life, cultures, and histories that colored my own South African upbringing in exile. I confronted V. Y. Mudimbe's "invention of Africa" with its colonial library in tow, an archive of nasty grand narratives that worked to obscure any possibility of African humanity, ignoring the fact of African agency. These libraries and archives tethered African history to European colonialism and did very little to provide the ordinary particularities of not only African lives but also the ways that Africans imagined alternatives to their political realities. These histories often redefined my relationship to South Africa simply because they knitted together pieces of a story that I was not privy to living since I remained in exile. The archives, whether written or oral, offered new information and perspectives particularly about the mounting resistance to oppression. These books radicalized me. These histories further cultivated a political consciousness that my parents had nurtured inside of me when I watched them resist authority and navigate deep forms of surveillance, all while surviving targeted violence through the shelter of the church.

Both apartheid and our resistance to it disturbed the fibers of our family life. It was soul-crushing to be bereft of our humanity on our soil. And yet, we lived. In fact, African peoples' dignified responses to some of the most painful and humiliating atrocities any soul could bear ushered in an unforgettable sacred space of devastating creativity. It is here that I learned of courage, integrity, and honor. More importantly, I learned that there were many stories like mine. This makes the efforts of historians who have diligently worked to capture the glorious measures of resistance that ordinary people took during the antiapartheid struggle all the more critical. These stories are often anchored by important political figures such as Oliver and Adelaide Tambo, Walter and Albertina Sisulu, Nelson Mandela and Winnie Madizikela Mandela, and Chris and Limpho Hani, among others. Many of them were members and founders of the African National Congress, the oldest political party on the African continent that led the nation to freedom. But there are fewer histories that capture vectors of leadership that operate outside of the formally recognized political realm. There are other stories of ordinary church leaders in the late twentieth century who took to the front lines when political leaders had been exiled, incarcerated, or killed; their disappearance and death invites us to imagine a kingdom come, a place space where faith forms and informs freedom.

NOTES

Introduction

1 The Anglo-Boer Wars began with the first war in 1880–1881, in which Boer farmers rebelled from British rule in the Transvaal and reestablished their independence. This war was followed by the Second Anglo-Boer War, from 1899 to 1902. In the end, the Boer Republics were converted to British colonies with limited *zelf-bestuur* (self-governance).

2 Adhikari, *The Anatomy of a South African Genocide*; Adhikari, *Not White Enough, Not Black Enough*; Goldin, *Making Race*; Lewis, *Between the Wire and the Wall*; Muzondidya, *Walking a Tightrope*; and Van Der Ross, *The Rise and Decline of Apartheid*.

3 Getachew, *Worldmaking after Empire*; and Swan, *Pasifika Black*.

4 For some discussions of "Coloured" identity, see Adhikari, "The Sons of Ham," 107–8; Bickford-Smith, *Ethnic Pride and Racial Prejudice in Victorian Cape Town*, 186–216; Keegan, *Colonial South Africa*, 281; and Lewis, *Between the Wire and the Wall*, 4.

5 Dubow, *Scientific Racism in Modern South Africa*; Evans, *Bureaucracy and Race*; Ferree, *Framing the Race*; Fields, "Ideology and Race in American History," 143–77; Marks and Trapido, *The Politics of Race, Class, and Nationalism in Twentieth Century South Africa*; Peberdy, *Selecting Immigrants*; Ross, *The Borders of Race in Colonial South Africa*; and Suzman, "Race

Classification and Definition in the Legislation of the Union of South Africa 1910–1960," 367.

One. "My Blood Is a Million Stories"

The chapter title was taken from a line in Talib Kweli's song "Black Girl Pain," which features South African–born rapper Jean Grae. In the song, Grae describes the complexity of her own African identity, which was once categorized as Coloured by the South African state. She notes that her blood is represented in different migratory paths from within South Africa, Mauritius, and St. Helena.

1   The Dutch East Indian Company was a chartered company of the United Provinces of the Netherlands. The area started as a refreshment station for the company's fleets heading east but soon grew to become the permanent home of Dutch settlers.

2   For some discussions of Coloured identity, see Adhikari, "The Sons of Ham," 107–8; Bickford-Smith, *Ethnic Pride and Racial Prejudice in Victorian Cape Town*, 186–216; Keegan, *Colonial South Africa*, 281; and Lewis, *Between the Wire and the Wall*, 4.

3   Erasmus, "Introduction," 13–28.

4   As Jemima Pierre has brilliantly shown, even though much of the scholarship on Africa seems to overlook race, both colonial and neocolonial forces are engaged in a process of racialization that constructs all Africans as Black. Her argument is helpful when considering South African historiography, because many scholars suggest that the contours of race were fleshed out in the scholarship. Yet, Pierre's notion of statecraft is helpful in considering the ways Coloured identity reflects this project of race making that ultimately erases the particularities of ethnicity. See Pierre, *The Predicament of Blackness*.

5   Geographer A. J. Christopher suggests the relevance of "bi-polar classifications" in colonial South Africa in "To Define the Indefinable," 402.

6   Bickford-Smith, *Ethnic Pride and Racial Prejudice in Victorian Cape Town*, 24. Bickford-Smith notes that an Afrikaner newspaper, *Het Volksbald*, conceded in 1876 that "many unmistakenly off-coloured have made their way into the higher ranks of society and are freely admitted to respectable situations and intermarriage with respectable families." Bickford-Smith is attentive to the "passing" phenomenon among Coloureds whose appearance made it possible for them to pass. George Frederickson also discusses Coloured passing in Frederickson, *White Supremacy*, 133.

7   Saul Dubow has astutely argued that European governments strove to "separate" rather than "segregate" the races. Separation was the primary rhetoric circulating in the late nineteenth century. It wasn't until the twentieth

century that "segregation" became the most dominating term in South African racial discourse. See Dubow, "Race, Civilisation, and Culture," 71–94; and Dubow, *Racial Segregation and the Origins of Apartheid in South Africa, 1919–1936.*

8 Fields, "Ideology and Race in American History," 143–77; and Suzman, "Race Classification and Definition in the Legislation of the Union of South Africa 1910–1960," 367.

9 Census Office, *Census of the Colony of the Cape of Good Hope* (1866).

10 The word "Kafir" did not carry the same pejorative weight it would possess later in the century.

11 The Immorality Amendment Act, 1950 (Act No. 21 of 1950), amended the 1927 act that forbade unmarried sexual intercourse between Europeans and Natives. The 1950 amendment extended the prohibition to Coloured and Asian populations. Wicomb, "Shame and Identity," 92, 100.

12 When these Indian Ocean histories have surfaced, they have focused on the ways these religious cultures fueled a Muslim presence among Coloureds. These histories have broadened our understanding of Coloured religiosity, but more research awaits.

13 The modern-day spellings for the ethnic group Fingo are "Fengu" and "Mfengu."

14 Census Office, *Census of the Cape of Good Hope* (1875).

15 Census Office, *Census of the Cape of Good Hope* (1892), xix.

16 Anonymous, "Ethnicity and Pseudo-Ethnicity in the Ciskei"; Giliomee and Mbenga, *New History of South Africa,* 106; Moyer, "A History of the Mfengu of the Eastern Cape"; and Webster, "Land Expropriation and Labour Extraction under Colonial Rule."

17 Census Office, *Census of the Cape of Good Hope* (1892), xix. The Fingo people were able to purchase land and began investing in businesses along the Cape frontier. Subsequently, the Fingos were seen as culturally sophisticated.

18 Census Office, *Census of the Cape of Good Hope* (1892), xix.

19 *St. Helena Guardian,* September 12, 1872, December 12, 1872, and November 13, 1873; and *Natal Mercury,* October 2, 1873.

20 *St. Helena Guardian,* September 12, 1872.

21 *Natal Mercury,* October 2, 1873.

22 *St. Helena Guardian,* May 1890.

23 As quoted in Yon, "Race-Making/Race-Mixing," 159.

24 Vinson, *The Americans Are Coming!,* 13.

25 Between 1886 and 1902 Americans had an incredible influence over the mining industry, and with that influence came an influx of Americans to Kimberly.

26 William Van Ness to Dr. Leyds, January 15, 1893, Consular Dispatches, Johannesburg General Records of the Department of State, record group 59,

T191, roll 15, National Archives of South Africa, Cape Town (hereafter cited as Johannesburg General Records).

27 Kadalie, *My Life and the ICU*, 220–21.

28 Vinson, "Citizenship over Race?," 2. Many African American missionaries settled in South Africa between 1910 and 1923.

29 Vinson, "Citizenship over Race?," 6.

30 Vinson, "Citizenship over Race?," 4.

31 George Hollis to Josiah Quincy, May 9, 1893, Johannesburg General Records. See also the African Methodist Episcopal foreign mission newspaper *Voice of Missions*, June 1, 1898; Van Ness to Leyds, September 18, 1893, Johannesburg General Records; John Ross to Leyds, September 16, 1893, Johannesburg General Records; Keto, "Black Americans and South Africa, 1890–1910," 387–88; Turner, "My Trip to South Africa"; and Gatewood, "Black Americans and the Boer War, 1899–1902," 231.

32 Dean, *The Pedro Gorino*, 69, 71. Clements Kadalie also mentions West Indian presence in the Cape in his autobiography. See Kadalie, *My Life and the ICU*. Other notable West Indians include Trinidadian barrister Henry Sylvester Williams, who participated in the first Pan-African Conference held in London in 1900. For information on Williams, see *The Cape Argus*, August 26, 1904; Saunders, "Henry Sylvester Williams in South Africa"; and Collis-Buthelezi, "Caribbean Regionalism, South Africa, and Mapping New World Studies," 37, 50–52.

33 *South African Spectator*, January 1, 1910; and *South African Spectator*, May 18, 1901.

34 Goldin, "Coloured Identity and Coloured Politics in the Western Cape Region of South Africa," 248.

35 Perbedy, *Selecting Immigrants*, 14.

36 Perbedy, *Selecting Immigrants*, 14; Collis-Buthelezi, "Under the Aegis of Empire," 116.

37 DeLoughrey, *Routes and Roots*, 42; and Davis, *Black Women, Writing, and Identity*.

38 Bhana and Brain, *Setting Down Roots*; Bhana and Pachai, *A Documentary History of Indian South Africans*; and Bradlow, "Immigration into the Union, 1910–1948."

39 Union of South Africa, *Parliament Debates (Hansard)* (Pretoria, South Africa: Government Printer, 1913), December 5, 1913, col. 2323; and Swan, *Gandhi*, 281–84.

40 Union of South Africa, *Parliament Debates (Hansard)*, 281–84.

41 Union of South Africa, *Parliament Debates (Hansard)*, 19–20.

42 Passenger immigrants are estimated at 1,000 in 1887, with a sharp increase to 6,000 by 1891. The 1911 census recorded 19,839 passenger Indians in Natal. Historians Surendra Bhana and Joy Brain, *Setting Down Roots*, suggest

that there were close to 16,000 in the remaining provinces by the time the Union of South Africa was established in 1910.

43   Census Office, *Census of the Natal Colony* (1891).

44   Census Office, *Census of the Cape Colony* (1905); Census Office, *Census of the Orange River Colony* (1905); Census Office, *Census of Natal Colony* (1905); and Census Office, *Census of the Transvaal and Swaziland Colony* (1906).

45   Sunderland, *Vlieland, British Malaya*, 73.

46   Census Office, *Census of the Cape Colony* (1905); Census Office, *Census of the Orange River Colony* (1905); Census Office, *Census of Natal Colony* (1905); and Census Office, *Census of the Transvaal and Swaziland Colony* (1906).

47   Christopher, "To Define the Indefinable," 404.

48   Newbury, "The March of Everyman," 80–101.

49   Census Office, *Census of the Union of South Africa* (1912), xxxiii.

50   Jeppe and Kotze, *De Locale Wetten der Zuid Afrikaansche Republiek 1849–1885* (1887), 1166.

51   Pretoria Census, 1912, 26.

52   Census Office, *Census of the Republic of South Africa* (1950), 277.

53   Stone, *When She Was White*, 109–15.

54   House of Assembly Debates, March 13, 1950, col. 2814, National Archives of South Africa, Pretoria.

55   The Population Registration Act of 1950 (Act No. 30 of 1950), Sec. 5(1). The act also defined ethnic subgroups within the Coloured and Bantu populations. For instance, Asians were considered a subgroup of the Coloured people.

56   This registry would also list important information about each citizen, including place of birth, residence, occupation, and marital status. According to an opposing minister of Parliament at the time, the registry was "going to be a history of everybody from the cradle to the grave" (Senate Debates, May 29, 1950, col. 3637).

57   House of Assembly Debates, March 16, 1950, col. 3419, National Archives of South Africa, Pretoria.

58   The Population Registration Act of 1950, Sec. 1, xv.

59   The notion that race is socially constructed is most evident in the institution of the Mixed Marriages Act of 1949, which prohibited interracial marriage. National government officials had instructed local administrative officers to use racial appearance and social habits rather than birth certificates to determine race. However, it was clear that the architects of apartheid recognized that race was socially constructed when they offered a loophole for reclassification of Natives who were sufficiently educated and cultured beyond the typical Native.

60 SAB NTS 1764 vol.2 53/276, Secretary of Native Affairs to Secretary Muar-
    rysburg Boere en WolwerksVereniging, May 3, 1951, National Archives of
    South Africa, Pretoria.

61 The Population Registration Act of 1950, Sec. 1, x.

62 The Population Registration Act of 1950, iii.

63 Adhikari, *Not White Enough, Not Black Enough*, 91.

64 Claiming a white identity could also mean that Coloureds could incur a
    personal, social, and cultural loss by denouncing their identity for political
    and economic status.

65 Posel, "Race as Common Sense," 98.

66 Posel, "Race as Common Sense," 98.

67 House of Assembly Debates, March 8, 1950, col. 2548, National Archives
    of South Africa, Pretoria; House of Assembly Debates, March 15, 1950, col.
    3610, National Archives of South Africa, Pretoria; House of Assembly De-
    bates, March 16, 1950, col. 3157, National Archives of South Africa, Pretoria.

68 House of Assembly Debates, March 15, 1950, col. 2972, National Archives of
    South Africa, Pretoria.

69 Union of South Africa, Senate Debates, May 30, 1950, col. 3687, National
    Archives of South Africa, Pretoria.

70 House of Assembly Debate, June 1, 1950, col. 3926, National Archives of
    South Africa, Pretoria.

71 An Afrikaans newspaper, *Die Burger*, went so far as to call the Population
    Registration Act of 1950 "an indispensable part of the machinery of a modern
    state." See also House of Assembly Debates, March 13, 1950, col. 2826, National
    Archives of South Africa, Pretoria; House of Assembly Debates, March 13,
    1950, col. 2794, National Archive of South Africa, Pretoria; House of Assembly
    Debates, March 13, 1950, col. 2837, National Archive of South Africa, Pretoria.

Two. Faith of Our Fathers

1 This scholarship runs parallel to the work on American Ethiopianism cov-
    ered by such scholars as Gayraud S. Wilmore, Eddie S. Glaude, and Alan
    Cobley or even Albert Clearge, James Cone, and Eric Lincoln.

2 Elphick, *The Equality of Believers*; Lahouel, "Ethiopianism and African Na-
    tionalism in South Africa before 1937"; Mills, "The Fork in the Road"; and
    Mills, "The Taylor Revival of 1866 and the Roots of African Nationalism in
    the Cape Colony."

3 Balia, *Black Methodists and White Supremacy in South Africa*; Campbell,
    Songs of Zion; and Wenzel, *Bulletproof*.

4 For many years, African evangelists served African people when mission-
    aries did not fulfill their ecclesiastical duties to their African congregants.
    These overburdened church leaders were severely underpaid and often

made less than their African congregants working in agriculture, business, and many other forms of skilled labor. African labor, even church work, changed drastically in the 1880s and 1890s when colonial governments introduced policies of racial restriction, land reservation, and heavy taxation. These changes were largely reflected in a larger capitalist agenda of state-sanctioned racial segregation that would be codified through the joint British and Afrikaner government of the Union of South Africa in 1910. See Etherington, *Preachers, Peasants, and Politics in Southeast Africa, 1835–1880*, 123.

5   Much of this work builds off of Mutero, whose early recognition and documentation of the transnational linkage between South Africans and African Americans serves as a critical building block for me to consider the impact of ecumenical solidarity.

6   On the role of ancestors, see Mills, "The Taylor Revival of 1866."

7   Maake Masango, interview by Tshepo Masango Chéry, Oral history (Johannesburg, South Africa, December 31, 2009).

8   African philosophers have affirmed my father's thinking. Their scholarship suggests that African names hold within them tensions of both history and the future. In fact, Dider Kaphagawani explains that first names and even surnames function as "storehouses of information be it historical, futuristic, descriptive, picturesque, or human." Quoted in Kaphagawani, "The Philosophical Significance of Bantu Nomenclature," 147. Other scholars arrive at similar conclusions. For details, see Atenga, Ellece, Litoseliti, and Sunderland, *Gender and Language in Sub-Saharan Africa*; Neethling, *Naming among the Xhosa of South Africa*; and Paulus, "Naming in Sesotho."

9   Quinn and Cuthbertson, *Presbyterianism in Cape Town*.

10   "Coloureds Leave," Saint Andrew's Church Minutes 1839, Tiyo Soga House, Uniting Presbyterian Church of Southern Africa, South Africa.

11   Methodist Missionary Society Archives, London (MMSA) H-2711/27, letter from Weavind to Society Headquarters, Missionary Correspondence, 29 August 1896; MMSA H-2710/8, Transvaal Synod Minutes of 1896.

12   Methodist Missionary Society Archives.

13   Mokone, *The Early Life of Our Founder*, 10–12.

14   Campbell, *Songs of Zion*, 118. Ministry in the Methodist Church became increasingly difficult for Mokone and his colleagues as racial segregation crystalized.

15   The highly contested acronym "AIC" stands for four related terms: African-instituted churches, African-initiated churches, African independent churches, and African Indigenous churches. I use AIC to describe African-initiated Churches, churches started on African soil even if they later became affiliated with independent bodies. See, for example, Hayes, "The African Independent Churches," 139–46.

16 Many Black Christians believed these words to be divine promises of their redemption. Historian George Shepperson argues that Black Christians worldwide identified with Ethiopians because they too sought God's promises of freedom (Ps. 68: 31, New International Version).

17 "A New Church and Possible Trouble"; and Lea, *The Native Separatist Church Movement,* 14.

18 Marks, *Reluctant Rebellion.*

19 Lea, *The Native Separatist Church Movement of South Africa,* 34.

20 SANAC, *Report of the Commission,* 2.

21 SANAC, *Report of the Commission,* 55.

22 SANAC, *Report of the Commission,* 55.

23 Rhodes University, Cory Library, Grahamstown, (RU) MS 14/787, Testimony of Father Hill, Native Separatist Churches, 1925.

24 Neame, "Ethiopianism," 258.

25 Neame, "Ethiopianism," 260.

26 Neame, "Ethiopianism," 258.

27 Taylor, "The Social Motive in Evangelism," 238–39.

28 Elphick, "The Benevolent Empire and the Social Gospel," 347. "Between 1884 and 1911, the numbers of Christians grew from 60,154 to 322,673 new converts. According to the 1911 census, 26 percent of Natives identified themselves as Christians. By the end of the twentieth century, more than 76 percent of South Africans identified as Christians."

29 SANAC, *Report of the Commission,* 462.

30 SANAC, *Report of the Commission;* and Neame, "Ethiopianism," 260.

31 Neame, "Ethiopianism," 262.

32 SANAC, *Report of the Commission,* 559.

33 SANAC, *Report of the Commission,* 174.

34 *Report of the Proceedings of the First Missionary General Missionary Conference, July 13–20, 1904,* 182.

35 Neame, "Ethiopianism," 259. Lea also compared Ethiopianism to the Haitian Revolution. See Lea, *The Native Separatist Church Movement in South Africa,* 34.

36 Hill and Pirio, "Africa for Africans," 209–53; and Vinson, *The Americans Are Coming!*

37 RU MS 14/787, Testimony of Reverend Thomas William Maitland, Native Separatist Churches.

38 *Report of the Proceedings of the First General Missionary Conference, July 13–20, 1904,* 182; and SANAC, *Report of the Commission,* 64.

39 Historian Wallace G. Mills has argued that most AICs were and continue to be apolitical. See Mills, "The Fork in the Road," 51–61. Conversely, Christopher Saunders argues that many Ethiopianists were extremely political. See Saunders, "African Nationalism and Religious Independency in the Cape Colony," 205–10.

40 Union of South Africa, Office of Census and Statistics, *Official Year Book of the Union*, 437–38. The Ethiopian movement incited a massive proliferation of AICs at the time. By 1919 there were more than seventy-six recognized sects; however, many more churches had not earned government recognition and were not accounted for in government records.

41 RU MS 14/787, Introduction and Content of Church Separatist Hearings, Native Separatist Churches, 1925.

42 SANAC, *Report of the Commission*, 2.

43 Tile was the first Native clergyman to withdraw his ministry from the Wesleyan Church to establish the Thembu national church with the help of Xhosa royalty. Ntiskana, a tireless evangelist and prodigious hymn writer, established the first Indigenous and autonomous Christian organization. See Hastings, *The African Church, 1450–1950*, 218; Hodgson, *Ntsikana's Great Hymn*; and Saunders, "Tile and the Thembu Church."

44 National Archives of South Africa, Pretoria (NASA) SAB JUS 528 6515/29, J. Erasmus, Secretary of the African People's Organization, enclosure in letter from Mossel Bay to South African Police Oudtshoorn, South African Police, August 26, 1921. For a comprehensive discussion of Coloured churches of Griqua and issues of nationalism, see Landau, *Popular Politics in the History of South Africa, 1400–1948*, 162–213.

45 Campbell, *Songs of Zion*, 114–15.

46 RU MS 14/787, Testimony of Reverend Thomas William Maitland, Native Separatist Churches; CL MS 14/787, Testimony of Reverend Peter David Serfontein, Native Separatist Churches, 1925.

47 RU MS 14/787, Testimony of Reverend Peter David Serfontein, Native Separatist Churches, 1925.

48 RU MS 14/787, Testimony of Charles Demas, Native Separatist Churches, 1925.

49 RU MS 14/787, Testimony of Thomas William Maitland, Native Separatist Churches, 1925.

50 RU MS 14/787, Testimony of Jeremiah Mothapi, Native Separatist Churches, 1925.

51 RU MS 14/787, Testimony of Joel David, Native Separatist Churches, 1925.

52 RU MS 14/787, Testimony of Ephraim Munyane, Native Separatist Churches, 1925.

53 Bickford-Smith, *Ethnic Pride and Racial Prejudice in Victorian Cape Town*, 2–6, 26–28. Despite claims that Cape Town was a bastion of British liberalism, Bickford-Smith refutes the idea that the Cape Province and in particular Cape Town were more liberal than the rest of the nation.

54 RU MS 14/787, Testimony from the Christian Evangelist Mission Church, Native Separatist Churches, 1925.

55 Landau, *Popular Politics in South Africa*, 203.

56 RU MS 14/787, Testimony of Abel Mnsangu, Native Separatist Churches, 1925.

57   RU MS 14/787, Testimony of Abel Mnsangu.

58   RU MS 14/787, Testimony of Thomas William Maitland, Native Separatist Churches, 1925.

59   RU MS 14/787, Testimony of Henry Butana Make, Native Separatist Churches, 1925.

60   Turner, "My Trip to South Africa," 809–13.

61   RU MS 781, Hendrik Palatsie versus African Mission Society, Court of the Sub-Native Commissioner, June 1920.

62   SANAC, *Report of the Commission*, 520.

63   Private Collection of Archbishop Motame, Alexandra Township (PCAM), "Historical Preface," Constitutions and Canons of the Ethiopian Catholic Church in Zion, 1919.

64   Vinson, "Sea Kaffirs."

65   PCAM, "Historical Preface," Constitutions and Canons of the Ethiopian Catholic Church in Zion, 1919.

66   Emory University, Pitts Theological Library, Atlanta EU RG 005/10/2, Photograph of Founders of the Ethiopian Catholic Church of Zion, Series V. Correspondence, 1919.

67   Donaldson, "Language Contact and Linguistic Change"; and Roberage, "The Formation of Afrikaans."

68   Great Britain, *Parliamentary Papers*, 85–87.

69   Transvaal, *Statutory Proclamations of the Transvaal, 1900–1902*, 129.

70   RU MS 14/787, Testimony of Reverend Thomas William Maitland, Native Separatist Churches, 1925.

71   RU MS 14/787, Testimony of Lucas Thomas Mdhleni Lungu, Native Separatist Churches, 1925.

72   RU MS 14/787, Testimony of Stephen Hotsnaal, Native Separatist Churches, 1925.

73   RU MS 14/787, Testimony of John George Philip, Native Separatist Churches, 1925.

74   Saunders, "Tile and the Thembu Church," 553–70; and Saunders, "African Nationalism and Religious Independency in the Cape Colony," 205–10.

75   RU MS 14/787, Testimony of Reverend Thomas William Maitland, Native Separatist Churches, 1925.

76   SANAC, *Report of the Commission*, 63.

77   RU MS 14/787, Testimony of Craig Davison, Native Separatist Churches, 1925.

78   RU MS 14/787, Testimony of Archbishop D. Abrams, Native Separatist Churches, 1925.

79   RU MS 14/787, Testimony of Solomon Mndaweni, Native Separatist Churches, 1925.

80   RU MS 14/787, Testimony of Reverend Jacob, Native Separatist Churches, 1925.

81 RU MS 14/787, Testimony of an unknown Coloured minister, Native Separatist Churches, 1925.

82 RU MS 14/787, Testimony of John George Phillip, Native Separatist Churches, 1925.

83 RU MS 14/787, Testimony of Samuel Blackston, Native Separatist Churches, 1925.

84 RU MS 14/787, Testimony of Peter David Serfontein, Native Separatist Churches, 1925.

85 RU MS 14/787, Testimony of Abel Mnsangu, Native Separatist Churches, 1925.

86 RU MS 14/787, Testimony of Revered Andrew Piet Oliphant, Native Separatist Churches, 1925.

87 MMSA H-2711/27, letter from Weavind to Society Headquarters, Missionary Correspondence, August 29, 1896; MMSA H-2710/8, Transvaal Synod Minutes of 1896.

88 RU MS 14/787, Testimony of Lucas Thomas, Native Separatist Churches, 1925.

89 Duncan, "'African Churches Willing to Pay Their Own Bills'" (my emphasis).

90 RU MS 14/ 787, Testimony of Joel David, Native Separatist Churches, 1925.

91 RU MS 14/ 787, Testimony of Joel David, Native Separatist Churches, 1925.

92 RU MS 14/787, Testimony of Samuel Jacobus Brander, Native Separatist Churches, 1925.

93 RU MS 14/787, Testimony of Samuel Jacobus Brander, Native Separatist Churches, 1925.

94 EU RG 005/12/10, Biography of Clergy, African Orthodox Church Clergy Records.

Three. In the Name of the Father

1 Campbell, *Songs of Zion*, 134; and Erlmann, *Music, Modernity, and the Global Imagination*, 107.

2 Charlotte is often described in South African national discourse as a mother figure. In fact, the National Museum Publications specifically described her as the mother of the Black freedom struggle. The term "Black freedom struggle" has many points of origin but is most commonly associated with African American scholarship. For a discussion of this historiography, see Arnesen, "Reconsidering the Civil Rights," 31–34; Cha-Jua and Lang, "The Long Movement as Vampire"; Hall, "The Long Civil Rights Movement: And the Political Uses of the Past"; Horne, "Towards a Transnational Agenda for African American History in the 21st Century"; Kelley, "But a Local Phase of a Global Problem"; Kelley and Lemelle, *Imagining*

Home; Slate, "From Colored Cosmopolitan to Human Rights"; Theoharis, "Black Freedom Struggles"; and West, Martin, and Wilkins, *Toussaint to Tupac*. The work of Keita Cha-Jua, Lang, West, Horne, and Kelley, among so many others, speaks to the consistent ways in which historically Black people worldwide understand themselves to be in a transnational struggle of freedom that precedes both the formal period of the civil rights movement and the antiapartheid movement. Charlotte's description on a national level as the mother of the Black freedom movement speaks to the ways historians, even those outside of the academy, understand the global dimensions of the freedom project. Charlotte functions as a bridge both temporally and geographically to struggles in the United States and beyond that constitute the Black freedom struggle. See Botes, "Charlotte Maxeke (1872–1939)."

3   Thozama April, "Theorising Women: The Intellectual Contributions of Charlotte Maxeke to the Struggle for Liberation in South Africa" (PhD dissertation, University of the Western Cape, 2012).

4   Madipoane J. Masenya states that "the repercussions of seeking to do justice to an African context in one's academic endeavours, including in one's endeavour to foreground not only Africa, but the experiences of African women, will earn one an insider/outsider status." Masenya, "For Ever Trapped?" Amathabile Masola makes a forceful insistence for the space of Black feminist faith in "I Cite a Little Prayer." For a bevy of scholarship on the topic that covers more specifically African women's experiences in faith but also more broadly the place of spirituality in the academy (especially Christianity), the most productive work has been with scholars who most readily engage theology. See Hetherington, "Women in South Africa"; Masenya, "African Womanist Hermeneutics"; Masenya, "For Ever Trapped?"; and Mashini, Ackman, and Draper, *Women Hold Up the Sky*. See also Elphick, "Writing Religion into History"; and Paris, *The Spirituality of African Peoples*.

5   Campbell, *Songs of Zion*, 271.

6   Erlmann, *African Stars*, 50.

7   Harris, "The Archival Sliver."

8   A creative reading of the Manye sisters' archive both relies on and invokes the pioneering scholarship of Tereisa Mbari Hinga, Mercy Amba Oduyoye, Isabel Phiri, Jualynne E. Dodson, Marla Frederick, Judith Weisenfield, Betty Collier-Thomas, R. Marie Griffith, and Barbara Savage, who insist on making visible women's contributions to religious institutions.

9   Schler, "Writing African Women's History with Male Sources," 319.

10   Saunders and Hodgson, "Soga and Dukwana"; and Shepperson, "Ethiopianism and African Nationalism."

11   Masola, "I Cite a Little Prayer."

12   The first district of the AME Church was established in West Africa in 1854. However, the growing congregations in southern Africa would make it the hub of the AME Church outside of the United States. This also began decades of Indigenous church development that is often described as church schisms. The literature on this process is prolific and deserves important consideration. See Hayes, "Issues of 'Catholic' Ecclesiology in Ethiopian-Type AICs." However, it is also useful to consider church merging and short-term affiliation of all these different churches as part of a larger process of African church creation that African leaders embraced as they developed different church governance structures.

13   Xuma, "Charlotte Maxeke (Mrs)," 7.

14   Anonymous, "Ethnicity and Pseudo-Ethnicity in Ciskei," 395.

15   Like historian Poppy Fry, I use the term "Fingo" rather than the anthropology-inspired ethnic nomenclature "Mfengu" to signal its constructed nature. See Fry, "Siyamfenguza."

16   Stapleton, "Valuable, Gallant, and Faithful Assistants."

17   Coquery-Vidrovitch, *Africa and Africans in the 19th Century*, 137; and Fry, "Siyamfenguza."

18   Peires, "Ethnicity and Pseudo-Ethnicity in Ciskei."

19   Fry, "Siyamfenguza."

20   Cobbing, "The Mfecane as Alibi"; Moyer, "Some Current Manifestations of Mfengu History," 145; Moyer, "A History of the Mfengu of the Eastern Cape," 290; Peires, "Ethnicity and Pseudo-Ethnicity in Ciskei," 262; and Webster, "The War of 1835 and the Emancipation of the Fingo."

21   McCord, *The Calling of Katie Makanya*, 8.

22   Historians had inaccurately described this migratory episode within a history of the notorious Zulu leader Shaka Zulu's Zulu expansion, referred to as the Mefecane. The idea of the Mefecane skews other histories of migration and displacement in this period that were largely ignited by the colonial settlement. Furthermore, because the Fingo migration was understood as part of the migration of people south from Natal, the Fingos were disparagingly associated with Zulu people.

23   "Margaret McCord Nixon, 87," *Chicago Tribune*, April 12, 2004.

24   McCord, *The Calling of Kaitie Makanya*, 11. In literary studies this is the trope of "the talking book." See Gates, *The Signifying Monkey*.

25   McCord, *The Calling of Katie Makanya*, 11.

26   Vernal, *Farmfield Mission*.

27   Deacon, Phillips, and van Heyningen, *The Cape Doctor in the Nineteenth Century*; and Lefèber and Voorhoeve, *Indigenous Customs in Childbirth and Care*.

28   Campbell, *Songs of Zion*, 252.

29   McCord, *The Calling of Katie Makanya*, 59.

30 Scholars William Beinart and Colin Bundy insist that there is no substantial distinction between Xhosa and Mfengu people. See Beinart and Bundy, *Hidden Struggles in Rural South Africa*, 10.

31 Campbell, *Songs of Zion*, 253.

32 McCord, *The Calling of Katie Makanya*, 61.

33 *The Life and Legacy of Charlotte Mannya-Maxeke: The Memory Project Inaugural Lecture*, 4.

34 *The Life and Legacy of Charlotte Manye-Maxeke.*

35 Hensman, *Cecil Rhodes*, 300.

36 Hensman, *Cecil Rhodes*, 299, 301.

37 McCord, *The Calling of Katie Makanya*, 23.

38 McCord, *The Calling of Katie Makanya*, 10.

39 Lawrance, Lynn Osborn, and Roberts, "Introduction," 4.

40 McCord, *The Calling of Katie Makanya*, 8.

41 Kallaway, "Introduction to the Study of Education for Blacks in South Africa," 8–9.

42 Gaitskell, "Race, Gender, and Imperialism," 1.

43 Gaitskell, "Race, Gender, and Imperialism," 4.

44 "1871 Annual Report," United Society for the Propagation of the Gospel in Foreign Parts, Women's Missionary Association, Bodleian Library, University of Oxford University, 10.

45 "1871 Annual Report," 10.

46 Noble, "British South Africa and the Zulu War," 126.

47 Gaitskell, "Race, Gender and Imperialism," 2.

48 Gaitskell, "Race, Gender and Imperialism," 168.

49 Skota, *The African Who's Who*, 195.

50 Johannes T. van der Kemp's legacy is encapsulated in a series of writings shortly after his death. See Brightwell, *The Friend of the Hottentot*; Smith, *Johannes van der Kemp*; Smith, *Heroes and Martyrs of the Modern Missionary Enterprise*; and van der Kemp, *Memoirs of the Rev. J. T. van der Kemp, M.D., Late Missionary in South Africa.*

51 *Christian Express*, August 1862, 10.

52 Opland, *Xhosa Poets and Poetry*, 111. See also Draper, *Orality, Literacy, and Colonialism in Southern Africa*, 12.

53 McCord, *The Calling of Katie Makanya*, 13.

54 McCord, *The Calling of Katie Makanya*, 161.

55 Gaitskell, "Housewives, Maids, or Mothers."

56 McCord, *The Calling of Katie Makanya*, 54.

57 McCord, *The Calling of Katie Makanya*, 26.

58 McCord, *The Calling of Katie Makanya*, 27.

59 "Letter from Mrs. Wilcox," *Rice County Journal* (Northfield, Minnesota), June 29, 1882.

60 "Letter from Mrs. Wilcox," *Rice County Journal* (Northfield, Minnesota), June 29, 1882.

61 Historical Papers Research Archive, University of Witwatersrand, ZA HPPRA AD843-S-S-38-S38.1, Preface, "What an Educated Girl Can Do," pamphlet and leaflets, 1930.

62 For substantive discussions on the African Choir and the Manye sisters' involvement, see Jaji, *Africa in Stereo*; Erlmann, *African Stars*; and Erlmann, *Music, Modernity, and the Global Imagination.*

63 McCord, *The Calling of Katie Makanya*, 12.

64 McCord, *The Calling of Katie Makanya*, 39, 45, 47.

65 McCord, *The Calling of Katie Makanya*, 32.

66 McCord, *The Calling of Katie Makanya*, 50.

67 McCord, *The Calling of Katie Makanya*, 54.

68 Xuma, "Charlotte Maxeke (Mrs.)."

69 Erlmann, *African Stars*, 45.

70 McCord, *The Calling of Katie Makanya*, 53.

71 McCord, *The Calling of Katie Makanya*, 60.

72 Skota, *The African Yearly Register*, 194–95.

73 Xuma, "Charlotte Maxeke (Mrs.)," 10.

74 McCord, *The Calling of Katie Makanya*, 11

75 Xuma, "Charlotte Maxeke (Mrs.)."

76 Xuma, "Charlotte Maxeke (Mrs.)," 5.

77 Xuma, "Charlotte Maxeke (Mrs.)," 5.

78 McCord, *The Calling of Katie Makanya*, 6.

79 McCord, *The Calling of Katie Makanya*, 13.

80 McCord, *The Calling of Katie Makanya*, 14.

Four. Ministries of Migration

1 *New York Times*, August 6, 1924, 3.

2 Césaire, *Discourse on Colonialism.*

3 Since Carl Schmitt established the field of political theology when he wrote *Political Theology: Four Chapters on the Concept of Sovereignty* in 1922, new interrogations of political theology engage race more readily and rigorously. Beyond America as the site of exploration, the work of Michelle Wolf (South Africa), Anthony G. Reddie (UK), Emmanuel Katongole (Africa), David Tonghou Ngong (Africa), and Kwok Pui Lan (Korea), among others, emphasizes that politics cannot be separated from religious practices, institutions, cultures, and histories. See Day, *Unfinished Business*; Katongole, *The Sacrifice of Africa*; Pui Lan, *The Hong Kong Protests and Political Theology*; Reddie, *Is God Colour Blind?*; Shulman, *American Prophecy*; Smith, *Weird John Brown*; Tonghou Ngong, *The Holy Spirit and Salvation in*

African Christian Theology; Walker, *A Noble Fight*; and Wolf, "Madonna and Child of Soweto."

4   Ilesanmi and Kane, "New Directions in African Political Theologies."

5   Walker, "The Race for Theology," 136.

6   Boesak, "A Restless Presence," 26.

7   Boesak, "A Restless Presence," 14.

8   Boesak, "A Restless Presence," 26.

9   Walker, "The Race for Theology," 137.

10   McGuire's ministry shows the critical ways that people of African descent contributed to the missionary enterprise. He was one of the earliest "reverse missionaries," what esteemed religious scholar Jacob Olupona describes as evangelists from the global South who work to revitalize Christianity in the West. Olupona's term, however, is contemporary in nature. It is a reflection on how the geographical center of Christianity is no longer the West but rather the global South. Yet his term "reverse missionary" is still useful even in this historical context because it describes McGuire's and even Maxeke's work.

11   Of the 203 Black men ordained or received between 1865 and 1918 in the Episcopalian Church, 93 of them were born overseas, but only 5 of the 93 were from the British West Indies.

12   Lewis, *Yet with a Steady Beat*, 86.

13   Hayden, "Black Ministry in the Episcopalian Church," 2.

14   High Church is a type of worship that emphasizes sacerdotal, ceremonial, liturgical, traditional, and Catholic elements. These practices center on the theology of word and sacrament.

15   Hayden, "Afro-Anglican Linkages, 1701–1900," 25.

16   The Church Missionary Society was led by missionaries of color who were more cognizant of the cultural worship distinctions among the populations they served. The missionaries who traveled and established missions primarily in East Africa were associated with Low Church practices.

17   In Jamaica, for example, about a quarter of the population was Anglican. See Caldecott, *The Church in the West Indies*, 221.

18   The Anglican Church was supreme throughout the Caribbean. It had complemented the slaveholding society prior to emancipation because it emphasized hierarchy, authority, and obedience. Even with emancipation, however, the Anglican Church represented British power. When the British agreed to foster a climate of religious freedom in the colonies at the Conference of Berlin (1884–1885), the Anglican Church still had the most adherents and represented British power.

19   Lampe, *Christianity in the Caribbean*, 116.

20   James, *Holding Aloft the Banner of Ethiopia*, 42.

21   Curtin, *The Rise and Fall of the Plantation Complex*. In the 1820s, British colonies accounted for more than half of the sugar produced in the Caribbean.

A century later, the production had decreased to a mere 6 percent. In the same period, however, Cuba increased production from 17 percent to just under 80 percent. A similar phenomenon unfolded in the smaller islands of Saint Kitts, Nevis, Montserrat, and Antigua.

22 James, *Holding Aloft the Banner of Ethiopia*, 42.

23 James, *Holding Aloft the Banner of Ethiopia*, 42.

24 Haynes, "West Indian Journalist Analyzes Chasm."

25 "Missionary Chronicle," 200.

26 This was done to urge the legislature to proceed with the disestablishment of the Anglican Church.

27 "George McGuire," *Who's Who in New York*.

28 The flagship campus of Mico Teacher's College was located in Kingston, Jamaica. Founded by abolitionist Sir Thomas Fowell Buxton with the express purpose of educating newly emancipated slaves, Mico Teacher's College became the largest college in the West Indies for the first half of the twentieth century.

29 Ford and Cudall, *The Handbook of Jamaica, 1908*, 318.

30 Jamaicans alone contributed 78,000 laborers for these efforts between 1889 and 1891. Another 91,000 Jamaicans migrated to Panama when the American-controlled Isthmus Canal Commission took over from 1891 to 1915.

31 Cronon, *Black Moses*, 15.

32 *Classified Digest of the Records of the Society for the Propagation of the Gospel in Foreign Parts, 1702–1882*, 240.

33 Westerman, "Historical Notes on West Indians," 342.

34 Westerman, "Historical Notes on West Indians," 343.

35 Walker, "The Race for Theology," 137.

36 Walker, "The Race for Theology," 137.

37 Westerman, "Historical Notes on West Indians."

38 Mather, *Who's Who of the Colored Race*, 226–27. Morgan studied at St. Aidan's Theological College and at King's College at the University of London.

39 Mather, *Who's Who of the Colored Race*.

40 Bragg, *History of the Afro-American Group in the Episcopal Church*, 273.

41 George McGuire appears most frequently in American historiography because of his clear affiliation with the UNIA. Morgan only recently has appeared in histories on the Orthodox Church, which he would later join. See Namee, "Father Raphael Morgan."

42 Bragg, *History of the Afro-American Group of the Episcopal Church*, 273.

43 St. Phillip's Episcopal Church, Richmond, VA, Private Church Records.

44 "Clergy List," St. Phillip's Episcopal Church, Richmond, VA, St. Phillip's Episcopal Archives.

45 White, "Patriarch McGuire and the Episcopal Church," 127. However, his findings about the relationship of these men gave us an unclear view of how

they both came to serve the Episcopalian Church. White even suggests that it was likely Morgan who introduced McGuire to the episcopate.

46 Terry-Thompson, *The History of the African Orthodox Church*, 49.

47 *New York Age*, January 26, 1928.

48 "Vicar H. C. Banks to Dear Friend," October 1943, ScMG 464, box 1, folder 3, James S. Watson Papers, Schomburg Center for Black Culture.

49 *New York Age*, January 26, 1928.

50 Bragg, *History of the Afro-American Group of the Episcopal Church*, 273.

51 Mather, *Who's Who of the Colored Race*, 226.

52 *The Gleaner*, July 22, 1913, 6.

53 Morgan, "Letter to the Editor," 380–82.

54 Namee, "Father Raphael Morgan," 457.

55 "Convocation of Arkansas," 161.

56 The Protestant Episcopal Church in the United States of America in the Court of Review, *In the Matter of the Presentment of Bishop William Montgomery Brown*.

57 Brown Montgomery, *The Catholic Church and the Color Line*, 11–12.

58 White, "Patriarch McGuire and the Episcopal Church," 154.

59 Bragg, "Untitled."

60 "Report of the Madison Square Garden Meeting," 508.

61 "Schools We Support," box 9, folder 2, RG 61, The Records of the American Church Institute of the Episcopalian Church and Church-Related Schools, Archives of the Episcopalian Church, Austin, Texas.

62 "Schools We Support."

63 White, "Patriarch McGuire and the Episcopal Church," 157.

64 Boesak, *Black and Reformed*, 26.

65 Johnson, *Black Manhattan*, 163.

66 Greater Federation of New York Churches, *Report of Negro Churches in Manhattan*, 25.

67 Putnam, *Radical Moves*, 71.

68 *Negro World*, November 6, 1920.

69 Terry-Thompson, *The History of the African Orthodox Church*, 51.

70 Terry-Thompson, *The History of the African Orthodox Church*, 53.

71 Terry-Thompson, *The History of the African Orthodox Church*.

72 Newman, "The Origins of the African Orthodox Church," xiv.

73 Newman, "The Origins of the African Orthodox Church," iii.

74 Newman, "The Origins of the African Orthodox Church," 52.

75 Best, "The South in the City," 303.

76 Best, "The South in the City," 304.

77 Terry-Thompson, *The History of the African Orthodox Church*, 52.

78 *New York Age*, April 16, 1930.

79 *New York Times*, April 19, 1914.

80 Terry-Thompson, *The History of the African Orthodox Church*, 53.

Five. Garvey's God

1   Garvey was greatly influenced by Booker T. Washington and the Tuskegee Normal and Industrial Institute after he read Washington's memoir, *Up
from Slavery*. In fact, the young Jamaican leader had actually sought Washington's support to establish an industrial school in Jamaica. According to
historian Robert A. Hill, the idea had been proposed two years prior at the
International Conference on the Negro, held at Tuskegee in 1912. See Hill,
Marcus Garvey and Universal Negro Improvement Association Papers, Vol. 2,
69.

2   Hill and Blair, *Marcus Garvey*, 319–39. Garvey proposed that "a certain class
of graduates from this Institute [the proposed Industrial Farm and Institute in Jamaica] will be used as missionaries to Africa in hope of helping to
bring millions of that wonderful Continent into the van of civilization." See
Marcus Garvey to W. E. B. Du Bois, "Dear Friend and Brother," New York,
April 25, 1916, W. E. B. Du Bois Papers, Special Collections and Archives,
University of Massachusetts Amherst Library. Garvey corresponded directly with Washington hoping to secure funding and support for his educational initiative. He appealed to Washington, saying "having organized
ourselves into a Society for the purpose of helping the struggling masses
of this community to a higher state of industry and self-appreciation, we
take the opportunity of acquainting you of our aims, and we hereby beg to
solicit your assistance in helping us carry out our most laudable work." Despite Washington's death, Garvey's ambitions took him to America, where
he would finally relocate his organization.

3   After World War I, thousands of African American men who had fought to
defend the principles of freedom and democracy returned to America to
experience intensified racism, discrimination, and prejudice. Garvey used
this disillusionment and frustration to draw thousands of followers. "The
Declaration of the Rights of the Negro Peoples of the World," a document presented and signed at the International Convention of 1920, was an
important statement concerning the key principles of the UNIA. Among a
list of fifty-four demands, religion abounds, including an important statement regarding freedom of religion. This is a turning point in Garvey's
overt declaration of Christianity in the UNIA. This new declaration is a reflection of the ecumenical composition of the UNIA.

4   Garvey, "The Destiny of the Negro" (written July/August 1914), 65–66.

5   In Harlem, between 1920 and 1930, there were friendly, fraternal, and benevolent associations for almost all Caribbean immigrants living in the United
States. These included the St. Vincent Benevolent Association, the St. Vincent Benevolent Society, Sons and Daughters of Christopher, the Bermuda
Benevolent Association, the British Virgin Island Benevolent Association,
the British Guiana Benevolent Association, the Antigua Progressive Society,

the Grenada Mutual Association, the Trinidad Benevolent Association of New York, the Jamaica Benevolent Association, the Jamaica Benevolent Society, the St. Lucia United Benevolent Association, the Tobago Benevolent Association, the American West Indies Ladies Aid Society, the Sons and Daughters of Barbados, the Montserrat Progressive Society, and the Danish West Indies Society, among many others. See note 16 in this chapter for more on the associations in Harlem at this time.

6   Garvey, "The Destiny of the Negro."

7   The idea to recolonize Africa was popular in the 1830s among men such as Paul Cuffe and James Forten. It was gradually appropriated by antislavery organizations such as the American Colonization Society.

8   *Negro World*, April 2, 1921.

9   Marcus Garvey to W. E. B. Du Bois, "Dear Friend and Brother," New York, April 25, 1916, W. E. B. Du Bois Papers, Special Collections and Archives, University of Massachusetts Amherst Library.

10   Pinkney, *Red, Black, and Green*, 44–45.

11   Anderson, *Imagined Communities*.

12   Rolinson, *Grassroots Garveyism*.

13   Scholars such as Mark Christian and Erik McDuffie make similar arguments about regionalism but with a focus on the Midwest. See Christian, "Marcus Garvey and the Universal Negro Improvement Association (UNIA), 424–34; and McDuffie, "'A New Day Has Dawned for the UNIA.'"

14   "Marcus Declares Himself," *Baltimore Observer*, May 1920.

15   These societies helped immigrants adjust to their new lives in the United States. They also helped West Indians maintain important cultural, social, and economic ties with their home islands. Their projects included offering scholarships, extending mortgages to members, helping with wages during periods of illness and death, and sending supplies to the Caribbean during natural disasters.

16   Martin, *Race First*; and Bandele, *Black Star*, 86. Some of the key scholars who define Black nationalism in African American history include Wilson Jeremiah Moses, John Bracey, Alphonso Pinkney, and Edwin S. Redkey. More recently, political scientists such as Robert A. Brown, Michael Dawson, and Todd C. Shaw also have contributed to the literature. See Bracey, Meier, and Rudwick, *Black Nationalism in America*; Carlisle, *The Roots of Black Nationalism*; Moses, *The Golden Age of Black Nationalism, 1890–1925*; Pinkney, *Red, Black, and Green*; and Redkey, *Black Exodus*. An emerging group of scholars offers new perspectives on Black nationalism by focusing on Garveyism rather than the towering figure of Garvey himself. Their works include Harold, *The Rise and Fall of the Garvey Movement in the Urban South, 1918–1942*; Jai Issa, "The Universal Negro Improvement Association in Louisiana"; Rolinson, *Grassroots Garveyism*; and Trent Vinson, *The Americans Are Coming!* In the realm of religion and Garveyism, the

work of Randall K. Burkett is unmatched. See Burkett, *Garveyism as a Religious Movement.*

17 Sylvester Johnson, *African American Religions, 1500–2000*, 294.

18 Platt, White, and Rushing turn to McGuire's work founding the African Orthodox Church in the United States, while Natsoulas, Newman, and Johnson are concerned with its spread to the African continent. See Platt, "The African Orthodox Church"; White, "Patriarch McGuire and the Episcopal Church"; Rushing, "A Note on the Origin of the African Orthodox Church"; Natsoulas, "Patriarch McGuire and the Spread of the African Orthodox Church to Africa"; Newman, "Archbishop Daniel William Alexander and the African Orthodox Church"; Newman; "The Origins of the African Orthodox Church"; and Johnson, *The African Orthodox Church.*

19 Burkett, *Garveyism as a Religious Movement*; and Burkett, *Black Redemption.*

20 Roderick McLean, Erlne P. Gordon, Brada Imani, Phillip Potter, Asad Walker, and Nancy Hurd Schluter make similar claims of Garvey being a theologian. They raise important points about Garvey understanding theology and being able to reinterpret it in an effort to raise race consciousness among Black people. See McLean, *The Theology of Marcus Garvey*; Gordon, "Garvey and Black Liberation Theology"; Imani, *The Gospel According to Marcus Garvey*; Potter and Walker, "Marcus Garvey and Reverend Albert B. Cleage Jr."; and Hurd Schluter, "Marcus Garvey as Theologian."

21 Bair, "Ethiopia Shall Stretch Forth Her Hands unto God," 39.

22 Bair, "Ethiopia Shall Stretch Forth Her Hands unto God," 43.

23 Historians such as Barbara Bair, Beryl Satter, Ula Y. Taylor, and Tony Martin provide foundational thinking on women's leadership within the UNIA, while the more recent work of Keisha Blaine, Natanya Duncan, and Melissa Castillo-Garsow extends this pioneering scholarship by examining gender, ethnicity, and international politics more deeply.

24 Burkett, *Garveyism as a Religious Movement*; Burkett, *Black Redemption*; Burlacioiu, "Expansion without Western Missionary Agency and Constructing Confessional Identities"; Gordon, "Garvey and Black Liberation Theology"; Imani, *The Gospel According to Marcus Garvey*; McLean, *The Theology of Marcus Garvey*, 43–44; Newman, "Archbishop Daniel William Alexander and the African Orthodox Church"; Platt, "The African Orthodox Church"; Johnson, *The African Orthodox Church*; Rushing, "A Note on the Origin of the African Orthodox Church," 37–39; and Wilmore, *Black Religion and Black Radicalism.* And even with these claims, preeminent Garvey historian Robert Hill argues that religion was never a fundamental part of the UNIA; see Hill, *Marcus Garvey and Universal Negro Improvement Association Papers*, Vol. 11.

25 Rushing, "A Note on the Origin of the African Orthodox Church," 37.

26 J. Lorand Matory contributed a methodological construction of "invented traditions of religions" and how religious practices have traveled back and

forth to Brazil. This is an example of another form of "invented traditions" that shows the breadth of diasporic religious practices and cautions us to not think that we are looking at the same thing at all times. See Matory, *Black Atlantic Religion*.

27   Dorman, *Chosen People*; Taylor, *The Promise of Patriarchy*; and Weisenfeld, *New World A-Coming*.

28   Putnam, *Radical Moves*, 72.

29   Best, *Passionately Human, No Less Divine*, 2.

30   Best, *Passionately Human, No Less Divine*, 2.

31   James, "Explaining Afro-Caribbean Social Mobility," 220.

32   Wallace Best makes a similar claim in his discussion of storefront churches during World War I. See Best, "The South and the City," 302.

33   Crumbley, *Saved and Sanctified*.

34   Quoted in Gates, *The Black Church*, 120.

35   Kropotkin, *Mutual Aid*; Maynard, "The Translocation of West African Banking"; and Watkins-Owens, *Blood Relations*.

36   *Negro World*, August 16, 1924; and *Negro World*, September 6, 1924.

37   "Representing Deity as Black," *New York Times*, August 17, 1924.

38   *Negro World*, April 2, 1921.

39   *Constitution and Book of Laws Made for the Government of the Universal Negro Improvement Association, Inc., and African Communities League, Inc., of the World* (New York, July 1918; revised and amended August 1922), 57; and Burkett, *Garveyism as a Religious Movement*, 82.

40   *Negro World*, April 2, 1921.

41   *Negro World*, April 2, 1921.

42   Burkett, *Garveyism as a Religious Movement*, 71.

43   McGuire, *The Universal Negro Catechism*; and McGuire, *The Universal Negro Ritual*.

44   Burkett, *Garveyism as a Religious Movement*, 21.

45   Burkett, *Garveyism as a Religious Movement*, 18.

46   Burkett, *Garveyism as a Religious Movement*, 20.

47   Burkett, *Garveyism as a Religious Movement*, 178.

48   Ford's contributions to Garveyism extended beyond music. Along with E. L. Gaines, Ford wrote the rules and regulations of the African Legion and the Black Cross Nurses. Ford's Hebraic influences also emerged center stage in these documents when he and Gaines created the African Legion along the same lines as the Zion Jewish Legion.

49   "Shine on, Eternal Light," box 59, MS 099 F853, Arnold Josiah Ford Papers, Special Collections Department, University of Delaware.

50   Ford and Rabbi Matthew Wentworth fiercely believed that they were descendants of the Israelites through the Ethiopian monarchy of Solomon. In the 1930s Ford would try to make good on the frequently chanted slogan of the UNIA, "Africa for the Africans," when he invited about six hundred of

his members to immigrate to Gondar, Ethiopia. His immigration to Africa, particularly his move to Ethiopia, was a reflection of Ethiopia's importance in the narrative of African redemption. See Kobre, "Rabbi Ford," 27.

51 "Biographical Sketch," SCM 97–9, box 1, folder 2, A. Matthew Wentworth Collection, Schomburg Center for Research in Black Culture.

52 King, "Some Notes on Rabbi Ford and New Black Attitudes to Ethiopia," 51.

53 Bishop Heber, who was a British missionary to India, is mainly known for his hymns and some of his poems. He wrote "From Greenland's Icy Mountains" in about 1809 after he had obtained his doctorate of divinity at Oxford University. See Chatterton, *A History of the Church of England in India*, 143. According to Chatterton, it was during this period that Heber wrote his best-known hymns, including "Holy, Holy, Holy," "The Son of God Goes Forth to War," "Brightest and Best of the Sons of the Morning," and the evangelical missionary hymn "From Greenland's Icy Mountains," which the UNIA adopted. Interestingly, Mahatma Gandhi, a well-known and documented anticolonialist, objected to the hymn. Gandhi claimed that it showed Christian aggression to Hinduism:

> You, the missionaries come to India thinking that you come to a land of heathens, of idolators, of men who do not know God. One of the greatest of Christian divines, Bishop Heber, wrote the two lines which have always left a sting with me: "Where every prospect pleases, and man alone is vile." I wish he had not written them. My own experience in my travels throughout India has been to the contrary. I have gone from one end of the country to the other, without any prejudice, in a relentless search after truth, and I am not able to say that here in this fair land, watered by the great Ganges, the Brahmaputra and the Jumna, man is vile. He is not vile. He is as much a seeker after truth as you and I are, possibly more so.

Gandhi, "Speech at a Meeting of Missionaries at the YMCA Calcutta."

54 Wilson, "Heber's Hymns," 622.

55 Heber, "From Greenland's Icy Mountains."

56 "Prayer for Guidance," 832.

57 McGuire, *The Universal Negro Ritual*, 10–14.

58 "A Collect for Guidance," 100.

59 *Negro World*, February 19, 1921.

60 McGuire, *The Universal Negro Ritual*, 21.

61 McGuire, *The Universal Negro Ritual*, 21.

62 *Negro World*, March 28, 1925; and Burkett, *Garveyism as a Religious Movement*, 7–8.

63 *Negro World*, August 13, 1927.

64 Van der Woud, "How Shall We Sing the Lord's Song in a Strange Land," 132–33.

65 Burkett, *Black Redemption*, 9.

66 Masango, "Money Matters."

67 Burkett, *Black Redemption*, 12.

68 Black liberation theology is a theological orientation in which Jesus's ministry on Earth is understood and interpreted as one in which God champions those who are oppressed. It foregrounds the Christian tradition as one in which Jesus's ministry can be understood uplifting all oppressed people. In the 1960s when Black liberation theology was formally defined, it focused on the African American experience. In the 1970s, these scholars aligned themselves with theologians all over the world as they examined US imperialism in Vietnam and apartheid in South African. Black liberation theology was formally introduced in the 1960s with the work of James H. Cone and Gayraud S. Wilmore, but it had been practiced generations before in UNIA meetings. See Cleage, *The Black Messiah*; Cone, *Black Theology and Black Power*; Cone, *A Black Theology of Liberation*; and Cone, *God of the Oppressed*.

69 Burkett, *Garveyism as a Religious Movement*, 87.

70 This was true for both the AOC and another church, called the House of Athyli, which had its headquarters in New Jersey.

Six. "We See on the Horizon the Sun of African Orthodoxy"

1 African Orthodox Archives, RG 005, box 9, folder 99, Correspondence, James Poyah, 1930–1945, Pitts Theological Library, Emory University.

2 United States Bureau of Census, *Religious Bodies* (Washington, DC: United States Government Printing Office, 1926), 45–49, 1070.

3 Burlacioiu, "Expansion without Western Missionary Agency and Constructing Confessional Identities," 86.

4 Collis-Buthelezi, "Caribbean Regionalism, South Africa, and Mapping New World Studies"; Vinson, "'Sea Kafirs,'" 281–303.

5 Magubane, *The Ties That Bind*, 90.

6 Masogha himself had organized another independent religious body with North American roots, the House of Athyli. Alexander, like Masogha, thought he was a good candidate to establish another independent church with North American support.

7 Josiah Semouse shared the stage with Charlotte and Katie Manye.

8 *Negro World*, April 2, 1921.

9 Banton, *More Auspicious Shores*, 326.

10 African Orthodox Church Archives, RG 005, box 3:38, Pitt Theological Library, Emory University; and Johnson, *Archbishop Daniel William Alex-*

ander and the African Orthodox Church, 1. Johnson's work is foundational in understanding the church history.

11 Dee, "Nyasa Leaders, Christianity and African Internationalism in 1920s Johannesburg," 387.

12 Scholars including Robert Edgar, Joel Cabrita, Nkosinathi Sithole, Isabel Mukonyora, and Carol Mueller have made important inroads in unpacking the histories of these healing churches and ministries. Anne Muller, *Rituals of Fertility and Sacrifice*; Cabrita, *The People's Zion*; Cabrita, *Text and Authority in the South African Nazaretha Church*; Edgar, *Finger of God*; Mukonyora, *Wandering a Gendered Wilderness*; and Sithole, *Isaiah Shembe's Hymns and the Sacred Dance in Ibandla LamaNazaretha Sacred Dance*. But the growth in churches also included the Pentecostal movement captured in the work of scholars such as Hathaway, "The Role of William Oliver Hutchinson and the Apostolic Faith Church in the Formation of British Pentecostal Churches"; and Maxwell, "Historicizing Christian Independency: The Southern African Pentecostal Movement, c. 1908–1960."

13 According to Samuel Brander, the church had at least 506 members across South Africa, Basutoland, and British Bechuanaland by as early as 1908. See Brander, *The South African Natives*, 207–8.

14 McGuire to Alexander, October 24, 1924, McGuire and Alexander correspondence.

15 African Orthodox Church Archives, RG 005, box 10, folder 119, Correspondence, James Poyah to Alexander, January 4, 1930, Pitts Theological Library.

16 African Orthodox Church Archives, RG 005, box 3, folder 38, The Primate's Charge, 1928.

17 West, "Ethiopianism and Colonialism."

18 African Orthodox Church Archives, RG 005, box 9, folder 99, Correspondence of James Poyah, 1930–1945, January 2, 1930.

19 *Negro World*, April 2, 1921; and Newman, "The Origins of the African Orthodox Church," x.

20 *Negro World*, July 16, 1921.

21 Gregor Cobley, "The 'African National Church,'" 357.

22 J. H. Pimm Papers, William Ballinger to J. H. Pimm, December 23, 1930, box 1/4/141, University of Witwatersrand Archives.

23 McGuire to Alexander, October 24, 1924, McGuire and Alexander correspondence, Pitts Library.

24 McGuire to Alexander, October 24, 1924, McGuire and Alexander correspondence, Pitts Library.

25 African Orthodox Church Archives, RG 005, box 9, folder 99, Correspondence of James Poyah, 1930–1945, January 2, 1930.

26 McGuire to Alexander, October 24, 1924, McGuire and Alexander correspondence, Pitts Library.

27 McGuire to Alexander, October 24, 1924, McGuire and Alexander correspondence, Pitts Library.

28 McGuire to Alexander, October 24, 1924, McGuire and Alexander correspondence, Pitts Library.

29 McGuire to Alexander, October 24, 1924, McGuire and Alexander correspondence, Pitts Library.

30 McGuire to Alexander, October 24, 1924, McGuire and Alexander correspondence, Pitts Library.

31 "The Fifth General Synod," 1–2; and "Commissary in South Africa," 2.

32 "Letter from the Very Right Rev. Daniel William Alexander to Patriarch McGuire," March 24, 1925, RG 005, box 9, folder 108, African Orthodox Church Collection, Pitts Theological Library, Emory University.

33 "Patriarch Alexander to the Very Right Rev. D. W. Alexander," March 17, 1925, RG 005, box 10, folder 14, African Orthodox Church Collection, Pitts Theological Library, Emory University.

34 "The Fifth General Synod," 1–2.

35 African Orthodox Church Archives, RG 005, box 9, folder 99, Correspondence of James Poyah, 1930–1945, July 7, 1951, Pitts Theological Library, Emory University.

36 Reverend Edwin Lewis's Report to the British Consul-General, F.O. 371/9633 213, Public Record Office, United Kingdom.

37 Conclusions of Lewis's Report to the British Consul-General, F.O. 115/3380, Public Record Office, United Kingdom.

38 McGuire to Alexander, October 24, 1924, McGuire and Alexander correspondence.

39 African Orthodox Church Archives, RG 005, box 3, folder 38, The Primate's Charge, 1928, Pitts Theological Library, Emory University.

40 African Orthodox Church Archives, RG 005, box 9, folder 99, Correspondence of James Poyah, 1930–1945, January 29, 1930, Pitts Theological Library, Emory University.

41 Kalu, "Ethiopianism and the Roots of Modern African Christianity," 588.

42 West, "Ethiophianism and Colonialism."

43 "Commissary in South Africa," 2.

44 Alexander to McGuire, March 25, 1925, McGuire and Alexander correspondence, African Orthodox Church Archives, RG 005, box 9, folder 108, Correspondence of the African Orthodox Church, 1923–1971, Pitts Theological Library, Emory University.

45 "Address of the Bishop-Elect of South Africa," 4.

46 Alexander, "A South African Abroad," 1.

47 Alexander, "A South African Abroad," 1.

48 Alexander, "A South African Abroad," 2.

49 British Consul Report, February 1929, F.O. 115/3380, Public Record Office, United Kingdom.

50   British Consul Report, February 1929, F.O. 115/3380, Public Record Office, United Kingdom.

51   "Lillian to Daniel William Alexander," undated, RG 005, box 2, folder 7, African Orthodox Church Collection, Pitts Theological Library, Emory University.

52   Alexander, "A South African Abroad," 2.

53   Alexander, "A South African Abroad," 2.

54   Alexander, "A South African Abroad," 6.

55   Alexander, "A South African Abroad," 7.

56   African Orthodox Church Archives, RG 005, box 10, folder 119, Alexander to the Commissioner of Immigration and Asiatic Affairs in Pretoria, Pitts Theological Library, Emory University.

57   African Orthodox Church Archives, RG 005, box 9, folder 99, Correspondence of James Poyah, 1930–1945, January 4, 1930, Pitts Theological Library, Emory University.

58   "Provincial News, South Africa," *Negro Churchman* 5 (March 1927): 2.

59   Alexander, "A South African Abroad," 2.

60   Alexander, "A South African Abroad," 2.

61   Alexander, "Greetings from South Africa," 2.

62   SANA NTS 1445 59/214 Gazaland Zimbabwe Ethiopian Church.

63   National Archives of Zimbabwe, Office of the High Commissioner, File A 3/18/11; and West, *The Rise of an African Middle Class*, 143–44.

64   West, *The Rise of an African Middle Class*, 142.

65   West, *The Rise of an African Middle Class*, 142.

66   Byfield, "Introduction: Rethinking the African Diaspora," 5.

67   UNIA branches that began with Kampara and Taylor soon extended beyond Evaton to Sophiatown, Waterpan, Pretoria, Johannesburg, and Cape Town as well as cities in Northern and Southern Rhodesia. Martin, *The Pan-African Connection*, 134–35.

68   Ncwana was greatly affected by the sinking of SS *Mendi* in which Isaac Wauchope, who had taught Charlotte and Katie Manye, died. In turn, Ncwana established the Mendi Memorial Club to honor the dead. "Mendi Memorial Club," *Umateteli wa Bantu*, November 20, 1920.

69   Frank Mothiba, "Greetings from the Natives of South Africa," *Negro World*, November 24, 1924.

70   "UNIA," *Umteteli wa Bantu*, November 7, 1925.

71   *Black Man*, August 20, 1920.

72   *Negro Churchman*, April 22, 1929.

73   West, *The Rise of an African Middle Class*, 143.

74   "Provincial News, South Africa," 2.

75   "Provincial News, South Africa," 2.

76   "Provincial News, South Africa," 2.

77   "Provincial News, South Africa," 3.

78   "Provincial News, South Africa," 3.

79   Alexander, "Address of the Bishop-Elect of South Africa," 6.

80   "Consecration Service," 7.

81   "Consecration Service," 7.

82   "Oath of Obedience," African Orthodox Church Collection, RG 005, Oversized Printed Material, Pitts Theological Library, Emory University.

83   "Consecration Service," 8.

84   Alexander, "Address of the Bishop-Elect of South Africa," 5 (my emphasis).

85   Alexander, "Address of the Bishop-Elect of South Africa," 4.

86   Alexander, "Address of the Bishop-Elect of South Africa," 4.

87   Alexander, "Address of the Bishop-Elect of South Africa," 5.

88   "Archbishop D. W. Alexander Returns," 6; and Principal Immigration Officer to Secretary of Native Affairs, March 20, 1928, NTS 11/214 African Orthodox Church, National Archives South Africa, Pretoria Campus.

89   Undated Diary Entry, RG 005, box 2, folder 6, African Orthodox Church Collection, Pitts Theological Library, Emory University.

90   "Return Fare to Africa," *Negro Churchman* 5 (November 1927): 8.

91   African Orthodox Church Archives, RG 005, box 9, folder 99, Correspondence of James Poyah, 1930–1945, July 7, 1951, Pitts Theological Library, Emory University.

92   Alexander, "The Separatist Church Movement," *Negro Churchman* 5 (December 1927): 3–4, and 6 (January 1928): 7–8.

93   African Orthodox Church Archives, RG 005, box 3, folder 38, The Primate's Charge, 1928, Pitts Theological Library, Emory University.

Seven. Seeds of Freedom

1   "The Prospectus for the Seminary of St. Augustine of Hippo," NTS 11/214 African Orthodox Church, National Archives of South Africa, Pretoria Campus.

2   African Orthodox Clergy List, Department of Bantu Administration and Development, 120/4/58, National Archives of South Africa, Pretoria Campus.

3   St. Augustine's Pro-Cathedral, RG 005, box 11, folder 11, African Orthodox Church Collection, Pitts Theological Library, Emory University.

4   Eugene Marshall to Alexander, March 22, 1929. African Orthodox Church Correspondence, 1926–1963, RG 005, box 11, folder 1, African Orthodox Church Collection, Pitts Theological Library, Emory University.

5   Eugene Marshall to Alexander, March 22, 1929, African Orthodox Church Correspondence, 1926–1963, RG 005, box 11, folder 1, African Orthodox Church Collection, Pitts Theological Library, Emory University.

6   Johnson, *Archbishop Daniel William Alexander and the African Orthodox Church*, 87.

7   Mandela, *A Long Walk to Freedom*, 364–68.

8   Kihali, *The Orthodox Christian Witness in East Africa*, 90.

9   "The Prospectus for the Seminary of St. Augustine of Hippo."

10   Despite the church's race consciousness, Alexander constantly sought funds from the De Beers Mining Consolidation. He even asserted to the company head that because Kimberley was a company town, it was the responsibility of De Beers to uplift the community.

11   "Provincial News, South Africa," 2.

12   Angell, *Bishop Henry Turner McNeal and African American Religion in the South*, 233–35.

13   "The Prospectus for the Seminary of St. Augustine of Hippo."

14   Duff, *Foreign Missions*, 38.

15   *Lovedale Missionary Institute Report for 1890*, 6–8; *Lovedale Missionary Institute Report for 1902*, 2.

16   Elkins, *The Imperial Reckoning*, 20.

17   "Syllabus of the St. Augustine of Hippo," African Orthodox Church Collection, RG 005, Oversized Printed Material, Pitts Theological Library, Emory University.

18   "Syllabus of the St. Augustine of Hippo," African Orthodox Church Collection, RG 005, Oversized Printed Material, Pitts Theological Library, Emory University.

19   "The Prospectus for the Seminary of St. Augustine of Hippo."

20   "The Prospectus for the Seminary of St. Augustine of Hippo," 2.

21   "The Prospectus for the Seminary of St. Augustine of Hippo," 2.

22   "Oath of Canonical Obedience," African Orthodox Church Collection, RG 005, Oversized Printed Material, Pitts Theological Library, Emory University.

23   "Oath of Canonical Obedience."

24   "Oath of Canonical Obedience."

25   Welbourn, *East African Rebels*, 78.

26   Welbourn, *East African Rebels*, 80.

27   Spartas, "The Patriarchal See in Africa," 3.

28   Spartas, "The Patriarchal See in Africa," 3.

29   Kihali, *The Orthodox Christian Witness in East Africa*, 54.

30   Kihali, *The Orthodox Christian Witness in East Africa*, 55.

31   SAB NTS, 1455, 111/214.

32   Kihali, *The Orthodox Christian Witness in East Africa*, 52.

33   Welbourn, *East African Rebels*, 77–102 (my emphasis).

34   Welbourn, *East African Rebels*, 101.

35   Mahmood Mamdani provides a critical engagement of how colonialism was a response to the ways white settler societies responded to the Native question. See Mamdani, *Citizen and Subject*; Mamdani, "Historicizing Power and Responses to Power"; and Mamdani, "Indirect Rule, Civil Society, Ethnicity."

36 Groves, *The Planting of Christianity in Africa*, 126.

37 Sundkler and Sneed, *A History of the Church in South Africa*, 557; and Thompson, "Capturing the Image," 7.

38 Elkins, *The Imperial Reckoning*, 20.

39 Tignor, *Colonial Transformation of Kenya*, 114.

40 Colonial policy imposed poll and hut taxes, which created revenue while forcing Africans into wage labor because taxes could be paid in cash or labor. Between 1906 and 1910, taxes doubled when the government made Kikuyu children taxable. British revenue jumped from 44,451 pounds in 1905–1906 to 105,000 pounds five years later. The real blow came another five years later when the colonial government earned 658,414 pounds from African poll and hut taxes.

41 Castello, *Black Tommies*; Moyd, *Violent Intermediaries*; and Samson, *World War I in Africa*.

42 Findley and O' Rourke, *Power and Plenty*, 429.

43 Cone Robertson, "Grassroots in Kenya"; Ewing, *The Age of Garvey*; Hetherington, "The Politics of Female Circumcision in the Central Province of Colonial Kenya, 1920–30"; Nyangweso Wangila, *Female Circumcision*; Thomas, *Politics of the Womb*; and Welbourn, *East African Rebels*.

44 Kenyatta, *Facing Mount Kenya*, 133.

45 Bunche, "The Irua Ceremony among the Kikuyu of the Kiambu District, Kenya."

46 Davison, *Voices from Mutira*, 40.

47 Bunche, "The Irua Ceremony among the Kikuyu of the Kiambu District, Kenya," 48.

48 Bunche, "The Irua Ceremony among the Kikuyu of the Kiambu District, Kenya," 61.

49 Bunche, "The Irua Ceremony among the Kikuyu of the Kiambu District, Kenya," 51.

50 Thomas, *Politics of the Womb*, 22.

51 Colony and Protectorate of Kenya, *Annual Report of Education Department, 1929*, 81–89.

52 *Memorandum on Education Policy in British Tropical African Dependencies*, 4.

53 Grogan and Sharp, *From Cape to Cairo*.

54 Quoted in Gorman, "The Development of Language Policy in Kenya with Particular Reference to the Educational System," 417.

55 KNA Provincial Commissioner/Central Province 8/5/3; and KNA Provincial Commissioner/Central Province 8/53

56 Tenure of Church and School Plots, 1930–1933, Maitland to Home, December 24, 1930; KNA Provincial Commissioner 8/48/7, KNA Provincial Commissioner/Central Province 8/7/1, Political situation in the province, 1929–1930; Fazan to Provincial Commissioner, December 24, 1929.

57   Simon Gikandi, *Ngugi Wa Thiong'o* (Cambridge: Cambridge University Press, 2000), 22.

58   Kihali insists that both organizations were established at the same time with similar political aims. He asserts that the political divisions reflected in the historiography is about the organizations' competing and revisionist histories.

59   *Corfield Report Cmd. 1030 and the Kenya Sessional Paper No. 5.1959–60,* (Nairobi: Government Printers, 1960), 39.

60   *Kenya Land Commission Evidence Volume I,* 220.

61   Kenyatta, *Kenya, Land of Opportunity,* 15.

62   As quoted in Mwakikagile, *Africa and the West,* 109.

63   Thomas, *Politics of the Womb,* 1.

64   Murray, "The CMS and Female Circumcision," 36.

65   Johana Kunyiha to Archbishop Daniel William Alexander, July 1, 1935. African Orthodox Correspondence, 1923–1971, African Orthodox Church Collection, RG 005, box 12, folder 14, Pitts Theological Library, Emory University.

66   From Archbishop Alexander's correspondence, Pitts Theological Library Archive, Emory University. Quoted also in Kimani Githieya, *The Freedom of the Spirit,* 97.

67   KNA:DC/FH/2/1/4, document 1/23, Letter of DC Fort Hall (WR Kidd) to PC Nyeri.

68   KNA:DC/FH/2/4, documents 1/15 and 1/8.

69   Black, "Offended Christians, Anti-Mission Churches and Colonial Politics: One Man's Story of the Messy Birth of the African Orthodox Church in Kenya," 273.

70   Sandgren, *Christianity and the Kikuyu,* 101.

71   Kimani Githieya, *The Freedom of the Spirit,* 101.

Epilogue

1   De Gruchy, "Grappling with a Colonial Heritage," 168.

2   The Freedom Charter, June 26, 1955, reprinted in *The Freedom Charter of South Africa,* 3, 7.

3   Historians Landau, *The Realm of the Word*; Landau, *Popular Politics in the History of South Africa*; Odendaal, *The Founders*. André Odendaal and Paul Landau even show that Africans, particularly the Griquas, had considered the relationship between the church and national formation as far back as the sixteenth century.

BIBLIOGRAPHY

"Address of the Bishop-Elect of South Africa." *Negro Churchman* 5 (October 1927): 4.

Adhikari, Mohamed. *The Anatomy of a South African Genocide: The Extermination of the Cape San Peoples.* Athens: Ohio University Press, 2011.

Adhikari, Mohamed. *Not White Enough, Not Black Enough: Racial Identity in the South African Coloured Community.* Columbus: Ohio University Press, 2005.

Adhikari, Mohamed. "The Sons of Ham: Slavery and the Making of Coloured Identity." *South African Historical Journal* 27, no. 1 (1992): 95–112.

Alexander, D. W. "Address of the Bishop-Elect of South Africa." *Negro Churchman* 5 (October 1927): 4–6.

Alexander, D. W. "Greetings from South Africa." *Negro Churchman* 5 (March 1927): 2.

Alexander, D. W. "The Separatist Church Movement." *Negro Churchman* 5 (December 1927): 3–4.

Alexander, D. W. "The Separatist Church Movement." *Negro Churchman* 6 (January 1928): 7–8.

Alexander, D. W. "A South African Abroad." *Negro Churchman* 5 (November 1927): 1.

Anderson, Benedict. *Imagined Communities: Reflections and Origins on the Spread of Nationalism.* London: Verso, 2006.

Angell, Stephen W. *Bishop Henry Turner McNeal and African American Religion in the South.* Knoxville: University of Tennessee Press, 1992.

April, Thozama. "Theorising Women: The Intellectual Contributions of Charlotte Maxeke to the Struggle for Liberation in South Africa." PhD dissertation, University of the Western Cape, 2012.

"Archbishop D. W. Alexander Returns." *Negro Churchman* 6 (March 1928): 6.

Arnesen, Eric. "Reconsidering the Civil Rights." *Historically Speaking* (April 2009): 31–34.

Atenga, Lilian Lem, Sibonile Edith Ellece, Lia Litoseliti, and Jane Sunderland. *Gender and Language in Sub-Saharan Africa: Tradition, Struggle and Change.* Philadelphia: John Benjamin Publishing, 2013.

Bair, Barbara. "'Ethiopia Shall Stretch Forth Her Hands unto God': Laura Kofey and the Gendered Vision of Redemption in the Garvey Movement." In *A Mighty Baptism: Race, Gender, and the Creation of American Protestantism,* edited by Susan Juster and Lisa MacFarlane, 38–61. Ithaca, NY: Cornell University Press, 1966.

Balia, Darryl. *Black Methodists and White Supremacy in South Africa.* Durban, South Africa: Madiba Publications, 1991.

Bandele, Ramla M. *Black Star: African American Activism in the International Political Economy.* Champaign: University of Illinois Press, 2008.

Banton, Caree A. *More Auspicious Shores: Barbadian Migration to Liberia, Blackness and the Making of an African Republic.* Cambridge: Cambridge University Press, 2019.

Beinart, William, and Colin Bundy. *Hidden Struggles in Rural South Africa: Politics and Popular Movements in the Transkei and Eastern Cape, 1890–1930.* Johannesburg: Raven, 1988.

Best, Wallace. *Passionately Human, No Less Divine: Religion and Culture in Black Chicago, 1915–1952.* Princeton, NJ: Princeton University Press, 2005.

Best, Wallace. "The South in the City: Black Southern Migrants, Storefront Churches, and the Rise of the Religious Diaspora." In *Repositioning North American Migration History: New Directions in Modern Continental Migration, Citizenship and Community,* edited by Marc S. Rodriguez, 302–27. Rochester, NY: University of Rochester Press, 2004.

Bhana, Surendra, and Joy B. Brain. *Setting Down Roots.* Johannesburg: Witwatersrand University Press, 1989.

Bhana, Surendra, and Bridglal Pachai. *A Documentary History of Indian South Africans.* Stanford, CA: Hoover Institution Press, 1984.

Bickford-Smith, Vivian. *Ethnic Pride and Racial Prejudice in Victorian Cape Town.* New York: Cambridge University Press, 2003.

Black, Joseph. "Offended Christians, Anti-Mission Churches and Colonial Politics: One Man's Story of the Messy Birth of the African Orthodox Church in Kenya." *Journal of Religion in Africa* 43 (2013): 261–96.

Boesak, Allan A. *Black and Reformed: Apartheid, Liberation, and the Calvinist Tradition.* Ossining, NY: Orbis Books, 1984.

Boesak, Allan A. "A Restless Presence: Church Activism and 'Post-Apartheid,' 'Post-Racial' Challenges." In *Conflicted Churches in the United States and South Africa,* edited by R. Drew Smith, William Ackah, Anthony G. Reddie, and Rothney S. Tshaka, 13–36. Jackson: University of Mississippi, 2015.

Botes, Marianna. "Charlotte Maxeke (1872–1939): 'Mother of Black Freedom in South Africa.'" National Museum Publications, August 4, 2020. https:// nationalmuseumpublications.co.za/charlotte-maxeke-1872-1939-mother-of -black-freedom-in-south-africa/.

Boyce-Davies, Carole. *Black Women, Writing, and Identity: Migrations of the Subject.* New York: Routledge, 1994.

Bracey, John H., Jr., August Meier, and Elliott Rudwick, eds. *Black Nationalism in America.* Indianapolis: Bobbs-Merrill, 1970.

Bradlow, Edna. "Immigration into the Union, 1910–1948." PhD Dissertation, University of Cape Town, 1978.

Bragg, George F., Jr. *History of the Afro-American Group in the Episcopal Church.* Baltimore: Church Advocate, 1922.

Bragg, George F., Jr. "Untitled." *Church Advocate,* March 1908.

Brander, Samuel. *The South African Natives: Their Progress and Present Condition.* London: J. Murray, 1908.

Brightwell, C. L. *The Friend of the Hottentot.* London: London Missionary Society, 1874.

Brown, Ras Michael. *African-Atlantic Cultures in Low-Country South Carolina.* Cambridge: Cambridge University Press, 2012.

Brown Montgomery, William. *The Catholic Church and the Color Line.* N.p.: 1910.

Bunche, Ralph J. "The Irua Ceremony among the Kikuyu of the Kiambu District, Kenya." *Journal of Negro History* 26 (January 1941): 46–65.

Burkett, Randall. *Black Redemption: Churchman Speak for the Garvey Movement.* Philadelphia: Temple University Press, 1978.

Burkett, Randall K. *Garveyism as a Religious Movement: The Institutionalization of Black Civil Religion.* Metuchen, NJ: Scarecrow, 1978.

Burlacioiu, Ciprian. "Expansion without Western Missionary Agency and Constructing Confessional Identities: The African Orthodox Church between the United States, South Africa, and East Africa, 1921–1940." *Journal of World Christianity* 6, no. 1 (2016): 82–98.

Byfield, Judith. "Introduction: Rethinking the African Diaspora." *African Studies Review* 43, no. 1 (2000): 1–9.

Cabrita, Joel. *The People's Zion: South Africa, the United States, and a Transatlantic Faith Healing Movement.* Cambridge, MA: Harvard University Press, 2018.

Cabrita, Joel. *Text and Authority in the South African Nazaretha Church.* Cambridge: Cambridge University Press, 2014.

Caldecott, Alfred. *The Church in the West Indies.* London: Society for Promoting Christian Knowledge, 1898.

Campbell, James. *Songs of Zion: The African American Episcopal Church in the United States and South Africa.* Chapel Hill: University of North Carolina Press, 1998.

Carlisle, Rodney. *The Roots of Black Nationalism.* Port Washington, NY: Kennikat, 1975.

Castello, Ray. *Black Tommies: British Soldiers of African Descent in the First World War*. Liverpool: Liverpool University Press, 2015.

Census Office. *Census of the Cape Colony* (1905).

Census Office. *Census of the Cape of Good Hope* (1875).

Census Office. *Census of the Cape of Good Hope* (1892).

Census Office. *Census of the Colony of the Cape of Good Hope* (1866).

Census Office. *Census of the Natal Colony* (1891).

Census Office. *Census of Natal Colony* (1905).

Census Office. *Census of the Orange River Colony* (1905).

Census Office. *Census of the Republic of South Africa* (1950).

Census Office. *Census of the Transvaal and Swaziland Colony* (1906).

Census Office. *Census of the Union of South Africa* (1912).

Césaire, Aimé. *Discourse on Colonialism*. Translated by Joan Pinkham. New York: Monthly Review Press, 2001.

Cha-Jua, Sundiata Keita, and Clarence Lang. "The Long Movement as Vampire: Temporal and Spatial Fallacies in the Black Freedom Movement." *Journal of African American History* 92, no. 2 (2007): 265–88.

Chatterton, Bishop Eyre. *A History of the Church of England in India: Since the Early Days of the East India Company*. London: Society for Promoting Christian Knowledge, 1924.

Christian, Mark. "Marcus Garvey and the Universal Negro Improvement Association (UNIA): With Special Reference to the 'Lost' Parade in Columbus, Ohio, September 25, 1923." *Western Journal of Black Studies* 28, no. 3 (2004): 424–34.

Christopher, A. J. "To Define the Indefinable: Population Classification and the Census in South Africa." *Area* 34, no. 4 (2002): 401–8.

Classified Digest of the Records of the Society for the Propagation of the Gospel in Foreign Parts, 1702–1882. London: Society Publishers, 1884.

Cleage, Albert B., Jr. *The Black Messiah*. Trenton, NJ: Africa World, 1989.

Cobbing, Julian. "The Mfecane as Alibi: Thoughts on Dithakong and Mbolompo." *Journal of African History* 29 (1988): 487–519.

"A Collect for Guidance." In *The Book of Common Prayer*. London: Everyman's Library, 1662.

Collis-Buthelezi, Victoria J. "Caribbean Regionalism, South Africa, and Mapping New World Studies." *Small Axe* 19, no. 1 (2015): 37–54.

Collis-Buthelezi, Victoria J. "Under the Aegis of the Empire: Cape Town, Victorianism, and Early Twentieth Century Black Thought." *Callaloo* 39, no. 1 (2016): 115–32.

Colony and Protectorate of Kenya. *Annual Report of Education Department, 1929*. Nairobi: Government Press, 1929.

"Commissary in South Africa." *Negro Churchman* 3 (April 1925): 2.

Cone, James H. *Black Theology and Black Power*. Maryknoll, NY: Orbis, 1997.

Cone, James H. *A Black Theology of Liberation*. Maryknoll, NY: Orbis, 2010.

Cone, James H. *God of the Oppressed*. New York: Seabury, 1975.

Cone Robertson, Claire. "Grassroots in Kenya: Women, Genital Mutilation, and Collective Action, 1920–1990." *Signs* 21, no. 3 (1996): 615–42.

"Consecration Service." *Negro Churchman* 5 (October 1927): 7–8.

Constitution and Book of Laws Made for the Government of the Universal Negro Improvement Association, Inc., and African Communities League, Inc., of the World. New York, July 1918, revised and amended August 1922.

"Convocation of Arkansas." *Living Church* 1, no. 36 (1907): 161.

Coquery-Vidrovitch, Catherine. *Africa and Africans in the 19th Century: A Turbulent History*. Abingdon, UK: Routledge, 2015.

Corfield Report Cmd. 1030 and the Kenya Sessional Paper No. 5.1959–60. Nairobi: Government Printers, 1960.

Covington-Ward, Yolanda. *Gesture and Power: Religion, Nationalism, and Everyday Performance in Congo*. Durham, NC: Duke University Press, 2015.

Cronon, E. David. *Black Moses: The Story of Marcus Garvey and the Universal Negro Improvement Association*. Madison: University of Wisconsin Press, 1955.

Crumbley, Diedre Helen. *Saved and Sanctified: The Rise of a Storefront Church*. Gainesville: University Press of Florida, 2012.

Curtin, Phillip D. *The Rise and Fall of the Plantation Complex*. Cambridge: Cambridge University Press, 1998.

Davis, Carol Boyce. *Black Women, Writing, and Identity: Migrations of the Subject*. New York: Routledge, 1994.

Davison, Jean. *Voices from Mutira: Changes in the Lives of Rural Kikuyu Women, 1910–1995*. Boulder, CO: Lynne Rienner, 1996.

Day, Keri. *Unfinished Business: Black Women, the Black Church, and the Struggle to Thrive in America*. Maryknoll, NY: Orbis Books, 2012.

Deacon, Harriet, Howard Phillips, and Elizabeth van Heyningen, eds. *The Cape Doctor in the Nineteenth Century: A Social History*. New York: Rodopi, 2004.

Dean, Harry. *The Pedro Gorino: The Adventures of a Negro Sea-Captain in Africa and on the Seven Seas in His Attempts to Found an Ethiopian Empire*. Yardley, PA: Westholme Publishing, 2011.

Dee, Henry. "Nyasa Leaders, Christianity and African Internationalism in 1920s Johannesburg." *South African Historical Journal* 70, no. 2 (2018): 383–406.

De Gruchy, John W. "Grappling with a Colonial Heritage: The English-Speaking Churches under Imperialism and Apartheid." In *Christianity in South Africa: A Political, Social, and Cultural History*, edited by Richard Elphick and Rodney Davenport, 155–72. Berkeley: University of California Press, 1997.

DeLoughrey, Elizabeth. *Routes and Roots: Navigating Caribbean and Pacific Island Literatures*. Honolulu: University of Hawai'i Press, 2009.

Donaldson, Bruce. "Language Contact and Linguistic Change: The Influence of English on Afrikaans." In *Language and Social History: Studies in South African Sociolinguistics*, edited by Rajend Meshtrie, 222–42. Claremont, South Africa: New Africa Books, 1995.

Dorman, Jacob S. *Chosen People: The Rise of American Black Israelite Religions*. Oxford: Oxford University Press, 2016.

Draper, Jonathan A. *Orality, Literacy, and Colonialism in Southern Africa*. Leiden, Netherlands: Brill, 2004.

Dubow, Saul. "Race, Civilisation, and Culture: The Elaboration of Segregationist Discourse in the Inter-War Years." In *The Politics of Race, Class, and Nationalism in Twentieth Century South Africa*, edited by Shula Marks and Stanley Trapido, 71–94. London: Routledge, 1987.

Dubow, Saul. *Racial Segregation and the Origins of Apartheid in South Africa, 1919–1936*. London: Palgrave Macmillan, 1989.

Dubow, Saul. *Scientific Racism in Modern South Africa*. New York: Cambridge University Press, 1995.

Duff, Alexander. *Foreign Missions: Being an Address Delivered before the General Assembly of the Free Church of Scotland*. Edinburgh, UK: Andrew Elliot, 1866.

Duncan, Graham. "'African Churches Willing to Pay Their Own Bills': The Role of Money in the Formation of Ethiopian-Type Churches with Particular Reference to Mzimba Secession." *African Historical Review* 45, no. 2 (2013): 52–79.

Duncan, Natanya K. "The 'Efficient Womanhood' of the Universal Negro Improvement Association: 1919–1930." PhD dissertation, University of Florida, 2009.

Edgar, Robert. *Finger of God: Enoch Mgijima, the Israelites, and the Bulhoek Massacre in South Africa*. Charlottesville: University of Virginia Press, 2018.

Elkins, Caroline. *The Imperial Reckoning: The Untold Story of Britain's Gulag in Kenya*. New York: Henry Holt, 2005.

Elphick, Richard. "The Benevolent Empire and the Social Gospel: Missionaries and South African Christians in the Age Segregation." In *Christianity in South Africa: A Political, Social, and Cultural History*, edited by Richard Elphick and Rodney Davenport, 347–69. Berkeley: University of California Press, 1997.

Elphick, Richard. *The Equality of Believers: Protestant Missionaries and the Racial Politics of South Africa*. Charlottesville: University of Virginia, 2012.

Elphick, Richard. "Writing Religion into History: The Case of South African Christianity." *Studia Historiae Ecclesiasticae* 21 (1995): 1–21.

Erasmus, Zimitri, "Introduction: Re-imagining Coloured identities in post-Apartheid South Africa." In *Coloured by History, Shaped by Place*, edited by Zimitri Erasmus, 13–28. Cape Town: Kwela Books, 2001.

Erlmann, Veit. *African Stars: Studies in Black South African Performance*. Chicago: University of Chicago Press, 1991.

Erlmann, Veit. *Music, Modernity, and the Global Imagination: South Africa and the West*. Oxford: Oxford University Press, 1999.

Etherington, Norman. *Preachers, Peasants, and Politics in Southeast Africa, 1835–1880: African Christian Communities in Natal, Pondoland, and Zululand*. London: Royal Historical Society, 1979.

Evans, Ivan. *Bureaucracy and Race: Native Administration in South Africa*. Berkeley: University of California Press, 1997.

Ewing, Adam. *The Age of Garvey: How a Jamaican Activist Created a Mass Movement and Changed Global Black Politics*. Princeton, NJ: Princeton University Press, 2014.

Ferree, Karen E. *Framing the Race in South Africa: The Political Origins of Racial Census Elections*. New York: Cambridge University Press, 2010.

Fields, Barbara J. "Ideology and Race in American History." In *Region, Race, and Reconstruction: Essays in Honor of C. Vann Woodward*, edited by J. Morgan Kousser and James M. McPherson, 143–77. New York: Oxford University Press, 1982.

"The Fifth General Synod." *Negro Churchman* 3 (July 1925): 1–2.

Findley, Ronald, and Kevin O' Rourke. *Power and Plenty*. Princeton, NJ: Princeton University Press, 2007.

Ford, Joseph C., and Frank Cudall. *The Handbook of Jamaica, 1908: Compromising Historical, Statistical, and General Information concerning the Island, Compiled from Official and Reliable Records*. Kingston, Jamaica: Government Printing Office, 1908.

Frederickson, George M. *White Supremacy: A Comparative Study of American and South African History*. New York: Oxford University Press, 1982.

The Freedom Charter of South Africa. New York: The United Nations Centre Against Apartheid, 1979.

Fry, Poppy. "Siyamfenguza: The Creation of Fingo-ness in South Africa's Eastern Cape, 1800–1835." *Journal of Southern African Studies* 36, no. 1 (March 2010): 25–40.

Gaitskell, Deborah. "Housewives, Maids, or Mothers: Some Contradictions of Domesticity for Christian Women in Johannesburg." *Journal of African History* 24, no. 2 (1983): 241–56.

Gaitskell, Deborah. "Race Gender, and Imperialism: A Century of Black Girls' Education in South Africa." In *Benefits Bestowed: Education and British Imperialism*, edited by J. A. Mangan, 150–73. London: Routledge, 1988.

Gandhi, Mahatma. "Speech at a Meeting of Missionaries at the YMCA Calcutta." *Young India* 27 (October 1925): 434–39.

Garvey, Marcus. "The Destiny of the Negro [written July/August 1914]." In *Marcus Garvey and Universal Negro Improvement Association Papers*, Vol. 1, edited by Robert A. Hill, 163. Berkeley: University of California Press, 1983.

Gates, Henry Louis, Jr. *The Black Church: This Is Our Story*. New York: Penguin, 2021.

Gates, Henry Louis, Jr. *The Signifying Monkey: A Theory of African American Literary Criticism*. Oxford: Oxford University Press, 1988.

Gatewood, Willard B. "Black Americans and the Boer War, 1899–1902." *South Atlantic Quarterly* 72, no. 2 (1976): 226–44.

"George McGuire." *Who's Who in New York City and State*. 9th ed. New York: Who's Who Publications Inc., 1929.

Getachew, Adom. *Worldmaking after Empire: The Rise and Fall of Self-Determination*. Princeton, NJ: Princeton University Press, 2020.

Gikandi, Simon. *Ngugi Wa Thiong'o*. Cambridge: Cambridge University Press, 2000.

Giliomee, Hermann, and Bernard K. Mbenga. *New History of South Africa*. Cape Town: Tafelberg, 2007.

Goldin, Ian. "Coloured Identity and Coloured Politics in the Western Cape Region of South Africa." In *The Creation of Tribalism in Southern Africa*, edited by Leroy Vail, 241–54. London: James Currey, 1989.

Goldin, Ian. *Making Race*. Cape Town: Maskew Miller Longman, 1987.

Gomez, Michael A. *Reversing Sail: A History of the African Diaspora*. Cambridge: Cambridge University Press, 2005.

Gordon, Ernle P. "Garvey and Black Liberation Theology." In *Garvey: His Work and Impact*, edited by Rupert Lewis and Patrick Bryan, 135–44. Trenton, NJ: Africa World, 1991.

Gorman, Thomas P. "The Development of Language Policy in Kenya with Particular Reference to the Educational System." In *Language in Kenya*, edited by Wilfred H. Whiteley, 397–453. Nairobi: Oxford University Press, 1974.

Great Britain. *Parliamentary Papers: House of Commons, Volume 56*. London, 1907.

Greater Federation of New York Churches. *Report of Negro Churches in Manhattan*. New York: Greater Federation of New York Churches, 1925.

Gregor Cobley, Alan. "The 'African National Church': Self-Determination and Political Struggle among Black Christians in South Africa 1948." *Church History* 60, no. 3 (September 1991): 356–71.

Grogan, Ewart, and Arthur H. Sharp. *From Cape to Cairo: The First Traverse of Africa from South to North*. London: Hurst and Blackett, 1900.

Groves, Charles P. *The Planting of Christianity in Africa*, Vol. 1, *1840*. Cambridge: James Clarke & Co., 2002.

Hall, Jacqueline Dowd. "The Long Civil Rights Movement: And the Political Uses of the Past." *Journal of American History* 91, no. 4 (March 2005): 1233–63.

Harold, Claudrena N. *The Rise and Fall of the Garvey Movement in the Urban South, 1918–1942*. New York: Routledge, 2007.

Harris, Verne. "The Archival Sliver: A Perspective on the Construction of Social Memory in Archives and the Transition from Apartheid to Democracy." In *Reconfiguring the Archive*, edited by Carolyn Hamilton, Verne Harris, Jane Taylor, Michele Pickover, Graeme Reid, and Razia Saleh, 135–51. London: Kluwer Academic, 2002.

Hastings, Adrian. *The African Church, 1450–1950*. Oxford: Oxford University Press, 1996.

Hathaway, Malcolm R. "The Role of William Oliver Hutchinson and the Apostolic Faith Church in the Formation of British Pentecostal Churches." *Journal of European Pentecostal Theological Association* 16 (1996): 40–57.

Hayden, J. Carleton. "Afro-Anglican Linkages, 1701–1900: Ethiopia Shall Soon Stretch Out Her Hands unto God." *Journal of Religious Thought* 44, no. 1 (1987): 25–34.

Hayden, John Carleton. "Black Ministry in the Episcopalian Church: An Overview." In *Black Ministry in the Episcopal Church: Recruitment, Training and Deployment*, edited by Adair T. Lummis and Franklin Turner, 1–20. New York: Executive Council of the Episcopal Church, 1979.

Hayes, Stephen. "The African Independent Churches: Judgment through Terminology?" *Missionalia* 20, no. 2 (1992): 139–46.

Hayes, Steven T. "Issues of 'Catholic' Ecclesiology in Ethiopian-Type AICs." In *Frontiers of African Christianity: Essays in Honour of Inus Daneel*, edited by Greg Cuthbertson, Hennie Pretorius, and Dana Robert, 137–52. Pretoria: University of South Africa Press, 2003.

Haynes, Samuel A. "West Indian Journalist Analyzes Chasm between West Indian and United States Negroes." *Philadelphia Tribune*, July 31, 1930.

Heber, Bishop Reginald. "From Greenland's Icy Mountains." Hymn, ca. 1809.

Hensman, Howard. *Cecil Rhodes: A Study of a Career*. New York: Harper & Brothers, 1901.

Hetherington, Penelope. "The Politics of Female Circumcision in the Central Province of Colonial Kenya, 1920–30." *Journal of Imperial and Commonwealth History* 26 (1998): 93–126.

Hetherington, Penelope. "Women in South Africa: The Historiography in English." *International Journal of African Historical Studies* 26, no. 2 (1993): 241–69.

Hill, Robert A., ed. *Marcus Garvey and Universal Negro Improvement Association Papers*, Vol. 1, *1826–August 1919*. Berkeley: University of California Press, 1983.

Hill, Robert A., ed. *Marcus Garvey and Universal Negro Improvement Association Papers*, Vol. 2, *August 1919–August 1920*. Berkeley: University of California Press, 1983.

Hill, Robert A., ed. *Marcus Garvey and Universal Negro Improvement Association Papers*. Vol. 11, June 1921–December 1922. Berkeley: University of California Press, 1995.

Hill, Robert A., and Barbara Blair, eds. *Marcus Garvey: Life and Lessons*. Berkeley: University of California Press, 1987.

Hill, Robert, and Gregory Pirio. "'Africa for Africans': The Garvey Movement in South Africa, 1920–1940." In *The Politics of Race, Class, and Nationalism in the Twentieth Century*, edited by Shula Marks and Stanley Trapido, 209–53. London: Routledge, 1987.

Hodgson, Janet. *Ntsikana's Great Hymn: A Xhosa Expression of Christianity in the Early 19th Century Eastern Cape*. Cape Town: University of Cape Town, 1980.

Hodgson, Janet. "Soga and Dukwana: The Christian Struggle for Liberation in the Mid 19th Century." *Journal of Religion in Africa* 3 (1986): 187–206.

Horne, Gerald. "Towards a Transnational Agenda for African American History in the 21st Century." *Journal of African American History* 91, no. 3 (Summer 2006): 288–303.

Hucks, Tracey E. *Yoruba Traditions and African American Religious Nationalism.* Albuquerque: University of New Mexico Press, 2012.

Hurd Schluter, Nancy. "Marcus Garvey as Theologian." PhD dissertation, Drew University, 2001.

Ilesanmi, Simeon, and Ross Kane. "New Directions in African Political Theologies." Political Theology Network, April 7, 2022. https://politicaltheology.com/new-directions-in-african-political-theologies/.

Imani, Brada. *The Gospel According to Marcus Garvey: His Philosophies and Opinions about Christ.* London: JKB Independent Publishers, 2013.

Issa, Jai. "The Universal Negro Improvement Association in Louisiana: Creating a Provisional Government in Exile." PhD dissertation, Howard University, 2005.

Jaffer, Zubeida. *Beauty of the Heart: The Life and Times of Charlotte Mannya Maxeke.* Bloemfontein, South Africa: University of the Free State, 2016.

Jaji, Tstisi Ella. *Africa in Stereo: Modernism, Music, and Pan-African Solidarity.* Oxford: Oxford University Press, 2014.

James, Winston. "Explaining Afro-Caribbean Social Mobility in the United States: Beyond the Sowell Thesis." *Comparative Studies in Society and History* 44, no. 2 (April 2002): 218–62.

James, Winston. *Holding Aloft the Banner of Ethiopia: Caribbean Radicalism in the Early Twentieth Century.* London: Verso, 1999.

Jeppe, Fred, and J. E. Kotze. *De Locale Wetten Der Zuid Afrikaansche Republiek 1849–1885.* Pretoria: J. F. Celliers/ Gouvernement der Z A Republiek, 1887.

Jeremiah Moses, Wilson. *The Golden Age of Black Nationalism, 1890–1925.* New York: Oxford University Press, 1978.

Johnson, James Weldon. *Black Manhattan.* New York: Da Capo, 1991.

Johnson, Morris R. *The African Orthodox Church.* San Francisco: International Scholars Press, 1999.

Johnson, Sylvester A. *African American Religions, 1500–2000: Colonialism, Democracy and Freedom.* Cambridge: Cambridge University Press, 2015.

Kadalie, Clements. *My Life and the ICU: The Autobiography of a Black Trade Unionist in South Africa.* London: Frank Cass, 1970.

Kallaway, Peter. "Introduction to the Study of Education for Blacks in South Africa." In *Apartheid Education: The Education of Black South Africans,* edited by Peter Kallaway, 1–44. Rondebosch, South Africa: University of Cape Town, 1984.

Kalu, Ogbu u. "Ethiopianism and the Roots of Modern African Christianity." In *The Cambridge History of Christianity, 1815–1914,* edited by Sheridan Gilley, 576–92. Cambridge: Cambridge University Press, 2006.

Kaphagawani, Didier N. "The Philosophical Significance of Bantu Nomenclature: A Shot at African Philosophy." In *Contemporary Philosophy: A New Survey,*

Vol. 5, *African Philosophy*, edited by Gutttorm Fløistad, 121–52. Dordtrecht: Martinus Nijhoff, 1987.

Katongole, Emmanuel. *The Sacrifice of Africa: A Political Theology for Africa*. Grand Rapids, MI: Eerdmans Publishing, 2011.

Keegan, Timothy. *Colonial South Africa and the Origins of Racial Order*. Charlottesville: University of Virginia Press, 1997.

Kelley, Robin D. G. "But a Local Phase of a Global Problem: Black History's Global Vision, 1950." *Journal of American History* (December 1999): 1045–77.

Kelley, Robin D. G., and Sidney Lemelle. *Imagining Home: Class, Culture, and Nationalism in the African Diaspora*. London: Verso, 1994.

Kenya Land Commission Evidence, Vol. I. Nairobi: Government Printers, 1933.

Kenyatta, Jomo. *Facing Mount Kenya: The Tribal Life of the Gikuyu*. London: Mercury, 1961.

Kenyatta, Jomo. *Kenya, Land of Opportunity*. Kenya: Central Bank of Kenya, 1991.

Keto, Clement T. "Black Americans and South Africa, 1890–1910." *Current Bibliography on African Affairs* 5, no. 4 (July 1972): 383–406.

Kihali, Elekiah Andago. *The Orthodox Christian Witness in East Africa*. Sheridan, WY: Eastern Light Publishing, 2020.

Kimani Githieya, Francis. *The Freedom of the Spirit: African Indigenous Churches in Kenya*. Atlanta: American Academy of Religion, 1997.

King, Kenneth J. "Some Notes on Rabbi Ford and New Black Attitudes to Ethiopia." In *Black Apostles: Afro-American Clergy Confront the Twentieth Century*, edited by Randall K. Burkett and Richard Newman, 49–56. Boston: G. K. Hall, 1978.

Kobre, Sidney. "Rabbi Ford." *The Reflex* 4, no. 1 (1929): 27.

Kropotkin, Peter Alekseyevich. *Mutual Aid: A Factor of Evolution*. London: William Heinemann, 1910.

Lahouel, Bahra. "Ethiopianism and African Nationalism in South Africa before 1937." *Cahiers d'Etude Africaines* 26, no. 104 (1986): 681–88.

Lampe, Armando, ed. *Christianity in the Caribbean: Essays on Church History*. Kingston, Jamaica: University of the West Indies, 1999.

Landau, Paul S. *Popular Politics in the History of South Africa, 1400–1948*. Cambridge: Cambridge University Press, 2010.

Landau, Paul S. *The Realm of the Word: Language, Gender, and Christianity in a Southern African Kingdom*. Portsmouth: Heinemann, 1995.

Lawrance, Benjamin N., Emily Lynn Osborn, and Richard L. Roberts. "Introduction: African Intermediaries and the 'Bargain of Collaboration.'" In *Intermediaries, Interpreters, and Clerks: African Employees in the Making of Colonial Africa*, edited by Benjamin N. Lawrance, Emily Lynn Osborn, and Richard L. Roberts, 3–34. Madison: University of Wisconsin Press, 2006.

Lea, Allen. *The Native Separatist Church Movement*. Cape Town: Juta, 1927.

Leeds, Asia. "Representations of Race, Entanglements of Power: Whiteness, Garveyism, and Redemptive Geographies in Costa Rica, 1921–1950." PhD dissertation, Berkeley University, 2001.

Lefèber, Yvonne, and Henk W. A. Voorhoeve. *Indigenous Customs in Childbirth and Care.* Netherlands: Van Gorcum, 1998.

Lewis, Gavin. *Between the Wire and the Wall: A History of South African "Coloured" Politics.* New York: St. Martin's, 1987.

Lewis, Harold T. *Yet with a Steady Beat: The African American Struggle for Recognition in the Episcopal Church.* Atlanta: Trinity Press International, 1996.

Lewis, Rupert. "The Contemporary Significance of African Diaspora in the Americas." *Caribbean Quarterly* 38, nos. 2–3 (1992): 73–80.

The Life and Legacy of Charlotte Mannya-Maxeke: The Memory Project Inaugural Lecture, September 23, 2015. South African Parliament. https://www
.parliament.gov.za/storage/app/media/ProjectsAndEvents/Inaugural
_Memory_Lecture_the_Life_and_Legacy_of_Charlotte_Mannya
_Maxeke/docs/programme_email2.pdf.

Lovedale Missionary Institute: Report for 1890. Lovedale: Lovedale Mission Press, 1891.

Lovedale Missionary Institute Report for 1902. Lovedale: Lovedale Mission Press, 1903.

Magubane, Bernard. *The Ties That Bind: African American Consciousness in Africa.* Trenton, NJ: Africa World, 1987.

Mamdani, Mahmood. *Citizen and Subject: Contemporary Africa and the Legacy of Colonialism.* Princeton, NJ: Princeton University Press, 1996.

Mamdani, Mahmood. "Historicizing Power and Responses to Power: Indirect Rule and Its Reform." *Social Research* 66, no. 3 (1999): 859–86.

Mamdani, Mahmood. "Indirect Rule, Civil Society, Ethnicity: The African Dilemma." *Social Justice: A Journal of Crime, Conflict, and World Order* 23, no. 1 (1996): 145–50.

Mandela, Nelson Rolihlahla. *A Long Walk to Freedom.* Boston: Little, Brown, 1994.

Marks, Shula. *Reluctant Rebellion: An Assessment of 1906–1908 Disturbances in Natal.* Oxford: Oxford University Press, 1970.

Marks, Shula, and Stanley Trapido. *The Politics of Race, Class, and Nationalism in Twentieth Century South Africa.* New York: Routledge, 1987.

Martin, Tony. *The Pan-African Connection: From Slavery to Garvey and Beyond.* Wellesley, MA: Majority Press, 1983.

Martin, Tony. *Race First: The Ideological and Organizations Struggles of Marcus Garvey and the Universal Negro Improvement Association.* Westport, CT: Greenwood, 1976.

Masango, Tshepo. "Money Matters: West Indian Benevolent Societies in New York City." Master's thesis, University of Pennsylvania, 2007.

Masenya, Madiopane J. "African Womanist Hermeneutics." *Journal of Feminist Studies in Religion* 11, no. 1 (1995): 149–55.

Masenya, Madiopane J. "For Ever Trapped? An African Voice on Insider/Outsider Dynamics within South African Old Testament Gender–Sensitive Frameworks." OTE 27, no. 1 (2014): 189–204.

Mashini, Emma, Denise Ackman, and Jonathan Draper. *Women Hold Up the Sky.* Pietermaritzburg: Cluster Publications, 1991.

Masola, Athambile. "I Cite a Little Prayer: Name Your Black Feminist Sources." *Sunday Times,* May 2, 2021.

Mather, Frank Lincoln, ed. *Who's Who of the Colored Race: A General Biographical Dictionary of Men and Women of African Descent, 1915.* Ann Arbor: University of Michigan Press, 2009.

Matory, J. L. *Black Atlantic Religion: Tradition, Transnationalism, and Matriarchy in the Afro-Brazilian Candomblé.* Princeton, NJ: Princeton University Press, 2005.

Maxwell, David. "Historicizing Christian Independency: The Southern African Pentecostal Movement, c. 1908–1960." *Journal of African History* 40, no. 2 (1999): 243–64.

Maynard, Edward S. "The Translocation of West African Banking: The Yoruba Esusu Rotating Credit Association in the Anglophone Caribbean." *Dialectical Anthropology* 21, no. 1 (1996): 99–107.

McCord, Margaret. *The Calling of Katie Makanya: A Memoir of South Africa.* Hoboken, NJ: Wiley, 1998.

McDuffie, Erik. "'A New Day Has Dawned for the UNIA': Garveyism, the Diasporic Midwest, and West Africa, 1920–80." *Journal of West African History* 2, no. 1 (2017): 73–113.

McGuire, George Alexander. *The Universal Negro Catechism.* New York: UNIA, 1921.

McGuire, George Alexander. *The Universal Negro Ritual.* New York: UNIA, 1921.

McLean, Roderick. *The Theology of Marcus Garvey.* Washington, DC: University Press of America, 1982.

Memorandum on Education Policy in British Tropical African Dependencies: Memorandum Submitted to the Secretary of State for Colonies by the Advisory Committee on Native Education in the British Tropical African Dependencies. Cmd. 2374. London: HMSO, 1925.

Mills, George Wallace. "The Fork in the Road: Religious Separatism versus African Nationalism in the Cape Colony, 1890–1910." *Journal of Religion in Africa* 10, no. 1 (1978): 51–61.

Mills, George Wallace. "The Taylor Revival of 1866 and the Roots of African Nationalism in the Cape Colony." *Journal of Religion in Africa* 8, no. 2 (1976): 105–22.

"Missionary Chronicle." In *The Official Year Book of the Church of England,* 199–247. London: Society for the Promotion of Christian Knowledge, 1885.

Mokone, J. M. *The Early Life of Our Founder.* Johannesburg: A.S. Hunt, 1935.

Morgan, Robert Josias. "Letter to the Editor." *Russian Orthodox American Messenger*, English supplement, October–November 1904.

Mothiba, Frank. "Greetings from the Natives of South Africa." *Negro World*, November 24, 1924.

Moyd, Michelle R. *Violent Intermediaries: African Soldiers, Conquest, and Everyday Colonialism in German East Africa.* Athens: Ohio University Press, 2014.

Moyer, R. A. "A History of the Mfengu of the Eastern Cape." PhD dissertation, London University, 1976.

Moyer, R. A. "Some Current Manifestations of Mfengu History." In *Collected Seminar Papers on the Societies of Southern Africa in the 19th and 20th Centuries (October 1971–June 1972)*, 144–54. London: University of London, Institute of Commonwealth Studies, 1973.

Mukonyora, Isabel. *Wandering a Gendered Wilderness: Suffering and Healing in an African Initiated Church.* New York: Peter Lang, 2007.

Muller, Carol Anne. *Rituals of Fertility and Sacrifice: Nazarite Women's Performance in South Africa.* Chicago: University of Chicago Press, 1999.

Murray, Jocelyn. "The CMS and Female Circumcision." In *The Making of Missionary Communities in East Africa*, edited by Robert W. Strayer, 136–55. Albany, NY: SUNY Press, 1978.

Muzondidya, James. *Walking a Tightrope: Towards a Social History of the Coloured People of Zimbabwe.* Trenton, NJ: Africa World, 2005.

Mwakikagile, Godfrey. *Africa and the West.* Huntington, NY: Nova Science Publishers, 2000.

Namee, Matthew. "Father Raphael Morgan: The First Orthodox Priest of African Descent in America." *St. Vladimir's Theological Quarterly* 53, no. 4 (2009): 447–60.

Natsoulas, Theodore. "Patriarch McGuire and the Spread of the African Orthodox Church to Africa," *Journal of Religion in Africa* 12, no. 2 (1981): 81–104.

Neame, E. "Ethiopianism: The Danger of a Black Church." *Empire Review* 10, no. 1 (1905): 256–65.

Neethling, Stephen J. *Naming among the Xhosa of South Africa.* New York: Edwin Mullen, 2005.

Newbury, Colin. "The March of Everyman: Mobility and the Imperial Census of 1901." *Journal of Imperial and Commonwealth History* 12, no. 2 (2008): 80–101.

"A New Church and Possible Trouble." *Christian Express* 27, no. 322 (1897): 49.

Newman, Richard. "Archbishop Daniel William Alexander and the African Orthodox Church." In *The Colonial Africa Epoch*, edited by Gregory Maddox, 65–80. London: Routledge, 1993.

Newman, Richard. "The Origins of the African Orthodox Church." In *The Negro Churchman*, edited by Richard Newman, iii–xxii. Millwood: Kraus Reprint, 1977.

Noble, John [clerk of the House of Assembly for the Cape Colony]. "British South Africa and the Zulu War." In *Proceedings of the Royal Colonial Institute,* Vol. 10, *1878–79,* 105–68. London: Sampson Low, Marston, Searle & Rivington, 1879.

Nyangweso Wangila, Mary. *Female Circumcision: The Interplay of Religion, Culture, and Gender.* Maryknoll, NY: Orbis Books, 2007.

Odendaal, André. *The Founders: The Origins of the ANC and the Struggle for Democracy in South Africa.* Lexington: University Press of Kentucky, 2015.

Opland, Jeff. *Xhosa Poets and Poetry: Publications of the Opland Collection of Xhosa Literature.* Cape Town: David Phillips, 1998.

Palmer, Colin A. "Defining and Studying the Modern African Diaspora." *Journal of Negro History* 85 (2000): 27–32.

Paris, Peter J. *The Spirituality of African Peoples: The Search for a Common Moral Discourse.* Minneapolis: Fortress, 1995.

Paulus, Mohome. "Naming in Sesotho: Its Socio-Cultural and Linguistic Basis." *Names* 20, no. 3 (1972): 171–85.

Peires, J. B. "Ethnicity and Pseudo-Ethnicity in Ciskei." In *The Creation of Tribalism in Southern Africa,* edited by Leroy Vail, 395–413. Berkeley: University of California Press, 1991.

Peires, J. B. "Ethnicity and Pseudo-Ethnicity in Ciskei." In *Segregation and Apartheid in the Twentieth Century,* edited by William Beinart and Saul Dubow, 256–84. New York: Routledge, 1995.

Perbedy, Sally. *Selecting Immigrants: National Identity and South Africa's Immigration Policies, 1910–2005.* New York: Cambridge University Press, 2019.

Pierre, Jemima. *The Predicament of Blackness: Postcolonial Ghana and the Politics of Race.* Chicago: University of Chicago Press, 2012.

Pinkney, Alphonso. *Red, Black, and Green: Black Nationalism in the United States.* Cambridge: Cambridge University Press, 1976.

Platt, Warren C. "The African Orthodox Church: An Analysis of Its First Decade." *Church History* 58, no. 4 (December 1989): 474–88.

Posel, Deborah. "Race as Common Sense: Racial Classification in Twentieth-Century South Africa." *African Studies Review* 44, no. 2 (2001): 87–114.

"Prayer for Guidance." In *The Book of Common Prayer,* 57. London: Everyman's Library, 1662.

The Protestant Episcopal Church in the United States of America in the Court of Review. *In the Matter of the Presentment of Bishop William Montgomery Brown: Appeal from the Court for the Trial of a Bishop.* Cleveland: Gates Legal Publishing, 1924.

"Provincial News, South Africa." *Negro Churchman* 5 (March 1927): 2.

Pui Lan, Kwok. *The Hong Kong Protests and Political Theology.* Lanham, MD: Rowman and Littlefield, 2021.

Putnam, Lara. *Radical Moves: Caribbean Migrants and the Politics of Race in the Jazz Age.* Chapel Hill: University of North Carolina Press, 2013.

Quinn, Frank, and Greg Cuthbertson. *Presbyterianism in Cape Town: A History of Saint Andrew's Church, 1829–1979*. Cape Town: St. Andrew's Presbyterian Church, 1979.

Reddie, Anthony G. *Is God Colour Blind? Insights from Black Theology for Christian Ministry*. London: SPCK, 2009.

Redkey, Edwin S. *Black Exodus: Black Nationalist and Back-to-Africa Movements, 1890–1910*. New Haven, CT: Yale University Press, 1969.

"Report of the Madison Square Garden Meeting." In *Marcus Garvey and Universal Negro Improvement Association Papers*, Vol. 2, edited by Robert A. Hill, 497–508. Berkeley: University of California Press, 1983.

Report of the Proceedings of the First Missionary General Missionary Conference, July 13–20, 1904. Johannesburg, 1905.

"Return Fare to Africa." *Negro Churchman* 5 (November 1927): 8.

Roberage, Paul. "The Formation of Afrikaans." In *Language and Social History: Studies in South African Sociolinguistics*, edited by Rajend Meshtrie, 68–88. Claremont, South Africa: New Africa Books, 1995.

Rolinson, Mary G. *Grassroots Garveyism: The Universal Negro Improvement Association in the Rural South, 1920–1927*. Chapel Hill: University of North Carolina Press, 2007.

Ross, Robert. *The Borders of Race in Colonial South Africa: The Kat River Settlement, 1829–1856*. New York: Cambridge University Press, 2013.

Rushing, Byron. "A Note on the Origin of the African Orthodox Church." *Journal of African American History* 57, no. 1 (1972): 37–39.

Samson, Anne. *World War I in Africa: The Forgotten Conflict among the European Powers*. London: Bloomsbury Academic, 2019.

SANAC. *Report of the Commission with Annexures and Appendices, South African Native Affairs Commission, 1903–1905*, Vol. I. Cape Town, 1905.

Sandgren, David P. *Christianity and the Kikuyu: Religious Divisions and Social Conflict*. Bern: Peter Lang, Inc., 1989.

Saunders, Christopher. "African Nationalism and Religious Independency in the Cape Colony: A Comment." *Journal of Religion in Africa* 9, no. 3 (1978): 205–10.

Saunders, Christopher. "From Trinidad to Cape Town: The first black lawyer at Cape." *Quarterly Bulletin of the National Library of South Africa* 55, no. 4 (2001): 141–61.

Saunders, Christopher. "Tile and the Thembu Church." *Journal of African History* 11, no. 4 (1970): 553–70.

Schler, Lynn. "Writing African Women's History with Male Sources: Possibilities and Limitation." *History in Africa* 31 (2004): 319–33. https://doi.org/10.1017/S036154130000351X.

Schmitt, Carl. *Political Theology: Four Chapters on the Concept of Sovereignty*. Chicago: University of Chicago Press, 2006.

Shepperson, George. "Ethiopianism and African Nationalism." *Phylon* 14, no. 1 (1953): 9–18.

Shulman, George. *American Prophecy: Race and Redemption in American Political Culture.* Minneapolis: University of Minnesota Press, 2008.

Sithole, Nkosinathi. *Isaiah Shembe's Hymns and the Sacred Dance in Ibandla LamaNazaretha Sacred Dance.* Leiden, Netherlands: Brill, 2016.

Skota, T. D. Mweli. *The African Who's Who: An Illustrated Classified Register and National Geographic Dictionary of Africans in the Transvaal.* Johannesburg: Frier & Munro, 1965.

Skota, T. D. Mweli. *The African Yearly Register: Being an Illustrated National Biographical Dictionary (Who's Who) of Black Folks in Africa.* Johannesburg: Frier & Munro, 1932.

Slate, Nico. "From Colored Cosmopolitan to Human Rights: A Historical Overview of the Black Freedom Struggle." *Journal of Civil and Human Rights* 1, no. 1 (2015): 3–24.

Smith, G. *Johannes van der Kemp: First Medical Missionary to Africa.* London: Nelson, 1900.

Smith, Lucius E. *Heroes and Martyrs of the Modern Missionary Enterprise: A Record of Their Lives and Labors.* Providence: Potter, 1856.

Smith, Ted A. *Weird John Brown: Divine Violence and Limits of Ethics.* Stanford, CA: Stanford University Press, 2014.

Sparta, Ruben S. S. Musaka. "The Patriarchal See in Africa(?)" *Negro Churchman* 6, no.11 (December 1928): 3.

Stapleton, Tim. "Valuable, Gallant, and Faithful Assistants: The Fingo (or Mfengu) as Colonial Military Allies during the Cape-Xhosa Wars, 1835–1881." In *Soldiers and Settlers in Africa, 1850–1918,* edited by Stephen Miller, 15–48. Leiden, Netherlands: Brill, 2009.

Stone, Judith. *When She Was White: The True Story of a Family Divided by Race.* New York: Miramax Books, 2008.

Sunderland, David, ed. *Vlieland, British Malaya: A Report on the 1931 Census.* New York: Routledge, 2014.

Sundkler, Bengt, and Christopher Sneed. *A History of the Church in South Africa.* Cambridge: Cambridge University Press, 2000.

Suzman, Arthur. "Race Classification and Definition in the Legislation of the Union of South Africa 1910–1960: A Survey and Analysis." South African Institute of Race Relations, 1961.

Swan, Maureen. *Gandhi: The South African Experience.* Johannesburg: Ravan Press of South Africa, 1985.

Swan, Quito. *Pasifika Black: Oceania, Anti-Colonialism and the African World.* New York: New York University Press, 2022.

Tambo, Oliver. *Preparing for Power: Oliver Tambo Speaks.* New York: George Braziller, 1988.

Taylor, J. Dexter. "The Social Motive in Evangelism." *South African Outlook* 1, no. 1 (1933): 239–40.

Taylor, Ula. *The Promise of Patriarchy: Women and the Nation of Islam*. Chapel Hill: University of North Carolina Press, 2017.

Terry-Thompson, A. C. *The History of the African Orthodox Church*. New York: Beacon, 1956.

Theoharis, Jeanne. "Black Freedom Struggles: Reimagining and Defining the Fundamentals." *History Compass* 4, no. 2 (2006): 348–67.

Thomas, Lynn. *Politics of the Womb*. Oakland: University of California Press, 2003.

Thompson, T. Jack. "Capturing the Image: African Missionary Photography as Enslavement and Liberation." Day Associates Lecture, New Haven, CT, Yale Divinity School Library. https://web.library.yale.edu/sites/default/files/files/CapturingtheImage.pdf.

Tignor, Robert L. *Colonial Transformation of Kenya: The Kamba, Kikuyu, and Maasai from 1900–1939*. Princeton, NJ: Princeton University Press, 1976.

Tonghou Ngong, David. *The Holy Spirit and Salvation in African Christian Theology*. New York: Peter Lang, 2010.

Transvaal. *Statutory Proclamations of the Transvaal, 1900–1902*. London, 1904.

Turner, Henry McNeal. "My Trip to South Africa." In *Respect Black: The Writings and Speeches of Henry McNeal Turner*, 178–81. New York: Arno, 1971.

"UNIA Declaration of Rights of the Negro Peoples of the World," New York, August 13, 1920. In *Marcus Garvey and Universal Negro Improvement Association Papers*, Vol. 2, edited by Robert A. Hill, 571–80. Berkeley: University of California Press, 1983.

Union of South Africa. *Parliament Debates (Hansard)*. Pretoria, South Africa: Government Printer, 1913.

Union of South Africa, Office of Census and Statistics. *Official Year Book of the Union*. Pretoria, 1919.

United States Bureau of Census. *Religious Bodies* (1926 ed.). Washington, DC: US Government Printing Office, 1926.

van der Kemp, Johannes. *Memoirs of the Rev. J. T. van der Kemp, M.D., Late Missionary in South Africa*. London: J. Dennett for the London Missionary Society, 1813.

Van Der Ross, Richard. *The Rise and Decline of Apartheid: A Study of Political Movements among the Coloured People of South Africa, 1880–1985*. Cape Town: Tafelberg, 1986.

van der Woud, Joanne. "How Shall We Sing the Lord's Song in a Strange Land." In *Psalms in the Early Modern World*, edited by Linda Phyllis Austern, Kari Boyd McBride, and David L. Orvis, 115–34. Burlington, VT: Ashgate, 2011.

Vernal, Fiona. *Farmfield Mission: A Christian Community in South Africa, 1838–2008*. Oxford: Oxford University Press, 2012.

Vinson, Robert Trent. *The Americans Are Coming! Dreams of African American Liberation in Segregationist South Africa*. Athens: Ohio University Press, 2012.

Vinson, Robert Trent. "Citizenship over Race? African Americans in American–South African Diplomacy." *Safundi: The Journal of South African and American Comparative Studies* 15 (April 2004): 13–32.

Vinson, Robert Trent. "'Sea Kaffirs': 'American Negroes' and the Gospel of Garveyism in Early Twentieth Century Cape Town." *Journal of African History* 47, no. 2 (2006): 281–92.

Walker, Asad. "Princes Will Come Out of Egypt: Marcus Garvey and Reverend Albert B. Cleage Jr." *Journal of Black Studies* 39, no. 2 (2008): 194–251.

Walker, Corey D. B. *A Noble Fight: Freemasonry and the Struggle for Democracy in America*. Champaign: University of Illinois Press, 2008.

Walker, Corey D. B. "The Race for Theology: Toward a Critical Theology of Freedom." In *Race and Political Theology*, edited by Vincent W. Lloyd, 134–55. Stanford, CA: Stanford University Press, 2012.

Watkins-Owens, Irma. *Blood Relations: Caribbean Immigrants and the Harlem Community, 1900–1930*. Bloomington: Indiana University Press, 1996.

Webster, Alan Charles. "Land Expropriation and Labour Extraction under Colonial Rule: The War of 1835 and the 'Emancipation' of the Fingo." Master's thesis, Rhodes University, 1991.

Weisenfeld, Judith. *New World A-Coming: Black Religion and Racial Identity during the Great Migration*. New York: New York University Press, 2016.

Welbourn, Frederick B. *East African Rebels: A Study of Some Independent Churches*. London: SCM Press, 1961.

Wenzel, Jennifer. *Bulletproof: Afterlives of Anticolonial Prophecy in South Africa and Beyond*. Chicago: University of Chicago Press, 2009.

West, Michael O. "Ethiopianism and Colonialism: The African Orthodox Church in Zimbabwe, 1928–1934." In *Christian Missionaries and the State in the Third World*, edited by Holger Bernt Hansen and Michael Twaddle, 237–54. Athens: Ohio University Press, 2002.

West, Michael O. *The Rise of an African Middle Class: Colonial Zimbabwe, 1898–1965*. Bloomington: Indiana University Press, 2002.

West, Michael O., William G. Martin, and Fanon Che Wilkins, eds. *Toussaint to Tupac: The Black International since the Age of Revolution*. Chapel Hill: University of North Carolina Press, 2009.

Westerman, George. "Historical Notes on West Indians on the Isthmus of Panama." *Phylon* 22, no. 4 (Winter 1961): 340–50. https://doi.org/10.2307/273537.

White, Gavin. "Patriarch McGuire and the Episcopal Church." *Historical Magazine of the Protestant Episcopalian Church* 38, no. 2 (June 1969): 109–41.

Wicomb, Zoë. "Shame and Identity: The Case of the Coloured in South Africa." In *Writing South Africa: Literature, Apartheid, and Democracy, 1970–1995*, edited by Derek Attridge and Rosemary Jolly, 91–107. New York: Cambridge University Press, 2011.

Wilmore, Gayraud S. *Black Religion and Black Radicalism: An Interpretation of the Religious History of African American Women.* Maryknoll, NY: Orbis Books, 1998.

Wilson, John. "Heber's Hymns." *William Blackwood's Edinburgh Magazine* 24 (November 1827): 622.

Wolf, Michelle. "Madonna and Child of Soweto: Black Life beyond Apartheid and Democracy." *Political Theology* 19, no. 7 (2018): 572–92.

Xuma, Alfred B. "Charlotte Maxeke (Mrs): What an Educated Girl Can Do." Johannesburg: African Methodist Episcopal. Women's Parent Mite Missionary Society, 1930.

Yon, Daniel A. "Race-Making/Race-Mixing: St. Helena and the South Atlantic World." *Social Dynamics* 33, no. 2: 144–63.

INDEX